PREFACE

1. Scope

This publication provides joint doctrine for mortuary affairs support in joint operations. It outlines procedures for the search, recovery, evacuation (to include tracking of human remains), tentative identification, processing, and/or temporary interment of remains. This publication addresses both the Department of Defense's mortuary affairs responsibilities in regards to civil support duties under United States Northern Command and to the other geographic combatant commanders. It further addresses decontamination procedures for handling contaminated human remains and provides for the handling of personal effects of deceased and missing personnel.

2. Purpose

This publication has been prepared under the direction of the Chairman of the Joint Chiefs of Staff. It sets forth joint doctrine to govern the activities and performance of the Armed Forces of the United States in joint operations and provides the doctrinal basis for interagency coordination and for US military involvement in multinational operations. It provides military guidance for the exercise of authority by combatant commanders and other joint force commanders (JFCs) and prescribes joint doctrine for operations, education, and training. It provides military guidance for use by the Armed Forces in preparing their appropriate plans. It is not the intent of this publication to restrict the authority of the JFC from organizing the force and executing the mission in a manner the JFC deems most appropriate to ensure unity of effort in the accomplishment of the overall objective.

3. Application

a. Joint doctrine established in this publication applies to the Joint Staff, commanders of combatant commands, subunified commands, joint task forces, subordinate components of these commands, and the Services.

b. The guidance in this publication is authoritative; as such, this doctrine will be followed except when, in the judgment of the commander, exceptional circumstances dictate otherwise. If conflicts arise between the contents of this publication and the contents of Service publications, this publication will take precedence unless the Chairman of the Joint Chiefs of Staff, normally in coordination with the other members of the Joint Chiefs of Staff, has provided more current and specific guidance. Commanders of forces operating as part of a multinational (alliance or coalition) military command should follow multinational doctrine and procedures ratified by the United States. For doctrine and procedures not ratified by the

United States, commanders should evaluate and follow the multinational command's doctrine and procedures, where applicable and consistent with US law, regulations, and doctrine.

For the Chairman of the Joint Chiefs of Staff:

WILLIAM E. GORTNEY
VADM, USN
Director, Joint Staff

SUMMARY OF CHANGES
REVISION OF JOINT PUBLICATION 4-06
DATED 05 JUNE 2006

• **Changes the publication title from *Mortuary Affairs in Joint Operations* to *Mortuary Affairs*.**

• **Expands on the role of mortuary affairs support for homeland defense and civil support operations and changes the chapter title from *Mortuary Affairs Support in the United States* to *Homeland Defense and Defense Support of Civil Authorities*.**

• **Removes the tactics, techniques, and procedures for decontamination of human remains and personal effects.**

• **Adds a chapter on Mortuary Operations.**

• **Removes chapter on Procedures for the Search and Recovery of Human Remains and placed the information in appropriate chapter locations.**

• **Removes chapter on Evacuation and Tentative Identification of Human Remains and placed the information in appropriate chapter locations.**

• **Adds a chapter on Mortuary Affairs Battlefield Operations.**

• **Replaces the term decontamination with contamination mitigation.**

• **Changes the name of the mortuary affairs decontamination collection point to mortuary affairs contaminated remains mitigation site.**

• **Removes appendix on International Agreements and Memorandums of Understanding.**

• **Removes appendix on Common Forms Used in Mortuary Affairs and placed the forms in the appropriate chapter locations.**

• **Adds appendix on Transportation of Contaminated Remains.**

• **Adds appendix on Mortuary Affairs Assets and Capabilities.**

• **Adds appendix on Foreign Humanitarian Assistance.**

• **Provides additional guidance on the recovery, handling, processing, and evacuation of portions to reflect current Armed Forces Medical Examiner guidance and Department of Defense (DOD) policy.**

• **Provides additional guidance on the recovery, handling, processing, and evacuation of US contractor remains to reflect current DOD policy.**

• **Provides updated guidance on the joint personal effects depot and its procedures and operations.**

• **Provides guidance on inventory officer responsibilities for the collection, inventory, and shipment of personal effects.**

TABLE OF CONTENTS

CHAPTER V
PERSONAL EFFECTS

CHAPTER VI
MORTUARY OPERATIONS

CHAPTER VII
HOMELAND DEFENSE AND DEFENSE SUPPORT OF CIVIL AUTHORITIES

CHAPTER VIII
CONTAMINATED HUMAN REMAINS AND PERSONAL EFFECTS

APPENDIX

GLOSSARY

FIGURE

EXECUTIVE SUMMARY
COMMANDER'S OVERVIEW

- **Describes the Mortuary Affairs (MA) Program**

- **Discusses MA Support in a Theater of Operations**

- **Explains MA Planning**

- **Discusses MA Battlefield Operations**

- **Provides Guidance on Handling Personal Effects**

- **Covers Mortuary Operations**

- **Addresses MA Support for Homeland Defense and Defense Support of Civil Authorities**

- **Outlines MA Operations in a Chemical, Biological, Radiological, and Nuclear Environment and Handling of Contaminated Human Remains and Personal Effects**

Mortuary Affairs Program

The Joint Mortuary Affairs Program provides support across the range of military operations.

The Joint Mortuary Affairs Program is a broadly based military program providing for the care and disposition of missing and deceased personnel, including personal effects (PE). Based on the guidance and direction of the Secretary of Defense (SecDef) and the Chairman of the Joint Chiefs of Staff, the Joint Mortuary Affairs Program provides guidance to the combatant commands and Services.

Mortuary Affairs Policy

Policy as stated in Department of Defense Directive (DODD) 1300.22, *Mortuary Affairs Policy,* is that the human remains of all members of the Armed Forces of the United States will be returned for permanent disposition in accordance with the decedent's will or the laws of the state (territory, possession, or country) of the decedent's legal residence as directed by the person authorized to direct disposition of human remains (PADD).

Joint Mortuary Affairs Program

During peacetime and peace operations, mortuary services are provided at the local level by regional

The program provides for professional mortuary services, supplies, and related services to statutorily eligible personnel.

Service mortuaries or through established Service contracts. During military operations when local support capabilities are exceeded or not available, the Department of Defense (DOD) can direct all human remains go to a specified mortuary, normally the Port Mortuary at Dover Air Force Base, Delaware. The specified mortuary will provide positive identification (ID) (if augmented by Armed Forces Medical Examiner System), mortuary services, and return human remains to a place designated by the PADD for permanent disposition.

Military Mortuary Affairs Support

Mortuary affairs (MA) support begins at the unit level. Commanders are responsible for the recovery and evacuation of human remains of assigned and attached personnel (military, DOD civilian and contractor) to the nearest MA facility (usually located at the nearest support area). The Air Force, Marine Corps, and Army have personnel with MA training and have the capability to establish and operate mortuary affairs collection points (MACPs). The Army, however, is the only Service with an Active Component dedicated MA force structure and the capability to provide backup support to all Services and is often tasked to operate MACPs on an area basis.

Roles and Responsibilities

The Secretary of the Army serves as the executive agent for MA for DOD.

Geographic combatant commanders (GCCs) give authoritative direction and guidance on providing MA support to all assigned and attached forces physically present in their area of responsibility (AOR).

In all cases, the direct initial contact with family members of deceased personnel is performed by the parent Service.

Commander, United States Transportation Command, provides strategic airlift to evacuate human remains from outside the continental US to a designated DOD mortuary.

Each **Service** is responsible for MA support, to include tentative ID and disposition of human remains and PE, for its own personnel unless otherwise directed by the GCC or mutual support agreements between the Services.

Mortuary Affairs Support in a Theater of Operations

Joint Mortuary Affairs Office

GCCs normally establish a joint mortuary affairs office (JMAO) within their commands to provide policy to their assigned Service components and support the joint force. The JMAO develops MA-specific directives and geographic specific operation orders for the GCC, while providing oversight of Service component MA operations and programs.

Operational Mortuary Affairs Support

Operational MA support can be broken down into four types of support:

- **Direct support** (DS) is to a specific force and authorizes the MA team to answer directly to the supported forces request for assistance.

- **Area support** is not a support relationship, but rather a method by which a unit may provide support.

- **General support** (GS) is a support relationship that can be established between units.

- **Inter-Service support** is support provided by another Service to support operations.

Command and Control of Army Mortuary Affairs Assets

The deployment and assignment of US Army MA assets are dynamic and can be readily tailored to meet operational requirements. The company structure allows for deployment of a collection team, an MA platoon, or the company as a whole.

Temporary Storage, Interment, and Disinterment Operations

Commanders are responsible for temporary storage, interment, and disinterment operations to ensure the preservation and accountability of human remains under their control. The primary objectives of these operations are to maintain morale and field sanitation and to comply with the law of war, international law, and international agreements.

Mortuary Affairs Support to Non-US Personnel

Existing standardization agreements should be used whenever possible to facilitate common policies and procedures among participating nations. MA personnel process adversary detainee human remains and PE in accordance with the Geneva Convention Relative to the Treatment of Prisoners of War.

Strategic Implications of Mortuary Affairs Interaction with the Death of Non-US Civilians and Noncombatants

While it is in the interest of US and multinational forces to not be involved in the handling of the human remains of civilian and noncombatant deaths, this is a situation with specific political and cultural sensitivities that cannot always be avoided. Civil affairs (CA) personnel can assist local agencies interfacing with US military assets providing support to transport the human remains. CA personnel advise the command on cultural traditions impacting the handling and transport of human remains.

Mass Casualty/Fatality Incident Considerations

GCCs are responsible for the proper execution of MA when such events occur within their AOR. Coordination with the Armed Forces Medical Examiner (AFME) is mandatory in all peacetime mass casualty/fatality incidents, no matter where the incident occurs.

Legal Considerations

The legal considerations for MA support in a theater of operation stem from the commanders' responsibility for health and public hygiene as well as articles of the law of war and the Geneva Conventions. The MA program should include the commander's guidance on the rules of the use of force or rules of engagement and rules for gathering evidence to the forces conducting MA operations.

Special Considerations

Special considerations should include: special religious and cultural considerations; and use of nonmilitary MA support.

Mortuary Affairs Planning

Planning Guidance

GCCs are responsible for developing policies for the overall supervision of all MA matters. **Subordinate commanders** are responsible for ensuring that the MA support guidance from higher headquarters is implemented in their overall operational concept of operations.

Planning Considerations

Commanders and MA support planners at all levels should consider the following during planning and execution: review or establish multinational agreements; number of expected fatalities; level of infrastructure development (e.g., port mortuary location, intratheater lines of communications, airfields, and other facilities); and operational requirements.

Religious Considerations

Religious beliefs and practices will influence the handling of human remains and may impact joint and multinational operations. Religious support teams can advise on specific religious practices associated with handling of the deceased and interment operations.

Environmental, Safety, and Occupational Health Considerations

While complete protection of personnel, equipment, facilities, and the environment during military operations may not always be possible, planners should carefully address environmental, safety, and occupational health considerations during joint operations.

Public Affairs

The public release of information on casualties during peacetime should be in accordance with the individual Service's policies and procedures. All requests for information on the deceased should be referred to the appropriate JMAO or medical examiners and/or coroners (ME/Cs), who will coordinate the release of the requested information though the public affairs office once authorized.

Mortuary Affairs Battlefield Operations

Unit-Level Operations

Unit-level operations consist of the initial search, recovery, and evacuation of unit deceased personnel to the nearest MACP. This is the first step in the MA process on the battlefield.

Search and Recovery of Human Remains

When searching for human remains, follow a systematic method. This allows team members to thoroughly cover a large area. Once the entire area has been searched and all relevant items marked, the team will begin the documentation and recovery process. Personnel designated to document and safeguard PE must thoroughly check the entire human remains for PE, including the hands, neck, pockets, boots, and load-carrying equipment. Once human remains, portions, and disassociated effects have been tagged and placed in human remains pouches, the human remains should be evacuated to the evacuation point. It is vital that all aspects of the recovery operation be documented. This documentation provides a spatial and contextual reference as to where human remains, artifacts, and other material evidence are found within the recovery site.

Mortuary Affairs Collection Point Operations

The MACP is the basic unit for modern day MA support. These MACPs provide DS and/or GS for receiving, refrigeration, processing, tentative ID, and evacuation of human remains and their accompanying PE.

Theater Mortuary Evacuation Point Operations

A theater mortuary evacuation point (TMEP) will be established with the primary mission of evacuating all human remains and accompanying PE to a military mortuary. Locate the TMEP at or adjacent to a major aerial port of embarkation. This arrangement will capitalize on all available aircraft and corresponding logistic support.

Personal Effects

General Guidance

Personal effects include all personal items the individual possesses at the time of death, excluding government property.

Disposition of PE includes the collection, receipt, recording, accountability, storage, and disposal of the PE of US military personnel, civilians under US military jurisdiction, and all deceased persons for whom the US provides mortuary services. All efforts are made to safeguard and protect PE from the elements and pilferage during the entire handling and transportation process.

Roles and Responsibilities

The GCC is responsible for the control and coordination of MA support. This includes PE support for all US military personnel, US civilians and others, multinational partner, local national, and adversary personnel.

The **theater MA officer** is responsible for determining the theater process for handling and evacuation of PE.

The **MACP** is responsible for inventorying, recording, safeguarding, and evacuating all decedent effects.

Each deployed unit is responsible for the appointment of a PE inventory officer. The unit is responsible for the collection, inventory, safeguarding, packaging, and evacuation of all PE for the unit member.

The **theater inventory officer** is the sole responsible designee that ensures there is a clear chain of custody from the moment of incident to the MACPs.

The **theater PE depot** is responsible for the receipt, safeguard, inventory (when required), storage, palletizing, and evacuation of PE back to the continental US PE depot. When a PE depot is established, the need for a Service to handle the disposition of PE is eliminated.

Joint Personal Effects Depot Operations in the Continental US

A joint personal effects depot (JPED) is structured into five main sections: receiving, administration, processing, inventory officer final inventory, and shipping. The Casualty and Mortuary Affairs Operations Center maintains a JPED as required to support DOD operations around the world.

Mortuary Operations

Overview

DOD installations provide mortuary services for authorized personnel through contract with local commercial vendors. When commercial mortuary services are not available or are cost prohibitive, DOD or the Services may establish regional mortuaries.

Port Mortuary

The port mortuary's mission is to fulfill the US commitment of ensuring dignity, honor, and respect to our fallen and provide care, service, and support to their families. The port mortuary is where the AFME's office often determines cause and manner of death and obtains positive ID of deceased personnel.

Department of Defense Regional Mortuaries

Regional mortuaries are strategically placed to support overseas installations and operations and provide the full spectrum of mortuary services for a geographical region to all personnel who are authorized DOD mortuary services.

Installation Mortuary Support

In the US, installation mortuary support is handled in accordance with Service and installation regulations and guidance. Installations establish contracts for mortuary services.

Homeland Defense and Defense Support of Civil Authorities

Defense Support of Civil Authorities

DOD may be required to provide defense support of civil authorities (DSCA) for domestic incidents as directed by the President or when consistent with military readiness and appropriate under the circumstances and the law as per Homeland Security Presidential Directive-5, *Management of Domestic Incidents,* and DODD 3025.18, *Defense Support of Civil Authorities (DSCA),* to support civilian entities following the occurrence of a natural, man-made, or terrorist incident.

United States Northern Command (USNORTHCOM) and United States Pacific Command (USPACOM) provide DSCA as directed by the President or SecDef, which is typically after local, state, tribal, and other federal resources are overwhelmed and civil authorities have requested DOD assistance.

Roles and Responsibilities

Within the Department of Defense, mortuary affairs capabilities exist at the Service level that can be called upon to support a defense support of civil authorities mission assignment.

The Department of Homeland Security (DHS) establishes federal response operations structures in Presidential declared disasters/emergencies including: the deployment of emergency response teams, establishment of joint field office, coordination of overall incident, provision of funds, and issuance of mission assignments to include those assigned for the MA mission. The Department of Health and Human Services provides oversight of Emergency Support Function (ESF) #8, the ESF applicable to mass fatality management, and is responsible for assisting the ME/C office in coordinating response activities.

National Response Framework

According to the National Response Framework (NRF) the responsibility for responding to disaster incidents begins at the local level, specifically the local government affected by the disaster. The NRF however, plays a key role in helping community leaders mitigate the effects of the disaster event by facilitating the involvement of state, federal, and private sector assets prepared to aid the local response effort. MA activities are included within ESF #8—Public Health and Medical Services.

National Mass-Fatality Management Framework

Once assets are deployed, DOD units must interface with civilian entities in accordance with the National

Incident Management System's Incident Command System (ICS). DOD assets will interface with civilian response units within the ICS. MA units will operate within the operations section, as part of a fatality management branch and under the DOD chain of command at all times.

Chemical, Biological, Radiological, and Nuclear Consequence Management

During chemical, biological, radiological, and nuclear (CBRN) events that go beyond the ability of a state to respond, USNORTHCOM or USPACOM will activate and deploy CBRN response forces tailored to the scale and scope of the incident. When authorized by SecDef, DOD MA assets can help mitigate the potential health risks posed by mass fatalities and assist in incident response and recovery operations.

Homeland Defense

GCCs are responsible for coordinating DOD MA operations within their AORs. In DSCA incidents, local, tribal, or state ME/Cs will usually maintain jurisdiction over both military and civilian fatalities, including decedents from mass fatality incidents.

Contaminated Human Remains and Personal Effects

Overview of Department of Defense Operations in a Contaminated Environment

CBRN consequence management is a US Government–level responsibility to which DOD will provide support as directed to DHS, the Department of State, or other appropriate departments and agencies in the conduct of CBRN response. All DOD installations develop and exercise CBRN response plans, which outline operations and give tasks to staff functions such as public health and medical services, public affairs, legal counsel, and MA.

Mortuary Affairs Operations in a Contaminated Environment

The primary MA mission in a CBRN environment is the establishment and operation of a mortuary affairs contaminated human remains mitigation site (MACRMS) to complete MA ID tasks and contamination mitigation. Unit personnel, wearing appropriate mission-oriented protective posture gear, are responsible for the recovery of deceased unit members while evacuating the area. The unit will establish a collection point (CP). The unit will transport the human remains to either the CP or to the MACRMS as directed. The MACRMS is an established location utilizing specialized equipment where MA personnel safely handle contaminated human remains and perform the MA tasks.

Theater Mortuary Evacuation Point Operations

The TMEP will receive all human remains processed and cleared for evacuation from the MA processing point for contaminated human remains. The TMEP will not process these human remains but rather act as a transfer point.

Port Mortuary

The port mortuary will receive the human remains from the TMEP and store them until coordination for final disposition can be made. The AFME will determine the handling procedures for human remains marked with CBRN labels on a case by case basis, based on contaminant and exposure levels.

CONCLUSION

This publication provides joint doctrine for MA support in joint operations. It outlines procedures for the search, recovery, evacuation (to include tracking of human remains), tentative ID, processing, and/or temporary interment of human remains. This publication addresses both the DOD's MA responsibilities in regards to civil support duties under Commander, USNORTHCOM and to the other GCCs. It further addresses decontamination procedures for handling contaminated human remains and provides for the handling of PE of deceased and missing personnel.

CHAPTER I
MORTUARY AFFAIRS PROGRAM

> *"Show me the manner in which a nation cares for its dead, and I will measure with mathematical exactness, the tender mercies of its people, their loyalty to high ideals, and their regard for the laws of the land."*
>
> **William Ewart Gladstone**
> **British Prime Minister (four times between 1864 and 1894)**

1. Introduction

The Joint Mortuary Affairs Program is a broadly based military program providing for the care and disposition of missing and deceased personnel, including personal effects (PE). Based on the guidance and direction of the Secretary of Defense (SecDef) and the Chairman of the Joint Chiefs of Staff (CJCS), the Joint Mortuary Affairs Program provides guidance to the combatant commands (CCMDs) and Services. The combatant commanders (CCDRs) develop implementation plans based on CJCS policy and doctrine. Each Service implements the doctrine. The Joint Mortuary Affairs Program provides support across the range of military operations for:

a. Search, recovery, identification (ID), evacuation, temporary interment, disinterment, contamination mitigation, and reinterment of deceased US military personnel, US civilians and others (when requested by the Department of State [DOS]), and multinational partner, third country, local national, and adversary personnel. These mortuary affairs (MA) functions may be performed, under the civil support construct, in support of federal, state, or tribal authorities when requested by a jurisdictional federal department or agency and authorized by SecDef.

b. Operating MA processing points during military operations. MA processing points include mortuary affairs collection points (MACPs), theater mortuary evacuation points (TMEPs), MA processing points for contaminated remains, temporary interment sites, PE depots, and Department of Defense (DOD) mortuaries.

c. Preparing and coordinating shipment of human remains to the place designated by the person authorized to direct disposition of human remains (PADD).

d. Operation of the port mortuary at Dover Air Force Base (AFB), Delaware, and DOD mortuaries outside the continental United States (OCONUS) for the preparation of human remains and coordination of final disposition. Establishment of other port mortuaries, if so directed.

Note: The Armed Forces Medical Examiner System (AFMES) may, for logistical or operational purposes, delegate the use of an OCONUS mortuary.

e. Collecting, inventorying, storing, and processing PE of deceased and missing US military personnel, US civilians and others (when requested by DOS), and multinational partner, third country, local national, and adversary personnel.

f. Developing standards and specifications for the preparation of human remains, cremation, caskets, and urns.

g. Compilation of records and other data to support search and recovery (S&R) of human remains during operations in the theater.

h. Developing standard policies and procedures for implementation of the Joint Mortuary Affairs Program.

2. Mortuary Affairs Policy

Policy as stated in Department of Defense Directive (DODD) 1300.22, *Mortuary Affairs Policy*, is that the human remains of all members of the Armed Forces of the United States will be returned for permanent disposition in accordance with the decedent's will or the laws of the state (territory, possession, or country) of the decedent's legal residence as directed by the PADD. OCONUS, geographic combatant commanders (GCCs) will determine if and when operational constraints necessitate a transition to a program of temporary interment in their area of responsibility (AOR) for United States Pacific Command (USPACOM); this applies to non-US portions of the USPACOM AOR. When military necessity or other factors prevent evacuation of human remains, the remains may be kept in refrigerated storage or temporarily interred according to established procedures. The GCC makes the temporary interment decision, and the responsibility may not be delegated to subordinate commanders. GCCs may implement temporary interment to accommodate the mandate of some religious communities for a timely interment. Such policy may not be identical between US, multinational partner, local national, or adversary personnel. Interments performed within the scope and direction of the GCC are temporary, except for at sea disposition and when human remains are contaminated and present an ongoing threat to the living. Disinterment may commence when evacuation of the human remains is operationally acceptable. The recovery, evacuation, tentative ID, and final disposition of deceased military and civilian personnel under the jurisdiction of the Armed Forces of the United States are command responsibilities. Unit commanders who sustain losses are responsible for the recovery and evacuation of human remains to the nearest MA site. For humanitarian, health, and morale reasons in foreign countries, this policy may be extended to the local populace fatalities. It is DOD policy that:

a. The human remains of all members of the Armed Forces of the United States will be provided permanent disposition to the extent authorized in their appropriate Service regulations or by federal statutes.

b. All human remains shall be handled with reverence, care, priority, and dignity befitting them and the circumstances, in accordance with Defense Transportation Regulation 4500.9-R, Part VII, *Human Remains Movement*.

c. To the extent possible, PE will be returned to the person eligible to receive effects (PERE) as rapidly as possible. Only custody of the PE is transferred from the Service concerned to the PERE. Any question of title or ownership must be determined by agreement among the interested parties, or, if necessary, the civil courts in the county, tribal, or state domicile of the deceased or missing person.

d. Every reasonable effort will be made to identify human remains and fully account for unrecovered human remains of US military personnel, government employees, government contractors, their dependents, and others who die in military operations, training accidents, and other fatality incidents.

e. Temporary interment is a last resort to protect unit health, safety, and sanitation. Temporary interment should be only considered after all other courses of action (COAs) have been explored. Authority for temporary interment in a theater resides with the GCC. Burial at sea may be authorized by the ship's captain only when a preservation capability is not available aboard ship or when transfer to shore is not operationally feasible. The commander of a geographic CCMD OCONUS may approve temporary interments when human remains are contaminated with chemical, biological, radiological, and nuclear (CBRN) hazards and adequate contamination mitigation is not possible without endangering other personnel. Human remains will be disinterred as soon as possible based upon operational and safety requirements.

f. The preservation of human remains and PE will be given the highest priority. Every effort will be made to preserve the condition of human remains including those recovered from past conflicts.

g. MA personnel afford human remains a uniformly high level of dignity and respect regardless of the status of the deceased, whether military or civilian, and regardless of the circumstances under which the fatalities occurred, whether combat or noncombat.

h. DOD may provide mortuary support for the disposition of human remains and PE upon the request of DOS. The Under Secretary of Defense for Personnel and Readiness will coordinate this support with DOS to include cost reimbursement, where appropriate.

i. The disposition of allied, multinational partner, combatant or noncombatant host nation (HN), or third country human remains will likewise be given the same dignity and respect afforded US personnel. Coordination for handover to the HN will reside with the GCC in coordination with, and in conjunction with, the DOS through the HN embassy or the International Red Cross or Red Crescent, as appropriate.

j. The policy for supplying MA support to civil authorities in the United States is discussed in Chapter VII, "Homeland Defense and Defense Support of Civil Authorities."

3. **Joint Mortuary Affairs Program**

a. **Local Support.** During peacetime and peace operations, mortuary services are provided at the local level by regional Service mortuaries or through established Service contracts. Human remains are prepared and returned to a place designated by the PADD for permanent disposition. Decedent's PE are shipped to the PERE in accordance with Service regulations and procedures.

b. **Military Operations.** During military operations when local support capabilities are exceeded or not available, DOD can direct all human remains go to a specified mortuary, normally the port mortuary at Dover AFB. The specified mortuary will provide positive ID (if augmented by AFMES), provide mortuary services, and return human remains to a place designated by the PADD for permanent disposition.

c. The Joint Mortuary Affairs Program further covers emergency situations, such as S&R efforts for mass fatality incidents and temporary interment of remains when no other option is available.

d. The program provides for professional mortuary services, supplies, and related services to statutorily eligible personnel.

4. **Military Mortuary Affairs Support**

a. **Unit Level.** MA support begins at the unit level. Commanders are responsible for the recovery and evacuation of human remains of assigned and attached personnel (military, DOD civilian and contractor) to the nearest MA facility (usually located at the nearest support area). The Marine Corps Personnel Retrieval and Processing (PRP) Company provides S&R teams in support of units within the Marine Corps operational area. Each Service will notify the next of kin (NOK) (this includes special operations forces and other personnel who may not be assigned to a Service component command). Service instructions for casualty matters such as notification are provided in Department of Defense Instruction (DODI) 1300.18, *Department of Defense (DOD) Personnel Casualty Matters, Policies, and Procedures.*

b. **Mortuary Affairs Collection Point.** The Air Force, Marine Corps, and Army have personnel with MA training and have the capability to establish and operate MACPs. The Army, however, is the only Service with an Active Component dedicated MA force structure and the capability to provide backup support to all Services and is often tasked to operate MACPs on an area basis. Once the MACP receives human remains from the evacuating unit, the human remains are logged in and a case file is established. At that time, all classified documents, hazardous materials, weapons, and munitions are removed. Investigative agencies may collect evidence as required and provide it to the AFMES as warranted. Human remains should be handled with great care in regard to preservation of forensic evidence. Organizational clothing and individual equipment should not be removed in the operational area without approval of the AFMES. The human remains should not be cleaned or fingerprinted except by authorized investigative authorities or at the direction of the AFMES. Investigative personnel should use non-invasive fingerprinting methods to obtain the fingerprints whenever possible. PE should be inventoried for accountability and chain of custody. PE should remain with the human remains during evacuation. The human remains are tagged and placed in a human remains pouch (HRP). The HRP is sealed with a metal, numeric seal if available. The seal number is recorded in the case file. The human remains are refrigerated in secure storage until transportation is coordinated and human remains are recorded for manifest. Human remains should be evacuated as quickly as possible, using air transport, when available, or retrograde convoys, to the TMEP. The TMEP is usually located in a secure area on, or near, an aerial port of embarkation (APOE).

Movement of human remains is situational and theater specific and should be accomplished in the most expedient manner possible.

c. **Theater Mortuary Evacuation Point Support.** The TMEP provides general support (GS) to all authorized personnel within the theater of operations, and can operate as an MACP for units in the area. Upon receipt at the TMEP, the human remains are received and processed utilizing quality control (QC) procedures to complete case files prior to evacuation from theater. Photographs are taken as required to document the human remains without removal of clothing or equipment, or further manipulation. After processing, the noncommissioned officer in charge (NCOIC) will make the determination if a new HRP is required to protect and preserve the human remains. PE are inventoried or re-inventoried as required. When discrepancies are found, an investigation will be initiated. Numeric seals will not be broken without approval of the theater mortuary affairs office (TMAO). Safety of personnel always has priority over procedures. HRPs will have a numeric seal affixed (when possible) prior to evacuation and the seal number recorded in the case file and in the Mortuary Affairs Reporting and Tracking System (MARTS). Chain of custody will be maintained or initiated by TMEP personnel.

d. **Servicing Mortuary.** Human remains are prepared for final disposition at a DOD mortuary after release by the cognizant medical authority. When human remains are received at the mortuary, they are positively identified and prepared for final disposition as directed by the PADD.

5. **Roles and Responsibilities**

a. **Secretary of the Army**

(1) Serve as the executive agent (EA) for MA for DOD consistent with the guidance in DODD 1300.22, *Mortuary Affairs Policy*.

(2) Maintain the Central Joint Mortuary Affairs Board (CJMAB) and appoint a chairman.

b. **Geographic Combatant Commanders**

(1) Give authoritative direction and guidance on providing MA support to all assigned and attached forces physically present in their AOR.

(2) Designate a Service component to serve as the lead Service for the theater MA support program at the AOR level. As necessary, designate a lead Service at selected subordinate joint force commander (JFC) levels and assign responsibilities, tasks, and assets.

(3) Assume lead responsibility and coordination for fatalities occurring within the commander's AOR and assign tasks and assets, and organize commands as necessary to execute the MA mission.

(4) Establish a joint mortuary affairs office (JMAO) to provide oversight of MA support within their AOR. The GCC is authorized to establish a TMAO when the JMAO has

an extended area of operation and a centralized office within a theater is needed for overseeing MA operations. The JMAO and/or TMAO is responsible for detailed MA planning, the execution of the MA support mission, guidance, and policy within the operational area.

(5) Provide MA support to other CCMDs when appropriate.

c. **Commander, United States Transportation Command (USTRANSCOM)** provides strategic airlift to evacuate human remains from OCONUS to a designated DOD mortuary.

d. **Services.** Each Service is responsible for MA support, to include tentative ID and disposition of human remains and PE, for its own personnel unless otherwise directed by the GCC or mutual support agreements between the Services. In all cases, the direct initial contact with family members of deceased personnel is performed by the parent Service.

(1) **US Army Responsibilities**

(a) Maintain an MA force structure capable of providing support to its units and GS to the other Services. The Army will provide collection and evacuation support to the other Services through its facilities. GS, as it relates to MA operations, is defined as activities related to the operation and maintenance of a central MACP, the handling of decedent PE, and any mutually agreed-upon support.

(b) Maintain the records and charter of the CJMAB.

(c) Provide technical assistance to other Services upon request.

(2) **US Navy Responsibilities**

(a) Maintain a force structure to provide MA support for its units. At sea, fatalities are handled by the ship's medical department.

(b) During peacetime, provide or arrange MA support for the Navy, Marine Corps, and Coast Guard when operating as part of the Department of the Navy. Maintain the capability to accomplish burials at sea.

(c) Appoint a member to serve on the CJMAB. The Secretary of the Navy may appoint an additional member from the Marine Corps to serve on the CJMAB.

(3) **US Air Force (USAF) Responsibilities**

(a) Maintain a trained MA force structure capability to provide support for its units.

(b) Appoint a member to serve on the CJMAB.

(c) Provide and maintain the capability to evacuate the deceased of all Services from OCONUS theaters to the specified DOD mortuary.

(d) Operate and maintain a port-of-entry mortuary within the continental United States (CONUS) and as required, establish other CONUS port-of-entry mortuaries in support of all Services.

(4) **US Marine Corps Responsibilities.** Maintain an MA force structure capability to provide support to Marine Corps units.

(5) **US Coast Guard Responsibilities**

(a) In the US and its possessions and territories, provide or arrange MA support for its own personnel.

(b) Manage an MA program using civilian providers. Maintain the capability to accomplish burials at sea.

e. **Central Joint Mortuary Affairs Board**

(1) The CJMAB functions as a coordinating board for MA policy, procedures, mobilization planning, recommendations on mortuary services during military operations and promotes uniform Service policies, procedures, plans, and records for the disposition of human remains and PE.

(2) The CJMAB meets at least twice a year or at the call of the Chairman of the CJMAB to support special incidents. In the case of prolonged hostile action, the Chairman of the CJMAB determines if there is a requirement to activate a full-time CJMAB. If activated, the CJMAB becomes the governing body from which MA wartime policy will be promulgated to the Services. However, as a governing body, the CJMAB does not exercise command and control (C2) over the Services' MA functions, personnel, and facilities. C2 responsibilities are retained by the individual Services.

(3) Functions of the CJMAB may include, but are not limited to, disposition of human remains, PE programs, and, as necessary, CONUS military mortuary expansion. Peacetime guidelines also include procedures for supporting mass casualty/fatality incidents (MC/FIs).

For additional information, refer to DODD 1300.22, Mortuary Affairs Policy.

f. **Joint POW/MIA [Prisoner of War/Missing in Action]Accounting Command (JPAC).** JPAC's mission is to achieve the fullest possible accounting of all Americans missing as a result of the Nation's past conflicts.

g. **Joint Mortuary Affairs Center (JMAC)**

(1) The US Army's JMAC provides comprehensive MA expertise and technical assistance to all Services and CCMDs; monitors current operations, exercises, and readiness;

interfaces with federal and DOD agencies on MA matters; and maintains MA records as required.

(2) The JMAC will provide recommendations to the CJMAB on changes in MA policy and procedures.

h. **Armed Forces Medical Examiner System**

(1) The roles and responsibilities of the AFMES are outlined in Title 10, United States Code (USC), Section 1471; DODD 5154.24, *Armed Forces Institute of Pathology (AFIP)*; DODI 5154.30, *Armed Forces Institute of Pathology Operations.*

(2) In general, the Armed Forces Medical Examiner (AFME) has the authority to conduct a forensic pathology investigation, including an autopsy, of the death of any military member serving on active duty where the US Government (USG) has exclusive jurisdictional authority, including where the circumstances surrounding the death are suspicious, unexpected, or unexplained. In wartime, the AFMES will review every case to determine the cause and manner of death to secure information for completion of military records, to obtain data for substantiating protective equipment, to protect the welfare of the military community (such as in the investigation of novel wounding agents or possible "friendly fire" incidents), or when the Service member is an aircrew member and the death occurs during flight operations (and not as a result of hostile fire). The AFME, in consultation with relevant law enforcement, intelligence, and safety agencies, and the GCC or subordinate JFC, has the authority to order such autopsies in the operational area or upon the return of human remains to other locations. The AFMES has the expertise in the fields of forensic sciences related to ID and is the DOD scientific authority for the ID of human remains in current deaths and other deceased individuals for whom a death certificate has not been issued. These techniques include, but are not limited to, anthropological examination, antemortem/postmortem dental comparison, deoxyribonucleic acid (DNA) analysis, and consultation with the Federal Bureau of Investigation (FBI) for antemortem/postmortem latent print comparison. The AFME also provides medical certification for cause of death and manner of death. Services and CCMDs may request from the AFME assistance in the ID of any human remains. Normally, the AFMES operates as a supporting agency to the supported CCDR. The AFME coordinates with the CCDR and Services to determine if AFMES support is required.

j. **Port-of-Entry Mortuary Facility.** The Air Force Mortuary at Dover AFB, Delaware, is the designated port-of-entry mortuary facility. It handles most human remains from OCONUS to include wartime fatalities. Human remains are embalmed (as required), dressed, casketed, and prepared for shipment. Coordination is made with the Services to arrange for the disposition of the human remains as directed by the PADD. During military operations or MC/FIs, the Air Force Mortuary at Dover AFB can be tasked to provide mortuary services to include autopsy, medical examination, positive ID, embalming, cremation, dressing, casketing, and preparation and shipment for final disposition when supported by the AFMES.

k. **Religious Support Team (RST) and Behavioral (Mental) Health Support.** Given the context of mortality surrounding MA and the hostile conditions that may exist, causing extreme stress, Service component RSTs and behavioral health professionals should be utilized for combat and operational stress control/management.

l. **Emergency Family Assistance Center (EFAC).** In an MC/FI, whether due to natural disaster or a terrorist event among the US population, a joint EFAC should be established to mitigate the suffering of families. MA needs to work closely with the EFAC in order to facilitate the collection of DNA, notification of NOK, and transfer of PE.

Intentionally Blank

CHAPTER II
MORTUARY AFFAIRS SUPPORT IN A THEATER OF OPERATIONS

"In Flanders Fields the poppies blow
Between the crosses, row on row,
That mark our place; and in the sky
The larks, still bravely singing, fly
Scarce heard amid the guns below.

We are the Dead. Short days ago
We lived, felt dawn, saw sunset glow,
Loved, and were loved, and now we lie
In Flanders Fields."

From the poem "In Flanders Fields"
By Lieutenant Colonel John McCrae, MD, (1872–1918)
Canadian Army

1. Joint Mortuary Affairs Office

a. **Geographic Combatant Command Level.** GCCs normally establish a JMAO within their commands to provide policy to their assigned Service components and support the joint force. The JMAO develops MA-specific directives and geographic-specific operation orders (OPORDs) for the GCC, while providing oversight of Service component MA operations and programs. For additional guidance on the preparation of appendix 3 (Mortuary Affairs) to annex D (Logistics), see Chairman of the Joint Chiefs of Staff Manual (CJCSM) 3122.03, *Joint Operation Planning and Execution System (JOPES), Volume II, Planning Formats.* The JMAO oversight responsibilities may include the following:

(1) Implementing procedures concerned with S&R, evacuation, tentative ID, and return of human remains. This may include providing operational guidance to Service components and to subordinate joint force or single-Service commands on the disposition of human remains of those personnel assigned or attached to multinational forces.

(2) In coordination with the Service components and Service logistic support commands, determine the appropriate levels of mortuary supplies and equipment in theater. The Services are responsible for maintaining the levels assigned to them.

(3) Providing procedural guidance concerning transfer of adversary, multinational military and civilian human remains and their PE to the custody of another government, including maintenance of records required by the Geneva Conventions.

(4) Coordinating the development of the MA support plan for the AOR. Ensuring all Service components are informed of support locations and comply with directives.

(5) Coordinating with Service component commands for data on the recovery status of deceased and missing personnel.

(6) Coordinating the establishment of other offices or multinational force liaisons, as required, to supervise MA activities for a Service component, subordinate joint force, or on a geographic basis.

(7) Designating port of embarkation (POE) holding facilities and surface and aerial evacuation routes of human remains and PE.

(8) Coordinating holding facilities, interment, disinterment, and reinterment of human remains within the AOR. In wartime, this includes providing a recommendation to the respective GCC regarding temporary disposition of human remains when return to the US has been operationally or logistically challenged or human remains pose a health concern.

(9) Maintaining a central records point for deceased personnel and PE.

(10) Continuing to function after periods of military operations to oversee Service efforts to resolve the status and effect the evacuation of human remains and PE not previously accomplished. The GCC determines if the JMAO will continue to function in support of efforts to process human remains and PE of non-US military personnel. The Service component's headquarters coordinates transfer of human remains and records to parent Service control in the US. Parent Service headquarters are responsible for final archiving of records. The JMAO assists Service headquarters in coordinating these actions.

(11) Monitoring established agreements with affected countries, multinational partners, USG, and nongovernmental organizations (NGOs). If agreements are not established, the JMAO may coordinate and negotiate for affected country support in coordination with host country laws, Service component mortuary office, or GCC. If agreements cannot be negotiated, MA support is performed under current US military procedures in coordination with host country laws.

(12) Maintaining liaison with the joint force public affairs office.

(13) Coordinating with the joint environmental management board on MA environmental protection activities as required.

(14) Publishing guidance on environmental protection requirements and references as required.

(15) Delegating responsibilities to and providing oversight of the TMAOs.

b. **JMAO at the Subordinate Joint Force Level**

(1) A subunified command or joint task force (JTF) may establish a JMAO.

(2) If determined necessary, the GCC may delegate MA support authority to the subordinate command, which will allow the commander to designate a lead Service component (usually the Army) to handle MA for the command. Additionally, the subordinate JFC may direct the logistics directorate of a joint staff (J-4) to establish and

operate a joint task force–mortuary affairs office (JTF-MAO). If established, the JTF-MAO should:

(a) Provide guidance to facilitate the conduct of MA programs.

(b) Maintain data pertaining to the recovery, tentative ID, and temporary disposition of all US deceased or missing in the designated operational area.

(c) Maintain data pertaining to the recovery, tentative ID, and temporary disposition of all other deceased in the operational area in accordance with the Geneva Conventions.

(d) Serve as an MA liaison between the subordinate JFC, the Service component MA offices, and the TMAO.

(e) Serve as the central clearing point for MA-related information.

(f) Monitor the deceased and missing personnel PE program.

(g) Perform planning, execution, technical, and management functions.

(h) Develop and disseminate standards and procedures as well as collect and present MA management statistical data.

2. Operational Mortuary Affairs Support

a. Clear command relationships, to include support relationships, must be defined and articulated to all concerned as MA assets are normally distributed throughout the operational area and may support several units simultaneously. MA teams will normally be assigned general or direct support relationships to their supported units. Command relationships are addressed in Joint Publication (JP) 1, *Doctrine for the Armed Forces of the United States;* JP 3-0, *Joint Operations;* and JP 5-0, *Joint Operation Planning*.

b. Operational MA support can be broken down into four types of support:

(1) Direct Support (DS). DS is to a specific force and authorizes the MA team to answer directly to the supported forces request for assistance (RFA). An example would be a specific S&R team assigned to a unit for a specified mission assignment. The S&R team would answer directly to the supported unit until the mission was completed.

(2) Area Support. Area support is not a support relationship, but rather a method by which a unit may provide support. A good example is a combat sustainment support battalion (CSSB). Within its capability, it may support all units operating within its operational area, hence area support.

(3) General Support. GS is a support relationship that can be established between units. The Army is to provide backup general MA support to all Services when the Service capability to handle its own MA functions is exhausted or not resident. GS is given to a

supported force as a whole and not to any particular subdivision thereof. The TMEP would be a GS asset.

(4) Inter-Service Support. Inter-Service support is support provided by another Service to support operations. Marine Corps intertheater air support for transport of remains between MACP and TMEP locations would be an inter-Service support asset. Inter-Service support relationships are usually spelled out in agreements or theater orders or directives.

3. **Command and Control of Army Mortuary Affairs Assets**

a. **Introduction**

(1) The deployment and assignment of US Army MA assets is dynamic and can be readily tailored to meet operational requirements. The company structure allows for deployment of a collection team, an MA platoon, or the company as a whole.

(2) Regardless of size of the deployed MA element, the gaining command must develop and publish the command relationship for MA within the operational area. When other Service MA assets are deployed, they may have a different C2 structure.

b. **Tailored Deployment**

(1) Tailored deployment of the MA company has been the norm for the majority of military operations over the past two decades. Operational considerations and constraints often limit the deployment of MA assets into the operational area. Forward collection platoons or even individual collection sections may be deployed into the operational area. Scarce MA assets will likely be controlled as a theater asset.

(2) An MA collection section will usually be under the operational control (OPCON) of a US Army sustainment brigade. When the MACP is physically separated from the sustainment brigade, it may be placed under the tactical control (TACON) of the logistics unit commander on the installation where it is located. TACON in this aspect may be limited to force protection and specific support requirements determined by operational mission analysis. The MACP would provide GS within the sustainment brigade's operational area.

c. **Company Deployment**

(1) Full deployment of the MA company may occur during a major area conflict. When this occurs, the unit does not remain as a whole during the deployment. The various MA platoons/sections will be distributed throughout the area of operations per JMAO/TMAO guidance. MA assets may be tasked to provide any level of support based on mission requirements and availability of assets. C2 of the various MA elements must be established to ensure mission success.

(a) The MA company is usually assigned, attached, or placed under the OPCON of a CSSB to provide GS to a sustainment brigade's operational area.

(b) The main collection platoon may be OPCON to a CSSB to provide GS to a sustainment brigade's operational area.

(c) An MA collection section may be OPCON to a different CSSB than the one controlling the company to provide GS to another sustainment brigade's operational area.

(d) An MA collection section may be TACON to a brigade support battalion providing DS to a brigade combat team.

(2) Once coordination is complete and MA sites are established, the locations are published to the units within the operational area. All human remains within the theater of operations or operational area will be evacuated through the TMEP. Therefore, this notification must be to all Services and supported multinational partners, not just Army forces.

(3) The TMEP and PE depot placement within the operational environment are based upon the TMAO guidance. Normally these platoons will be OPCON to a sustainment brigade within the theater. Regardless of the size of the operational area, a TMEP and PE depot are usually established to coordinate evacuation of human remains and PE out of the operational area.

4. **Temporary Storage, Interment, and Disinterment Operations**

a. Commanders are responsible for temporary storage, interment, and disinterment operations to ensure the preservation and accountability of human remains under their control. The primary objectives of these operations are to maintain morale and field sanitation and to comply with the law of war, international law, and international agreements. However, human remains are to be evacuated as long as the operational situation permits. The exception to this is the evacuation of adversary human remains, which will be interred unless they are turned over to the HN or the Red Cross/Red Crescent. If they are interred, the site must be noted on accountability records as an interment site.

(1) The GCC is responsible to ensure that all US human remains that are temporarily interred are disinterred and returned to the US for disposition to the extent possible based on operational and public health and safety considerations. This responsibility is carried out by the JMAO. In the event that the human remains of multinational partner personnel are present at the interment site, it should be maintained if operationally feasible until custody of the site can be transferred to the appropriate government. The JMAO is responsible for monitoring, coordinating, and providing special guidance during disinterment operations.

(2) It is the responsibility of the designated MA lead Service component commander to coordinate and supervise disinterment operations within the designated operational area. The MA lead Service normally provides specialized equipment, personnel, and other support as necessary to accomplish the mission. Each individual component commander's MA office coordinates with the JMAO and obtains records and reports of temporary interments that will be necessary during the disinterment.

(3) Handling US dependent and/or US civilian fatalities will be conducted in the same manner as US military personnel. The same records and reports are used.

(4) When conducting interment/disinterment operations, it is important to take religious considerations into account when feasible.

(5) Interment and disinterment records to include burial at sea are forwarded to the JMAC upon completion of military operations. The JMAC will maintain historical records of all interment and disinterment operations to include burial at sea during military operations conducted by US MA forces.

b. **Temporary Storage.** Temporary storage of US, multinational partner, third country, local national, and adversary human remains is necessary to slow down decomposition while waiting processing or transportation. Refrigerated storage maintained at a temperature between 34 and 40 degrees Fahrenheit or 1.1 and 4.4 degrees Celsius should be pushed as far forward as possible. If refrigerated storage is not available, then keep the human remains stored under a tent or inside a hardened structure out of the elements. Never stack human remains when they are in an HRP only. Transfer cases containing human remains may be stacked for storage transportation purposes when operationally necessary (such as for security reasons or when there are limited refrigeration storage or transportation assets). When temporary storage or transport is not an option, temporary interment may be authorized by the GCC.

c. **Temporary Interment**

(1) The expedient and respectful repatriation of deceased personnel to the PADD is the top priority of the joint MA program. However, during extreme tactical or logistic situations that leave no alternatives, a program of temporary interment may be implemented. All interments, whether performed at the unit level or by MA personnel, are considered temporary except for committal at sea.

(2) Temporary interment of US or multinational partner human remains outside the respective national borders is the least preferred method. Every effort should be made to return human remains to the respective nation as soon as possible. When interment sites are established, separate sites should be established for the temporary interment of US, multinational partner, and adversary deceased. Unit commanders must obtain permission from the GCC to conduct temporary interment operations. In extreme circumstances, when a unit is cut off and has no means to communicate with higher headquarters, the senior commander is responsible for deciding whether temporary interment will be utilized after all known support options have failed. When operational or logistic circumstances prohibit the evacuation of human remains and the temporary interment of human remains is necessary, recovery operations should be conducted as soon as possible. For further guidance, see Appendix B, "Mass Interment."

d. **Isolated Interments**

(1) When the tactical situation requires a unit to move out of an area in an expedient manner without evacuating human remains, the unit may request permission

through command channels from the GCC to conduct isolated interments. Isolated interments are individual shallow graves constructed to prevent leaving human remains unattended in open areas. Inter all PE and other ID media with the human remains. Do not remove the ID tags or the ID card from the human remains under any circumstances. Attempt to mark the interment site in a manner that is easily distinguishable for future recovery teams.

(2) The unit prepares and submits an incident report on the isolated interment to higher headquarters as soon as time permits. This report should then be forwarded through channels to the joint MA office. Timely and accurate documentation from the unit is vital in ensuring that all human remains are recovered and evacuated in a timely manner. At a minimum, the incident report should include the following: 10-digit grid coordinates (by Global Positioning System [GPS]), the number of isolated graves, the tentative ID of each human remains, and how each isolated grave is marked.

e. **Committal at Sea.** When death occurs aboard ship, or when human remains are recovered from the sea, the human remains should be preserved for burial on land. This is applicable whether the human remains are US, multinational partner, or adversary. Committal at sea is permissible only when refrigerated storage facilities cannot be made available aboard ship and transfer to shore cannot be accomplished within a reasonable time or is operationally inadvisable.

(1) Prior to committal, the ship's commanding officer ensures that the human remains are identified. When feasible the commanding officer should contact the AFMES for guidance on obtaining ID media and biological samples prior to committal. Examine ID tags and then securely place them on the human remains. Remove PE from the human remains and examine them for ID value. Establish an ID case file, which consists of a statement of recognition from two individuals and a certificate of death signed by a medical officer. If assets are available, take fingerprints, dental x-rays, and a blood or tissue sample (for DNA) and place into the ID case file. Include any onboard medical and/or dental records in the ID case file.

(2) The ship's commanding officer appoints an officer to be in charge of the committal. The officer in charge (OIC) is responsible for accurately recording all facts, to

"The Mexican War (1846–1847) provided the first real test of the Army's ability to care for its war dead, but with results that were far from satisfactory. In one instance, General Zachary Taylor saw to it that the dead were properly collected and buried on the battlefield following his celebrated victory at Buena Vista. Unfortunately, he neglected to mark the site of the burial on the map accompanying his official report. Years later, when the US Government sought to erect a monument to honor the fallen heroes, no burial site could be found. A similar experience marked the campaign of General Winfield Scott, whose troops landed at Vera Cruz and marched overland to Mexico City. Of the hundreds who died and were buried along the way, only a fraction were located afterward."

Dr. Steven E. Anders
Quartermaster Professional Bulletin, September 1988

include the exact latitude and longitude, on the committal in the ship's log and for ensuring that due respect and honors be paid to the deceased. Prepare the deceased for committal by covering or shrouding the human remains with an HRP or other suitable material. The human remains are then weighted to ensure rapid submersion. For the human remains of US military personnel, drape the human remains with the US flag, hold religious services, and conduct military honors as authorized according to applicable regulations. The flag is used to drape the human remains prior to interment; it is not interred with the human remains, nor is it committed to the sea. If the human remains' identity is unknown, no US or other national flag shall drape the body. The human remains may be committed to the sea with the words appropriate for the individual being committed.

(3) The OIC is responsible for ensuring that all PE belonging to the deceased are gathered, inventoried, packaged, sealed, and safeguarded until proper disposition is arranged. Depending on the MA program and the support structure that is in place, the PE are either shipped to the PE depot, to the TMEP, or if the PE have been properly screened, directly to the PERE. Upon committal at sea, the OIC sends the ID case file and a report containing the facts of the committal, to include the distribution of the PE, through higher headquarters to the JMAO.

f. **Disinterment.** Disinterment operations should be conducted as soon as the tactical situation on the ground permits. When disinterment occurs and when arrangements are made to transfer human remains to the TMEP, host country, or a multinational partner, commanders will maintain accountability records and provide information for US, adversary or multinational partner deceased transferred from temporary interment sites for which they have responsibility.

5. **Mortuary Affairs Support to Non-United States Personnel**

a. **Interment of Multinational Forces.** Existing standardization agreements should be used whenever possible to facilitate common policies and procedures among participating nations. If agreements do not exist and the US is the lead nation, US policy and doctrine have primacy. If agreements do not exist and another nation is charged with lead nation responsibility, US policy would apply only to US forces and citizens, unless otherwise adopted by the multinational force. The GCC should exercise situational judgment if required to blend MA throughout the multinational force. The following procedures are applicable where no other guidance is available.

(1) When possible, the same records and reports as for US military personnel are accomplished and maintained.

(2) When interment is required, separate interment sites should be established for the burial of multinational and adversary dead. Separate sections are provided for US, multinational, and adversary deceased when circumstances require interment in a US interment site.

(3) PE of multinational personnel are processed in accordance with standing agreements. In the absence of agreements, PE are processed in accordance with US MA procedures.

b. **Interment of Detainees.** MA personnel process adversary detainee human remains and PE in accordance with the Geneva Convention Relative to the Treatment of Prisoners of War. In addition, a copy of the interment or disinterment records to include operational burial at sea records will be forwarded to the JMAC upon completion of military operations. MA personnel process civilian detainees in accordance with the Geneva Convention relative to the Protection of Civilian Persons in Time of War.

6. **Strategic Implications of Mortuary Affairs Interaction with the Death of Non-US Civilians and Noncombatants**

a. While it is in the interest of US and multinational forces to not be involved in the handling of the human remains of civilian and noncombatant deaths, this is a situation with specific political and cultural sensitivities that cannot always be avoided.

b. While not responsible for MA, civil affairs (CA) personnel can act as intermediaries between affected organizations and local government or families.

c. CA personnel can assist local agencies in interfacing with US military assets providing support to transport the human remains. This can include assistance with customs; location of storage facilities, burial sites, transportation options; and providing linguists. CA personnel advise the command on cultural traditions impacting the handling and transport of human remains.

d. Another special case is MA support to contractors and employees from third countries, unrelated to the ongoing theater of operation, that were employed by a USG contract. CA has been useful in interacting with the US embassy and foreign embassies in order to facilitate return of human remains to the home country.

For further guidance, refer to JP 3-57, Civil-Military Operations.

7. **Mass Casualty/Fatality Incident Considerations**

a. GCCs are responsible for the proper execution of MA when such events occur within their AOR. This may include coordinating the supervision and execution of matters pertaining to the search for, recovery, and evacuation of human remains to a military mortuary, either within their AOR or in the US, and for the collection and processing of the PE of the dead. This also includes coordination with the HN, DOS, and the country team.

b. Coordination with the AFME is mandatory in all peacetime MC/FIs, no matter where the incident occurs.

c. In determining the evacuation of human remains from a peacetime MC/FI event overseas, consideration should be given to transporting the human remains from the place of incident to a US mortuary for ID and preparation. The GCC, in coordination with the applicable Services and the AFME, is the final authority for this decision.

d. The GCC in whose AOR the loss of personnel occurs is responsible for executing the recovery phase of the operation, regardless of the Service of the deceased. To the extent possible, the GCC notifies the commander of the deceased concerning all evacuation actions.

e. The GCC of the AOR where the military mortuary is located is responsible for executing the ID processing and preparation phase of the MC/FI operation, regardless of the Service of the deceased.

f. DOS or other federal departments and agencies may request DOD assistance in MC/FIs that do not involve military personnel. Coordination among the CCMDs, CJCS, and federal department or agency representatives will be made to determine appropriate jurisdiction. The requesting agency provides appropriate funding for military support.

g. Requests for special transportation for MC/FIs are coordinated with USTRANSCOM.

h. Interagency and inter-Service coordination of assets is key to success. Depending on the location and incident, agencies such as the FBI (criminal/terrorist activity), Red Cross/Red Crescent (natural disaster), and federal, state, tribal, and local health and human services agencies will be involved as well as law enforcement at all levels. Depending on the location and incident, federal departments and agencies may also have jurisdiction over the mission or operation.

i. Specialized support personnel may be required, accessing capabilities within the Services (e.g., Seabees, engineers, CBRN) to assist in processing the scene or extracting deceased personnel. How support personnel are identified and sourced is a Service responsibility.

8. Legal Considerations

a. The legal considerations for MA support in a theater of operation stem from the commanders' responsibility for health and public hygiene as well as articles of the law of war and the Geneva Conventions. The MA program should include the commander's guidance on the rules of the use of force or rules of engagement and rules for gathering evidence to the forces conducting MA operations. This guidance will safeguard not only the forces conducting MA operations but also safeguard the site and evidence for future criminal investigations or site exploitation.

b. Commanders are responsible for the recovery and transport of US and multinational partner human remains to the nearest MACP or for requesting S&R support, if required. During an operational pause, the commander is required to recover and transport or inter HN or adversary human remains for morale, safety, and health and public hygiene reasons. A trained MA specialist may be required to handle human remains to avoid possible contamination from infectious diseases.

For further guidance on the handling of potentially infectious human remains, see United States Army Center for Health Promotion and Preventive Medicine (USACHPPM) Technical Guide 195, Safety and Health Guidance for Mortuary Affairs Operations: Infectious Materials and CBRN Handling.

c. The JTF-MAO should attempt to coordinate with the members of the Red Cross or Red Crescent for the return of deceased local nationals to local governmental control. Depending on the mission and the political climate of the operation, the JTF may receive limited assistance from the Red Cross or Red Crescent.

d. Disposition of PE must be in accordance with the decedent's will and/or the laws of the country, state, territory, or tribe in which the decedent legally resided and will be as directed by the PERE.

e. Legal investigations are required for deaths of US military personnel except for combat deaths that are unequivocally the result of engagement with opposing forces.

f. Legal investigations are required on all suspected law of war violations, detainee deaths, or war atrocities.

g. MA personnel will not release information on deceased personnel to anyone other than the JMAO or TMAO. Dissemination of information on deceased personnel will be handled through the office of the JMAO/TMAO or AFME.

9. **Special Considerations**

a. **Special Religious and Cultural Considerations**

For information regarding religious and cultural considerations during MA operations refer to Chapter III, "Mortuary Affairs Planning," paragraph 4, "Religious Considerations," and Appendix E, "Religious Support to Mortuary Affairs."

b. **Use of Nonmilitary MA Support.** The use of host-nation support (HNS), local national support, or third country national support should be limited to general labor, administration, transportation, and facility support. Only US military, USG civilians, or DOD contracted civilians should be utilized to accomplish search, recovery, and processing of US human remains and inventory of PE. If an agreement cannot be negotiated, MA support is performed under current US military procedures.

Intentionally Blank

CHAPTER III
MORTUARY AFFAIRS PLANNING

"Logistic considerations belong not only in the highest echelons of military planning during the process of preparation for war and for specific wartime operations, but may well become the controlling element with relation to timing and successful operation."

Vice Admiral Oscar C. Badger, US Navy
Address to the Naval War College, 1954

1. Introduction

During any military operation, MA should be planned in detail and included in plans, orders, and standard operating procedures (SOPs). The plans and orders should cover procedures for employing, shifting, and resourcing MA personnel and equipment throughout the operational area.

2. Planning Guidance

a. **GCCs** are responsible for developing policies for the overall supervision of all MA matters. Additionally, the command's MA plans and orders should include the following:

(1) Broad guidance to component commanders on MA matters that include the interface and coordination required with all concerned parties (e.g., higher headquarters and support headquarters staffs and the AFME), especially in terms of reporting requirements, handling, processing, tracking, and accounting for human remains and their PE.

(2) Designate a lead Service responsible for the implementation of the MA support plan. Circumstances warranting the re-designation of the lead Service from one Service to another should be included.

(3) Establish procedures for operating a JMAO and subarea offices as necessary.

(4) Provide procedural guidance concerning the transfer of the human remains of US military personnel, US civilians and others (when requested by DOS), and multinational partner, third country, local national, and adversary personnel and their accompanying PE to the custody of appropriate governments.

b. **Subordinate commanders** are responsible for ensuring that the MA support guidance from higher headquarters is implemented in their overall operational concept of operations (CONOPS). Planning at the subordinate command levels is more detailed and should facilitate the following:

(1) Designate units and staff agencies responsible for the implementation of the MA CONOPS.

(2) Assign responsibility, authority, and working relationships for each assigned task.

(3) Provide specifics on how to execute the MA CONOPS.

(4) Provide specifics on logistic support required.

(5) Provide methods to monitor the flow of and account for human remains into and out of all MA facilities on a daily basis.

3. Planning Considerations

MA support must be responsive and be able to provide support across the full range of military operations. Prior coordination with USTRANSCOM should be made to arrange for evacuation of human remains. Units capable of providing MA support should be scheduled on the time-phased force and deployment list to arrive at the beginning of any operation. Active Component MA units should be able to sustain operations until Reserve Component MA forces arrive. The lack of MA support during the initial stages of the operation could adversely affect ID, physical condition of the human remains, troop morale, expeditious return of human remains to their families, and personnel replacement system.

a. The MA CONOPS should be developed during the planning process. The appendix may be developed using the guidelines found in Appendix A, "Sample Format for Mortuary Affairs Appendix to an Operation Plan." The MA CONOPS is based on and designed to support the operational requirements of the command. Therefore, MA CONOPS may differ in scope, detail, objectives, and available resources between commands.

b. Commanders and MA support planners at all levels should consider the following during planning and execution.

(1) Review or establish:

(a) North Atlantic Treaty Organization (NATO) standardization agreements (STANAGs).

(b) Quadripartite standardization agreements.

(c) Multinational forces agreements (mortuary).

(d) International Committee of the Red Cross or Red Crescent.

(e) HNS requirements (mortuary).

(f) Acquisition and cross-servicing agreements.

(g) Religious practices associated with the faith of the deceased.

(h) HN laws and territorial or legal jurisdiction.

(i) Status-of-forces agreement.

(2) The number of personnel in the operational area and its size and location will have a large impact on the type of support that will be allocated.

(3) Number of expected fatalities. The manpower and personnel directorate of a joint staff (J-1) prepares a personnel estimate that should contain a casualty estimate. A casualty estimate is formulated by each Service in accordance with individual Service directives to support operations planning, future force planning, and training. Service components comprising a joint force will provide casualty estimates to the joint force J-1 who will then make the information available to the operations directorate of a joint staff, J-4, and the plans directorate of a joint staff. The exact number of fatalities that US military forces will suffer in military operations can never be accurately predicted; therefore, planning for MA support should be continuous and flexible enough to adjust to unanticipated situations. Plans and orders should be reviewed and amended as new facts become available, resources change, and other variables become apparent. The MA CONOPS should be kept simple, be achievable, and provide timely and useful information to those involved.

(4) In any theater, the level of infrastructure development (e.g., port mortuary location, intratheater lines of communications, airfields, and other facilities) will affect sustainment operations. Resources not available are usually brought into the theater via strategic lift resources.

(5) An MA support plan for the AOR must tailor MA support requirements to operational requirements. Operational requirements determine the size of the unit required to support the MA mission. MA support needs to be modular and scalable to meet mission requirements. This concept allows for the deployment of multifunctional teams to perform several MA functions simultaneously (e.g., collection point [CP] and TMEP operations) during small-scale operations. Some operations are politically sensitive, and the number of troops allocated may require special consideration.

(6) When planning operations involving humanitarian assistance (HA)/disaster relief missions, the establishment of an MA liaison officer (LNO) to coordinate between DOD and outside agencies, such as DOS, the Department of Health and Human Services (DHHS), NGOs, and local governments on MA issues, authorities, and COAs, is recommended. The GCC can request JMAC assets to provide the LNO and also provide reachback assistance to the commanders in developing COAs, planning, and analysis.

c. When plans and orders are created, the CONOPS, unit structure and capabilities, unit locations/relocations, and the number of troops being supported must be considered. Unit responsibilities must be specified for the S&R and evacuation of human remains to MACPs and/or the TMEP. These considerations are crucial to planning mission success and should be considered and planned for in meticulous detail. This part of the support plan is based on the high value used as a planning factor for determining numbers of projected fatalities during the initial stages of a conflict. The base plan should address how these problems will be handled until MA support arrives.

For additional guidance on the preparation of appendix 3 (Mortuary Affairs) to annex D (Logistics), see CJCSM 3122.03, Joint Operation Planning and Execution System (JOPES), Volume II, Planning Formats.

d. **Special considerations for operation plan (OPLAN) development are:**

(1) Develop procedures for the handling and transfer of deceased local nationals. Consult the command staff judge advocate (SJA) or command legal advisor and CA personnel on matters pertaining to deceased local nationals (for example, PE and responsibility for disposition). Deaths of persons in US care, such as dislocated civilians seeking help at sites under US control, create other obligations, such as medical certification and recording of deaths. When the HN has the capability, death records should be registered with the host government. If not, US forces should maintain records for later transmittal to host government officials.

(2) Requirements for MA in a CBRN environment include: personnel, equipment, facilities, and established procedures for both the non-MA unit and the MA personnel. For operating procedures for a mortuary affairs contaminated remains mitigation site (MACRMS), contact the JMAC for applicable tactics, techniques, and procedures (TTP). Refer to Appendix G, "Key Points of Contact," for contact information. Also refer to Chapter 8 "Contaminated Human Remains and Personal Effects." Additional guidance on safe handling, mitigation, and management of human remains can be found in USACHPPM Technical Guide 195, *Safety and Health Guidance for Mortuary Affairs Operations: Infectious Materials and CBRN Handling.*

(3) Develop procedures for MA support to USG agencies such as the FBI.

(4) Establish DOD and CCMD reporting procedures in coordination with the SJA for alleged violations of the law of armed conflict resulting in fatalities. Consult the command SJA or command legal advisor to incorporate procedures for safeguarding evidence for future criminal investigations or site exploitation.

(5) Review the current directives regarding handling and repatriation of DOD contractor personnel authorized to accompany the force (CAAF) and non-CAAF personnel for compliance with current directives and/or agreements as these procedures are subject to change.

(6) The GCC's plan may request an additional MA team for S&R capability to support catastrophic incidents or MACRMS operations during the initial phase. If this additional team is in theater, it could alleviate the need for the unit to conduct S&R operations for a catastrophic loss such as a downed aircraft or incident with multiple fatalities.

(7) Integrity of chain of custody of human remains and PE should be a priority for commanders with MA assets. When planning for MA assets, commanders should evaluate requirements and request assets to maintain the chain of custody and asset visibility at air hubs.

e. **Other Planning Considerations**

(1) C2 of the MA operation (reporting officials, chain of command, communications equipment, and administrative requirements).

(2) Number and location of MACPs, TMEPs, and PE depots required.

(3) Location of major road networks, alternate routes, rail lines, airports, and seaports.

(4) Time required for MA to become fully operational.

(5) Time required to call-up MA forces of the Reserve Component.

(6) The use of MA contractor support (only US will process US human remains).

(7) Coordinating intra-theater transportation requirements.

(8) Capability of USTRANSCOM to provide assets for evacuating human remains to the US.

(9) Coordination with mortuaries in and out of the AOR.

(10) Any alliances or agreements with HN and/or multinational forces.

(11) Climatic conditions.

(12) Environment, safety, and sanitation.

(13) HN facilities. What capabilities can the HN provide?

(14) Need for a joint security area threat evaluation plan.

(15) Security for personnel, equipment, sites, facilities, and convoys.

(16) Interface with public affairs, chaplain, legal, medical, and logistic points of contact (POCs).

(17) Interface with NGOs, intergovernmental organizations, embassy officials, and other USG personnel.

(18) During HA, defense support of civil authorities (DSCA), or homeland defense operations, the use of MA investigation teams has proven to be effective to support the MA mission. Investigation elements are trained to interview area personnel and conduct on-site assessment of requirements to conduct recovery operations. Planners should consider requesting the appropriate MA assets to support investigative teams.

(19) Strategic Planning. Request or review the appropriate site and/or country surveys for MA assets and facilities resident in the country identified for US use. If a

country survey has not been conducted or is not current, request one be conducted to determine refrigerated container and refrigerated facility support, morgues, and embalming capabilities, and identify current MA procedures already resident in the country that apply to US forces.

(20) The MA plan should support the commander's communications strategy by addressing public affairs topics such as casualty press releases and photographing and/or video recording the evacuation of human remains.

(21) Contract Support. Use of contract support for MA operations may include contract support for such items as ice and refrigerated storage as well as cadaver dogs to support S&R operations for mass fatality or collapsed structure recovery operations.

(22) Communications support for MARTS.

(23) Requirement for MA mitigation procedures, personnel, equipment, and facilities in the event of a CBRN incident.

4. Religious Considerations

Religious beliefs and practices will influence the handling of human remains and may impact joint and multinational operations. RSTs can advise on specific religious practices associated with handling of the deceased and interment operations. The RST can function as a liaison between the command and local clergy. The RST also counsels joint forces affected by the loss of comrades or constantly dealing with the deceased.

For additional information on religious support (RS) considerations to MA, see Appendix E, "Religious Support to Mortuary Affairs," and JP 1-05, Religious Affairs in Joint Operations.

5. Mortuary Affairs Facilities

a. Once initial military operations are completed, MA operations often transition to semi-permanent facilities. MACPs operating on an area basis and TMEPs are good examples of MA operations that can easily transition into a building or facility, once security improves and infrastructure becomes available.

b. Planners should contact their engineering support personnel to review existing MA facility plans in the engineering database, rather than design a new facility. These designs are generally less expensive alternatives than contract construction or leasing and are built using readily available materials in the DOD supply system.

6. Environmental, Safety, and Occupational Health Considerations

While complete protection of personnel, equipment, facilities, and the environment during military operations may not always be possible, planners should carefully address environmental, safety, and occupational health considerations during joint operations. Infectious organisms may be associated with human remains, regardless of postmortem condition, and could contaminate the storage and processing areas. Using standard precautions, all human remains should be handled as though they are potentially infectious. (See USACHPPM Technical Guide 195, *Safety and Health Guidance for Mortuary Affairs Operations: Infectious Materials and CBRN Handling,* for further information on the handling of potentially infectious human remains.) Therefore, each MA activity must ensure that strict personal health, hygiene, and sanitation procedures are constantly followed. In addition, MA personnel need to have a hazardous waste disposal plan that follows current environmental safety guidelines.

a. **Environmental Considerations.** GCCs are responsible for protecting the environment in which US military forces operate to the greatest extent possible consistent with operational requirements. They should ensure that environmental considerations are an integral part of the planning and decision-making processes.

For more guidance on annex L (Environment Considerations), see CJCSM 3122.03, Joint Operation Planning and Execution System (JOPES), Volume II, Planning Formats.

b. **Safety Considerations**

(1) To reduce the chance of becoming infected, personnel conducting MA functions should adhere to prescribed standard precautions when dealing with human remains. Planning considerations should include the requirement to obtain and sustain resources used by MA personnel to perform their mission in a safe environment.

(a) Personal protective equipment (PPE)—items, size, quantity, resupply.

(b) Water source—for sanitation of workstations as well as personnel.

(c) Medical support requirements—how to access the nearest medical unit or medical treatment facility in the event of occupational exposure, injury, or illness.

(d) Cleaning supplies—cleaning solutions and brushes for decontamination of equipment.

(e) Explosive ordnance disposal (EOD) inspection procedures.

(2) In accordance with biohazard material disposal procedures as required by the US Code of Federal Regulations for Environmental Compliance, established government-to-government agreements, or GCC interim operational policy for environmental compliance, use of proper PPE and following established safety and sanitation guidelines is critical to mission success.

(3) In accordance with biohazard material disposal procedures as required by the US Code of Federal Regulations for Environmental Compliance, established government-to-government agreements, or GCC interim operational policy for environmental compliance, incinerate all disposable protective clothing, bandages, dressings, sheets, towels, and other items coming into direct contact with the human remains or body fluids. The plan should address how the MA personnel are to dispose of hazardous waste if an incinerator is not available at their location.

c. **Occupational Health Considerations**

(1) The implementation of personal health and sanitation procedures as outlined in USACHPPM Technical Guide 195, *Safety and Health Guidance for Mortuary Affairs Operations: Infectious Materials and CBRN Handling,* will help prevent the following:

(a) The spread of diseases from human remains to personnel working in or located at an MA facility.

(b) The contracting of diseases from the MA facility's environment (e.g., walls and floors, protective clothing, equipment, and supplies that are used to handle or process human remains) by individuals who work in or visit an MA facility.

(c) The spread of disease from individuals who have contracted or are carriers of diseases to other susceptible individuals with whom the infected individuals come in contact.

(2) Occupational health and preventive medicine measures should be incorporated into the MA plan to identify occupational health and preventive medicine requirements and resources available to the MA personnel.

(a) Identify procedures for reporting blood-borne pathogen exposure to medical authorities. Annual blood-borne pathogen training is required for all MA personnel.

(b) Identify mental health professional assets available to MA personnel and establish procedures for accessing that capability. This includes critical debriefing and interventional counseling assets.

(c) Identify occupational health or preventive medicine support available to MA personnel and establish procedures for accessing that capability. This includes direction on proper maintenance and care of PPE and respiratory protection program requirements.

(d) Identify immunization requirements for the theater of operation for MA personnel. Immunization requirements for medical personnel and MA personnel will usually be the same. Baseline immunization requirements and testing should include at a minimum, HEP B [hepatitis B], HIV [human immunodeficiency virus], TB [tuberculosis]. Additional immunizations may be required based on the hazards in the region; check with your immunization department for a complete list of recommended immunizations.

7. **Communications and Interoperability**

a. An effective communications system is vital to planning and conducting successful MA programs. The MA unit should be able to communicate directly with the casualty reporting personnel, and the communications system should be compatible with other Service and multinational systems. In established alliances, specialized agencies and procedures exist to address MA. In other multinational operations, MA arrangements should be established.

b. During multinational military operations, difficulties could be encountered in establishing an MA system. Existing STANAGs should be used whenever possible. Differences in doctrine, training, equipment, culture, and language must be resolved and teamwork and trust developed. Interpreters may be required.

8. Public Affairs

The public release of information on casualties during peacetime should be in accordance with the individual Service's policies and procedures. If the incident occurs in the US, then the public release of information should be in accordance with DOD policies and procedures or local medical examiners and/or coroners (ME/Cs) if they have jurisdiction. In the event of war, the public release of information should be in accordance with DOD policies and procedures. These policies and procedures should preclude the public release of casualty information until the NOK have been notified. Therefore, in cases where there is or may be news media or public interest, the Service's procedures should ensure that the appropriate public affairs officer is advised when the NOK have been notified. The photographing of human remains is prohibited unless specifically authorized for official use. Photographs that identify individual human remains (e.g., photographs of case files and grave markers) are not authorized for public affairs use. Official photographs taken by MA personnel or by the AFME are authorized. (Note: Official photographs are part of the deceased official case file and will not be released except by the AFMES. AFMES will release official photographs upon request to either the NOK or appropriate investigative entities with a need to know.) All requests for information on the deceased should be referred to the appropriate JMAO or ME/C who will coordinate the release of the requested information through the public affairs office once authorized.

For more information, see JP 3-61, Public Affairs.

9. Training

a. The GCC has the authority and responsibility to conduct sufficient joint training for MA within the command to ensure effective conduct of joint operations. Subordinate JFCs ensure that assigned forces have been sufficiently trained in MA to prepare them for effective employment. A JFC who is also a Service component commander retains the responsibilities for Service training. The procedures for MA should be evaluated in CJCS- and CCMD-sponsored exercises.

b. The JMAC is available to assist in evaluating exercises and provide training support to all Services for MA. Refer to Appendix G, "Key Points of Contact," for contact information.

Intentionally Blank

CHAPTER IV
MORTUARY AFFAIRS BATTLEFIELD OPERATIONS

"I will never leave a fallen comrade."

United States Army Soldier's Creed

1. Unit-Level Operations

Unit-level operations consist of the initial search, recovery, and evacuation of unit deceased personnel to the nearest MACP. This is the first step in the MA process on the battlefield. Unit commanders will select personnel within their unit to perform this mission. The commander is responsible for ensuring that those personnel are identified, trained, and equipped to conduct these tasks. The unit S&R team should be familiar with all of the appropriate forms, PPE, and procedures associated with conducting an S&R, and preparing and preserving the human remains on the scene and in transit. The unit will designate a member of the team to accompany the human remains to the MACP and be prepared to provide tentative ID of the human remains. When a unit is unable to recover its own human remains, the unit coordinates with the appropriate higher headquarters to request S&R support from a supporting MA activity. Note: There are Service-specific differences as to when a unit should request S&R support from the MA activity. During the handling of human remains, care is taken to avoid exposure to blood or body fluids in accordance with USACHPPM Technical Guidance 190, *Managing Occupational Exposure to Bloodborne Pathogens*, and USACHPPM Technical Guide 195, *Safety and Health Guidance for Mortuary Affairs Operations: Infectious Materials and CBRN Handling*. Rubber gloves, aprons, N95 high efficiency particulate air (HEPA) respirators, and eye protection must be worn when working with or recovering human remains. If contact is made, the area is washed immediately with disinfectant and/or soap solution and the supervisor is notified right away. If there is a chance of aerosolization of body fluids, then minimal respiratory protection would be an N95 HEPA respirator or the military field protective mask. Surgical masks will not protect against disease-containing microdroplets. If N95 or greater is assessed as the hazard remediation, then fit testing will be required along with training.

2. Search and Recovery of Human Remains

a. **Search.** When searching for human remains, follow a systematic method. This allows team members to thoroughly cover a large area. Ensure each team consists of a team leader, two flankers, and enough people to adequately cover the search area. Equip the team with a GPS, compasses, sketch maps, appropriate PPE (minimum of gloves and masks to protect against depleted uranium, asbestos fibers, carbon fibers, and other associated hazards), and possibly a machete or hand ax, if required to clear ground brush.

(1) Once the S&R team has arrived at the designated dismount point, the team leader should first conduct a leader reconnaissance of the site prior to deploying the team. This assessment is used to establish boundaries, identify danger areas, coordinate security boundaries, and establish the search methodology to be used. Additional personnel may be required to stay at the dismount point for security and/or to relay communications. The team

should move single file, with the team leader and communications operator in the center of the formation. Once the team leader has determined that the team is within approximately 100 meters of the given recovery site location, the team will assemble into either an open search formation (double-arm interval), used for open or sparsely vegetated areas, or a closed formation (single-arm or close interval), used for densely vegetated areas or difficult terrain with limited visibility. The fields of view of adjacent searchers should overlap. The team should then use the "straight-line box" search method (see Figure IV-1), that is; the team leader will be in the rear-center of the formation. The S&R team will move in the direction of the recovery site in a slow and steady pattern, searching side-to-side for items pertaining to the operation. The team leader should ensure that the team maintains proper intervals, moves in the direction of the recovery site, and always stays online.

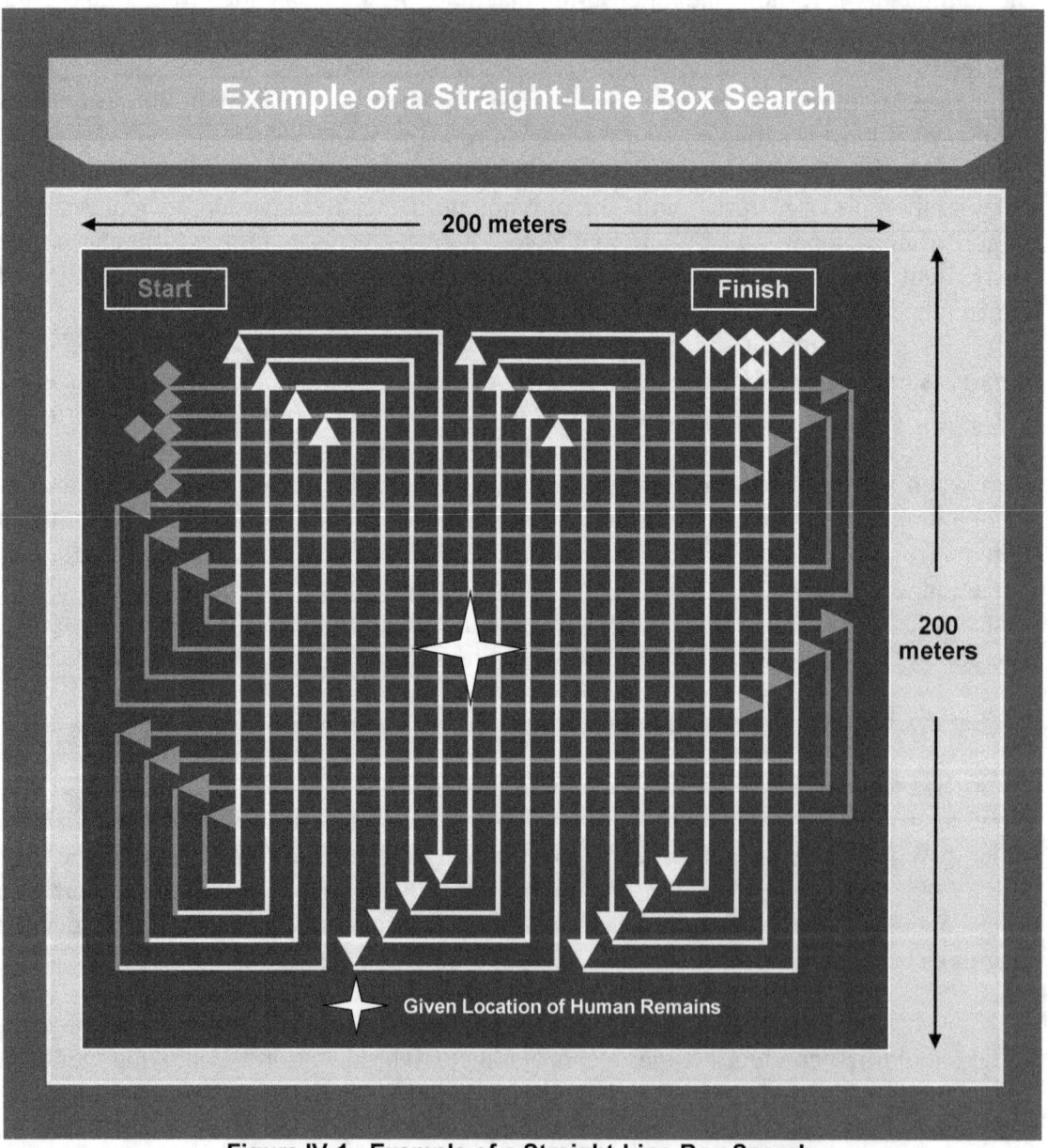

Figure IV-1. Example of a Straight-Line Box Search

(2) When team members observe an item that may be relevant to the search, the team member will use a predetermined verbal or hand-and-arm signal to alert the team to halt. The team leader will examine the item(s) and if the item is deemed to be human remains, portion of human remains, or disassociated PE, the team leader will mark the item with a predetermined color pin flag or other suitable marking method. Team leaders will mark any item that could be associated with the event; when in doubt, collect and return to AFMES for examination. The team leader will mark the pin flag using a grease pencil with the proper sequential "R" number for human remains, "E" number for disassociated PE, or "P" number for a portion of human remains. The team leader will then annotate the number assigned to the item and a description in a field notebook.

Note: An "R" number will be assigned to any item found that constitutes more than 50 percent of a human body and includes a majority of the torso. The team leader will make this determination. If there are no items representing more than 50 percent, each portion will receive a sequential "P" number. A torso will be marked as human remains. Body regions such as an isolated head or legs, even if attached at the pelvis, will be marked as a portion.

(3) This search and marking method will continue until the team has reached a point at least 100 meters past the last marked item. The team leader will then halt the team and direct the left or right flanker to perform an about-face, depending on which direction the search will proceed. The remaining team members will pivot around the flanker, remaining online until the team is facing in the opposite direction. The team leader will move to the rear-center of the formation and direct the movement of the team. This search pattern will continue until there is at least a 100-meter buffer in each direction around the defined recovery area.

(4) Team members search until they find all human remains or until the team leader determines there are no human remains in the area. Team members must be aware of areas where human remains may be located. Team members should also search unusual ground disturbances that may be due to emergency interments, collapsed bunkers, or fighting positions. Unusual odors, congregation of insects, scavenger birds, or animals should be investigated as they might lead to hidden human remains.

b. **Recovery**

(1) Once the entire area has been searched and all relevant items marked, the team will begin the documentation and recovery process. During combat, human remains and disassociated PE should be considered boobytrapped. Thus, proper precautions should be taken prior to handling any human remains, portions, or PE. Small portions and disassociated PE can be checked for possible booby traps by close examination prior to handling. Human remains represent a higher probability of being boobytrapped, so visual inspection may not always locate the presence of these devices.

(2) The recommended method to check human remains for booby traps is for one team member to attach a rope or strong cord to the side of the human remains opposite from the direction that he/she will pull the rope. After taking cover and with the remaining team members at a safe distance and behind cover, the designated personnel will pull the rope

until the human remains are rolled over and moved slightly away from its original position. All team members will stay behind cover for at least one minute, after which the human remains can be assumed safe to handle.

(3) If an explosive device discharges and causes fragmentation of the human remains and/or disassociation of PE, these items should be placed in an HRP with the human remains, as all preexisting disassociated evidence would have already been marked. Logically, these items were associated with the human remains prior to the explosion. All personnel handling human remains, portions, or effects must wear the proper protective equipment. Selection of PPE must be based on the exposure potential, that is, the probability of contact with blood and other potentially infectious materials, the likely amount of contact, and the expected duration of contact. Predesignated team members should complete the following tasks:

(4) **Recording PE**

(a) Personnel designated to document and safeguard PE should be the first personnel to come into contact with the human remains after booby trap checks are complete. These personnel must thoroughly check the entire human remains for PE, including the hands, neck, pockets, boots, and load carrying equipment. (Note: Pay particularly close attention to locating the ID tags and the ID card. Leave ID tags/card in place on the human remains. Use official ID media found as a basis for establishing tentative ID. Leave all ID media, PE, clothing, and organizational equipment on the human remains for forensic analysis. Inventory PE and record these items on Department of Defense [DD] Form 1076 [Military Operations Record of Personnel Effects of Deceased Personnel].)

(b) Provide ID media to team members completing other documentation.

(c) Place PE in a plastic slide closure bag, then place in a PE bag.

(d) Secure the PE bag to the left wrist of the human remains, if possible. If not, securely attach PE bag(s) to another location on the human remains.

(e) Sign the DD Form 1076. This becomes the chain of custody document for the PE.

(f) Place the DD Form 1076 in a slide closure plastic bag with the PE.

(5) **Recording ID media**

(a) Personnel designated to locate and record items of official ID media should thoroughly check all areas of the human remains' clothing and equipment. Any items or markings such as uniform nametape, laundry marks, helmet band marks, uniform and equipment sizes, serial numbers and markings on items of unit-issued equipment, Armed Forces ID Card, ID tags, rank insignia, and uniform patches should be annotated on DD Form 567 (Record of Search and Recovery); see Figure IV-2. (Note: No items of PE are annotated on this form.)

RECORD OF SEARCH AND RECOVERY	1. DATE *(YYYYMMDD)*

PRIVACY ACT STATEMENT

AUTHORITY: 10 USC Sections 1481 through 1488, EO 9397, Nov. 1943 (SSN).

PURPOSE AND USE: This form is used to establish initial identification of deceased personnel.

DISCLOSURE: Personal information provided on this form is given on a voluntary basis. Failure to provide this information, however, may result in improper identification of the deceased person and person making visual identification.

2. DECEDENT

a. NAME *(Last, First, Middle Initial) (or Unidentified)*	b. RANK	c. SSN	d. RACE	e. ORGANIZATION

3. TYPE OF SEARCH	4. DATE OF MISSION *(YYYYMMDD)*	5. FIELD SEARCH NUMBER	6. SEARCH AND RECOVERY NUMBER

7. EVACUATION NUMBER	8. DATE OF RECOVERY *(YYYYMMDD)*	9. NATIONALITY	10. ESTIMATED DATE OF DEATH *(YYYYMMDD)*

11. PLACE OF RECOVERY *(Indicate map sheet number, grid coordinates, name of nearest village or town; name, description, or number of roads, mountains or other landmarks; type of grave (shallow, deep, surface); type of position (artillery, infantry). If recovered from a vehicle, tank or plane, give position therein.)*

12. IDENTIFICATION MEDIA FOUND IN GRAVE AND/OR SURROUNDING AREA *(include serial numbers found on vehicles, tanks, aircraft and weapons.)*

13. OTHER REMAINS RECOVERED ON THIS MISSION *(Use continuation sheet if necessary.)*		14. RECOVERY TEAM MEMBERS		
SEARCH AND RECOVERY NO. a.	SEARCH AND RECOVERY NO. b.	NAME *(Last, First, Middle Initial)* a.	RANK b.	ORGANIZATION c.

15. TEAM LEADER

a. NAME *(Last, First, Middle Initial)*	b. RANK	c. ORGANIZATION
d. SIGNATURE		e. DATE SIGNED *(YYYYMMDD)*

16. RECEIVING OFFICIAL

a. NAME *(Last, First, Middle Initial)*	b. RANK	c. ORGANIZATION
d. SIGNATURE		e. DATE SIGNED *(YYYYMMDD)*

DD FORM 567, JUL 1998 (EG)   PREVIOUS EDITION MAY BE USED.   Designed using Perform Pro, WHS/DIOR, Jun 98

Figure IV-2. DD Form 567, Record of Search and Recovery

(b) All equipment (except weapons, ordnance, or unit-essential equipment) is transported with human remains. All equipment is annotated on DD Form 890 (Record of Identification Processing). Body armor is recorded on both the DD Form 890 and as a specific entry item in the MARTS case file for accountability and tracking purposes.

(c) Unload all weapons and remove explosive ordnance from human remains. Return these items to the unit armorer.

(6) Obtaining statements of recognition.

(a) When there are S&R team members or other personnel in the recovery area who can visually identify the human remains, a designated team member should complete a DD Form 565 (Statement of Recognition of Deceased); see Figure IV-3.

(b) The S&R team member completing the form will annotate as much information as possible using information provided by the acquaintance out of sight of the human remains. Once these blocks are completed, after verifying that the human remains are identifiable, the team member will escort the acquaintance to the human remains and determine if the human remains can be visually recognized. Any discrepancies found during the viewing with the descriptions provided prior will be annotated in the "remarks" block of the form. (Note: Human remains will not be washed or have clothing removed to aid the recognition process.)

(c) Complete all remaining blocks and have the acquaintance sign in the appropriate block.

(d) The team member completing the form will sign in the "witness" block.

(7) Questioning local inhabitants.

(a) When local civilians are encountered during the search or during recovery operations who may have information pertaining to the loss, a designated team member should attempt to complete a DD Form 1074 (Questionnaire of Local Inhabitants); see Figure IV-4.

(b) A linguist or interpreter may be needed to accomplish this task.

(c) Attempt to gain information on other unrecovered human remains in the area.

(d) Forward this report to the JMAO with other documents, even when no human remains are found.

(8) Completing tags for human remains, portions, and disassociated PE.

(a) A designated team member should prepare two S&R tags for each human remains, and one tag for each portion and disassociated PE.

(b) The S&R tags for human remains (see Figure IV-5) should have the S&R number on one side that consists of the mission number, the branch of Service of the recovering unit, the unit designation, and the number assigned to the human remains. Example: 001/AR311thQM/2 of 3 would be the S&R number for the first S&R mission for the Army's 311th Quartermaster Company. These human remains would be the second of three human remains recovered on this mission, or "R-2."

STATEMENT OF RECOGNITION OF DECEASED

PRIVACY ACT STATEMENT

AUTHORITY: 10 USC Sections 1481 through 1488, EO 9397, Nov. 1943 (SSN).

PURPOSE AND USE: This form is used to establish initial identification of deceased personnel.

DISCLOSURE: Personal information provided on this form is given on a voluntary basis. Failure to provide this information, however, may result in improper identification of the deceased person and person making visual identification.

1. TENTATIVELY IDENTIFIED DECEDENT		
a. NAME *(Last, First, Middle Initial) (or Unidentified)*	b. RANK	c. SSN
d. ORGANIZATION	e. SERVICE	

2. I HAVE PERSONALLY VIEWED THE REMAINS TENTATIVELY IDENTIFIED ABOVE. RECOGNITION IS BASED ON THE FOLLOWING.			
a. SEX	b. APPROXIMATE AGE *(Years)*	c. APPROXIMATE HEIGHT	d. RACE
e. HAIR COLOR *(If brown, indicate light or dark, as applicable)*		f. BUILD/MUSCULARITY *(Slender, medium, heavy or obese)*	
g. IDENTIFYING MARKS *(Fully describe by type and location ALL known scars, tattoos, birthmarks, amputations or other body markings to support the identification.)*			
h. REMARKS			

3. DETAILS OF VIEWING		
a. DATE *(YYYYMMDD)*	b. TIME	c. PLACE

4. PERSON MAKING VISUAL IDENTIFICATION		
a. NAME *(Last, First, Middle Initial)*	b. RANK	c. SSN
d. ORGANIZATION	e. SIGNATURE	f. DATE SIGNED *(YYYYMMDD)*
g. RELATIONSHIP TO DECEASED *(CDR, ISG, Friend, Relative, etc.)*	h. LENGTH OF TIME YOU KNEW DECEASED *(Number of months or years)*	

5. WITNESS			
I certify that the individual identified in Item 4 has viewed the remains in my presence, and that to the best of my knowledge and belief the above statements are true.			
a. NAME *(Last, First, Middle Initial)*	b. RANK	c. TITLE	
d. ORGANIZATION	e. SIGNATURE		f. DATE SIGNED *(YYYYMMDD)*

DD FORM 565, JUL 1998 (EG)   PREVIOUS EDITION MAY BE USED.   Designed using Perform Pro, WHS/DIOR, Jun 98

Figure IV-3. DD Form 565, Statement of Recognition of Deceased

(c) The reverse side of the S&R tag is left blank, except for human remains recovered from aircraft crashes or vehicles. For human remains from aircraft crashes, the reverse side of the tag would be marked "ACM," for advanced composite materials (see Figure IV-6). This marking will alert receiving MA personnel that the human remains may contain hazardous residue and special handling precautions may be warranted.

QUESTIONNAIRE OF LOCAL INHABITANTS

PRIVACY ACT STATEMENT

AUTHORITY: 10 USC Sections 1481 through 1488, EO 9397, Nov. 1943 (SSN).

PURPOSE AND USE: This form is used to establish initial identification of deceased personnel.

DISCLOSURE: Personal information provided on this form is given on a voluntary basis. Failure to provide this information, however, may result in improper identification of the deceased person and person making visual identification.

1. PERSON INTERVIEWED a. NAME *(Last, First, Middle Initial)* | b. ADDRESS

c. OCCUPATION | d. DATE INTERVIEWED *(YYYYMMDD)*

2a. ARE THERE REMAINS BELIEVED TO BE U.S. FORCES INTERRED IN THIS AREA? *(If Yes, complete 2b., c., d., and e.)* YES NO | b. WHO INTERRED THE REMAINS?

c. DATE OF DEATH *(YYYYMMDD)* | d. DATE OF INTERMENT *(YYYYMMDD)* | e. WHERE WERE THE REMAINS INTERRED? *(Include grid coordinates)*

3a. ARE THERE REMAINS BELIEVED TO BE U.S. FORCES ABOVE GROUND IN THIS AREA? *(If Yes, complete 3b., c., and d.)* YES NO | b. WHO FOUND THE REMAINS?

c. WHERE ARE THE REMAINS NOW? *(Include grid coordinates)* | d. DATE OF DEATH *(YYYYMMDD)*

4. WAS THE PERSON WHO FOUND THE REMAINS A WITNESS TO THE DEATH? YES NO | 5. WERE REMAINS RECOVERED FROM AN AIRCRAFT OR ARMORED VEHICLE? *(If Yes, describe type, marking, and crew position.)* YES NO

6. IS THE AREA WHERE REMAINS ARE LOCATED MINED AND/OR BOOBYTRAPPED? *(If Yes, describe in Item 12.)* YES NO

7a. WERE THE REMAINS TENTATIVELY IDENTIFIED PRIOR TO BURIAL? *(If Yes, complete 7b.)* YES NO

b. PERSON WHO TENTATIVELY IDENTIFIED THE REMAINS: (1) NAME *(Last, First, Middle Initial)* | (2) TITLE | (3) ADDRESS

8a. WERE PERSONAL EFFECTS RECOVERED WITH REMAINS? *(If Yes, complete 8b. and describe in Item 12.)* YES NO | b. WHERE ARE EFFECTS NOW?

9a. WAS GOVERNMENT PROPERTY FOUND AND/OR RECOVERED WITH REMAINS? *(If Yes, complete 9b. and describe in Item 12.)* YES NO | b. WHERE IS PROPERTY NOW?

10a. WERE U.S. FORCES PERSONNEL GIVEN MEDICAL TREATMENT PRIOR TO DEATH? *(If Yes, complete 10b., c., and d.)* YES NO | b. WHO PROVIDED MEDICAL AID?

c. NAME OF MEDICAL FACILITY | d. LOCATION OF MEDICAL FACILITY

11a. WERE U.S. FORCES PERSONNEL MISTREATED PRIOR TO OR AFTER DEATH? *(If Yes, complete 11b. and c. and explain in Item 12.)* YES NO | b. WHO MISTREATED THE PERSONNEL?

c. WITNESS TO MISTREATMENT (1) NAME *(Last, First, Middle Initial)* | (2) ADDRESS

12. ADDITIONAL INFORMATION *(Use continuation sheet if necessary)*

13. PREPARING OFFICIAL a. NAME *(Last, First, Middle Initial)* | b. RANK | c. ORGANIZATION | d. SIGNATURE | e. DATE SIGNED *(YYYYMMDD)*

DD FORM 1074, JUL 1998 (EG) PREVIOUS EDITION MAY BE USED. Designed using Perform Pro, WHS/DIOR, Jun 98

Figure IV-4. DD Form 1074, Questionnaire of Local Inhabitants

(d) The reverse side of S&R tags for human remains recovered from any vehicle suspected to contain depleted uranium should be marked “DU” for depleted uranium as a precaution.

(e) S&R tags for portions (see Figure IV-7) and effects (see Figure IV-8) should have the number assigned to the item annotated on one side and the reverse side should be left blank.

(f) One S&R tag will be attached to each human remains and the other to the zipper tab of the HRP.

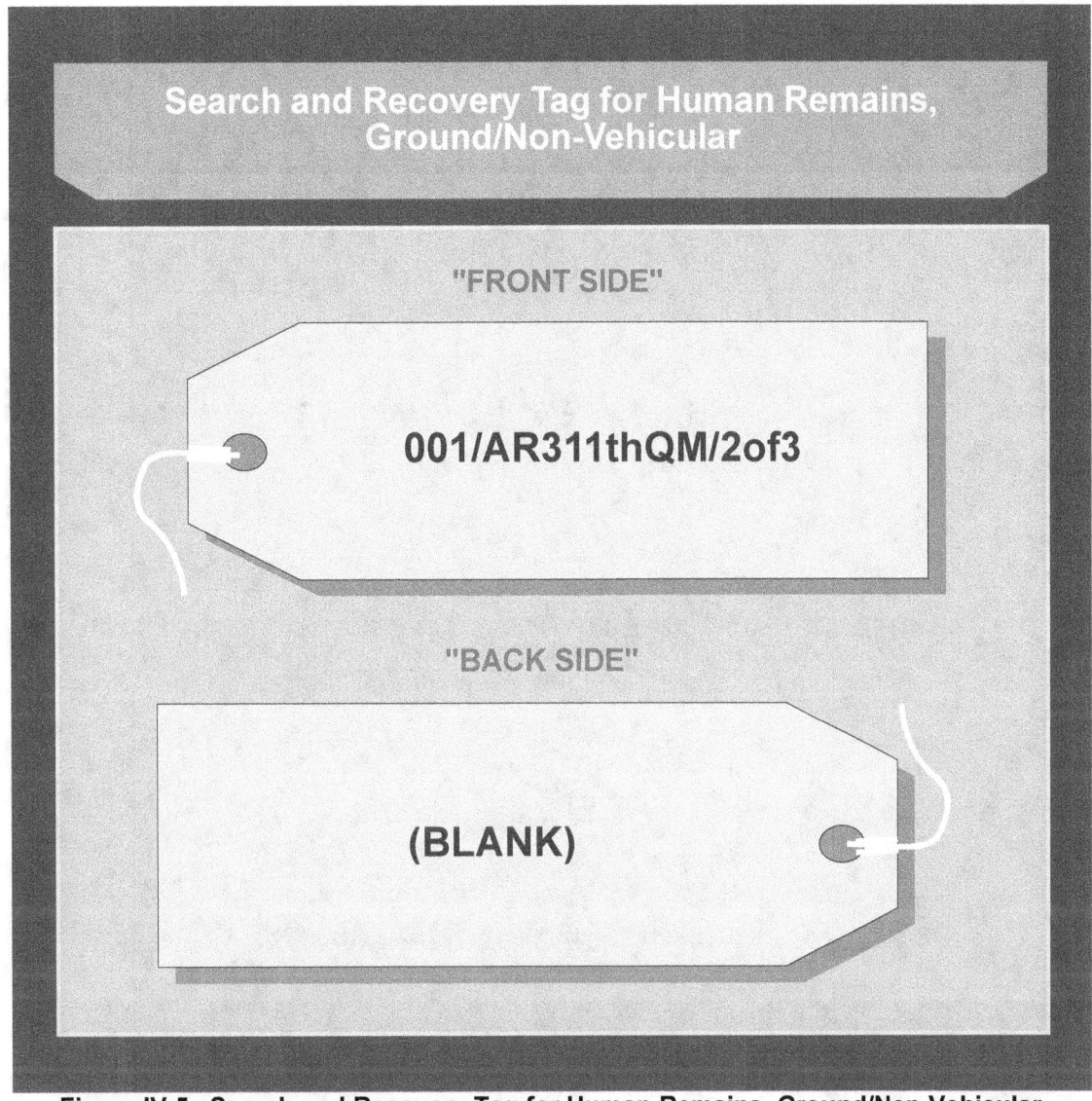

Figure IV-5. Search and Recovery Tag for Human Remains, Ground/Non-Vehicular

(g) Portions recovered from the same general location should not be individually bagged, unless there is a strong presumption that the human remains belong to a distinct "believed-to-be" (BTB) or that the location of recovery (provenience) information for where each portion was recovered is critical to an investigation. When at all possible, maintain skeletal integrity and keep skeletal remains together. Place the portions in an HRP for evacuation. The outside of the HRP will be marked "portions." A tag, or automated identification technology (AIT) device, will be placed inside a clear zip-closure bag or a sealed, watertight container and placed inside the HRP, or attached to the outside of the HRP. Disassociated effects will be recovered and placed in an HRP for evacuation; the outside of the HRP will be marked "effects." A tag or AIT device will be placed inside the HRP or attached to the outside of the HRP. If commingling is suspected, place the portions together in an HRP. The AFMES anthropological staff will examine and sort. Portions recovered from geographically and/or incidentally distinct areas should not be placed in the

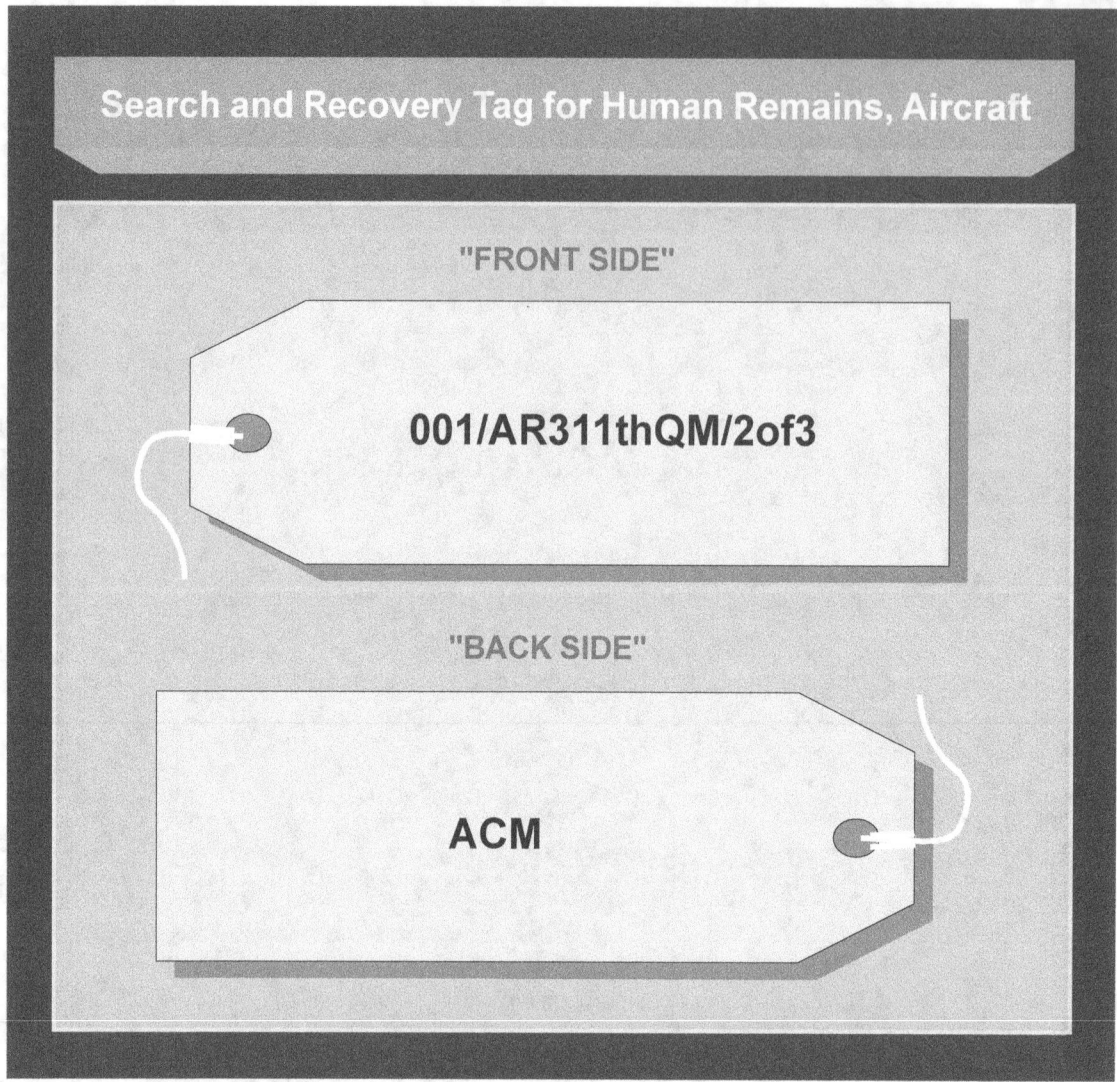

Figure IV-6. Search and Recovery Tag for Human Remains, Aircraft

same HRP or transfer case. Never combine portions transported from different S&R locations within the same HRP or transfer case.

(h) The documents prepared for each human remains will be put into a sealed, watertight container or clear zip-closure bag and placed inside the proper HRP.

c. **Evacuation Operations.** Once human remains, portions, and disassociated effects have been tagged and placed in HRPs, the human remains should be evacuated to the evacuation point. Human remains should always be:

(1) Carried feet first.

(2) Treated with dignity, reverence, and respect.

(3) Loaded head first onto fixed-wing aircraft.

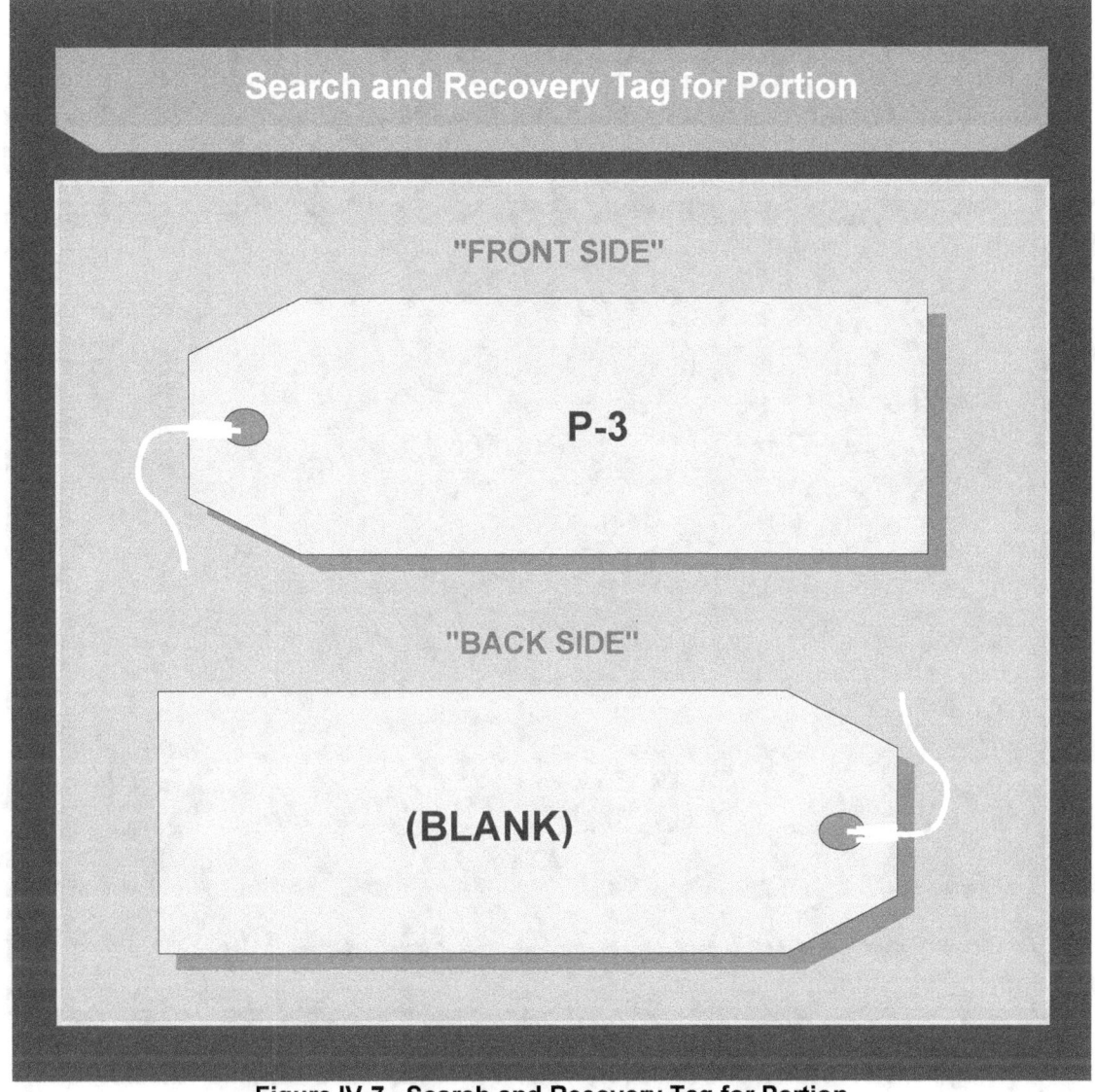

Figure IV-7. Search and Recovery Tag for Portion

(4) Loaded feet first onto vehicles or rotary-wing aircraft.

(5) Escorted to the most convenient MA facility.

d. **Post-Combat and Area-Clearance Phase Recovery Site Operations**

(1) Recovery site operations conducted by individual units or MA personnel during the post-combat or area-clearance phases of a military operation are usually more thorough and better documented than those conducted during the combat phase. Recovery sites are defined as areas where human remains or other material evidence have been deposited, or are believed to have been deposited.

(2) MA personnel may be available to supervise or conduct these types of operations, but the procedures outlined may be used by non-MA personnel whenever MA personnel are not available and the tactical situation permits. In addition to the

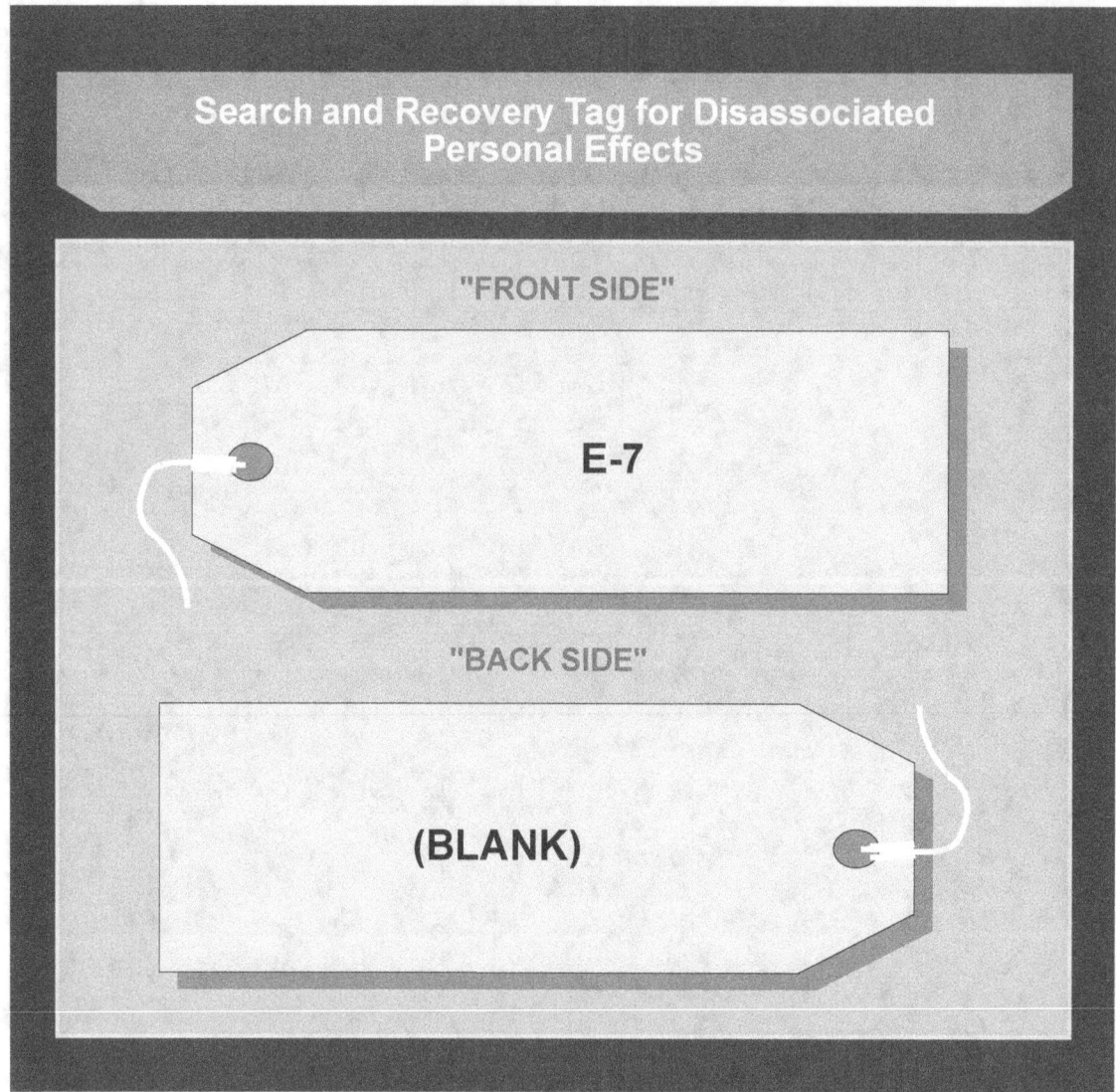

Figure IV-8. Search and Recovery Tag for Disassociated Personal Effects

aforementioned search procedures, the following search methods may be employed based on available resources and the area being searched.

(a) Strip or line search—usually used for covering large or open areas.

(b) Zone or sector search—area to be searched is divided into zones or sectors.

(c) Point to point search—is used in small confined areas.

(d) Spiral or circular search—typically used for outdoor scenes with one to two personnel conducting the search.

(e) Clockwise search and counter-clockwise search—inside search pattern with two personnel conducting the search.

(3) Use of additional special skills personnel. After cessation of major hostilities, it is more likely to have a greater availability of specialized personnel to assist during S&R operations. These personnel may include, but are not limited to:

(a) Linguists.

(b) Life support technicians.

(c) EOD.

(d) CBRN.

(e) MA.

(f) Medical personnel.

(g) Canine search teams.

(h) Anthropologists.

(i) Archaeologists.

(4) Gridding the recovery site. Use of the union grid system will ensure a more thorough and accurate documentation of the recovery site.

(a) Selecting the Datum. Once the area has been searched and all items marked, a permanent point of reference or "datum" is selected. This datum should be in the southwest corner of the defined recovery site. There should be no known human remains, portions, or effects located to the south or west of this position. Before evacuating human remains from the recovery site, the datum should be marked so as to be easily located in the future. This can be done in several ways, such as by driving a metal stake into the ground or even by stacking rocks. If there is already a nearby prominent object in the southwest corner that can be used as a datum, mark it so that it is easily distinguishable from other like items in the area.

(b) Meridian Line Placement. The line from the datum running due north (0 degrees) is called the meridian line. This line extends in uniformed increments (meters) until it surpasses the northernmost marked item in the recovery area. (Note: The smaller the increments, the more accurately the site will be documented.) Wood or metal stakes are placed at the proper increments in a direct line from the datum to the northernmost boundary of the recovery area.

(c) Baseline Placement. The line from the datum running due east (90 degrees) is called the baseline. This line extends in the same increments as the meridian line until it surpasses the easternmost marked item in the recovery area. (Note: The length of the baseline is rarely the same as the length of the meridian line.)

(d) Building the Grid Interior. Once the meridian and baselines have been emplaced, a measuring tape or rod is extended north from the first stake east of the datum on the baseline and east from the first stake north of the datum on the meridian line. An additional stake is placed at the point where these two devices intersect. This process is continued northward until the end of the meridian line is reached. The devices are moved over one stake to the east and the process repeated. This process is continued until the entire recovery area is gridded. This process will create a graph-like appearance comprised of small boxes, which are called "units." Twine or engineer tape can be strung between the stakes to better define these units.

(e) Checking the Accuracy of Units. The Pythagorean theorem is used to check the squareness of the units. The units are measured diagonally and the theorem $A^2 + B^2 = C^2$ is used. Example: A 4-meter (m) × 4-m unit measured diagonally should be 5.657 m.

(f) Numbering the Units. The numbering system that will be used to define each unit within the recovery site begins with the datum. The datum should always be numbered N500/E500. The numbers for each unit north and east of the datum will ascend in the increments the units were emplaced. Example: If each unit is 2 m × 2 m, then the first stake north of the datum on the meridian line will be numbered N502/E500, since it is 2 m north and 0 m east of the datum. Likewise, the first stake east of the datum on the meridian line will be numbered N500/E502, since it is 2 m east and 0 m north of the datum. The unit to which these numbers correspond will be the unit directly north and east of the stake.

(g) Unit Quadrants. Each unit is comprised of four individual quadrants: northwest (NW), northeast (NE), southwest (SW), and southeast (SE). Indicating in which quadrant of a particular unit an item was found will make documentation of the recovery more accurate. Example: If it were noted that item P-7 was found in N512/E504 on a recovery site comprised of 2-m × 2-m units, the variance of marking the location during a site recreation would be 2 m. But if it were noted that item P-7 was found in the SW quadrant of N512/E504, the variance would be reduced to only 1 m.

(5) Excavating a Recovery Site. In order to recover human remains from burial sites, collapsed bunkers, and especially aircraft crashes, excavation of soil within the recovery site may be required. The equipment used for excavation can vary from large earth-moving machines, to small hand trowels and toothbrushes. It is important to always recover as much of the human remains as possible. With modern technological and scientific methods, it is possible to make a positive ID using a small portion of soft tissue, or hard tissue found amongst thousands of fragments from several different individuals. During catastrophic events, often all that is recoverable are minuscule pieces of human anatomy. Sometimes these portions can be present as scattered surface materials, or buried at a depth of several feet interspersed with aircraft debris, foliage, and soil. Excavations of these types of recovery sites usually employ the methods of archaeology and are often very slow, deliberate operations. If the tactical situation permits, all recoverable human remains and portions of human remains should be recovered and evacuated to help ensure ID and proper repatriation of all individuals involved in the loss.

(6) Excavation and recovery operations employ several types of strategies, methods, and techniques.

(a) Basic Excavation Strategies. Excavation strategies employed on a recovery site must be flexible and adaptable to environmental, cultural, and physical challenges. There are two types of excavation strategies; strategy-discovery and strategy-recovery.

1. Strategy-Discovery. This strategy is employed when the exact location of human remains within a defined perimeter remains unknown after all information has been gathered. The excavation methods used are usually trenching and large-scale testing.

2. Strategy-Recovery. This strategy is employed whenever information gathered points to a specific location within the recovery site. The preferred excavation method is block-excavation.

(b) Basic Excavation Methods. Excavation methods employed within a recovery site are determined by the circumstances of the loss and the information gathered. There are four basic excavation methods; large-scale testing, trenching, block-excavation, and collection.

1. Large-Scale Testing. This excavation method consists of excavating alternate same-sized units throughout the recovery site by the use of a random numbering system. These "test pits" are usually 50 centimeters (cm) × 50 cm and dug to a depth determined by the team leader or recovery leader.

2. Trenching. This excavation method consists of digging long, linear units parallel to each other. Large areas of the recovery site can be examined for soil profiles and material evidence. The unexcavated areas between rows, or balks, should be uniform in width, usually no more than 50 cm, and be removed from areas where human remains or other material are found.

3. Block-Excavation. This is the preferred excavation method and consists of excavating contiguous units within the recovery site. All units are dug to a "sterile" depth. Sterile soil is soil that is undisturbed and free of human remains, artifacts, or other material evidence.

4. Collection. This excavation method is employed whenever no soil is present and all human remains, artifacts, and material evidence is located on the surface, such as on a rock-slope.

(c) Basic Excavation Techniques. There are three basic types of excavation techniques that are employed on a recovery site; fine-scale, coarse-scale, and mechanical.

1. Technique Fine-Scale. This excavation technique consists of the use of hand tools, including but not limited to hand trowels, toothbrushes, dental picks, paintbrushes, and bamboo picks. It is usually used when human remains or other material evidence are located and adjacent soil must be removed.

<u>2</u>. Technique Coarse-Scale. This excavation technique consists of the use of hand tools, such as picks and shovels. It is the most common technique for excavating recovery sites and is used when large amounts of soil must be removed and screened. It is often mixed with fine-scale excavation when human remains or soil disturbances are located.

<u>3.</u> Technique Mechanical. This excavation technique consists of the use of mechanical equipment, including but not limited to bulldozers, belly scrapers, and front-end loaders. It is normally employed when large amounts of overburden, or soil that has been deposited on top of the recovery site, must be removed to proximate the location or human remains and material evidence.

(d) Basic Recovery Techniques. Recovery techniques are the methods used to recover human remains and other material evidence during excavations. There are three types of basic recovery techniques: collection, dry-screening, and wet-screening.

<u>1.</u> Recovery Technique Collection. This recovery technique is employed when no soil needs to be excavated and all human remains, artifacts, and material are present on the surface, such as on a rock-slope.

<u>2.</u> Recovery Technique Dry-Screening. This recovery technique is employed when conditions permit the conveyance of excavated soil to a location outside of the recovery site, and the soil is placed into ¼-inch wire-meshed screens in an attempt to locate human remains, artifacts, or other material evidence. The soil passes through the screen by shaking or pressing by hand. All material evidence is placed in a clear plastic bag and checked periodically or prior to closing the unit.

<u>3.</u> Recovery Technique Wet-Screening. This recovery technique is employed when conditions will not allow soil to pass through the screen without assistance. Soil from the recovery site is conveyed to an outside area, placed in a screen, and water pressure is used to degrade the soil to a point where it will pass through the screen, leaving behind any material evidence and organic matter larger than the diameter of the wire mesh.

e. **Documentation of the Recovery Site.** It is vital that all aspects of the recovery operation be documented. This documentation provides a spatial and contextual reference as to where human remains, artifacts, and other material evidence are found within the recovery site. The recovery operation is documented in three manners; maps, field notebooks, and photos.

(1) **Mapping the Recovery Site.** Making accurate maps of every recovery site is essential. A map of the recovery site showing the locations of human remains, portions, and PE in relation to the datum can be used for future excavations and re-creation of the recovery site (see Figure IV-9). A detailed recovery site map should include:

(a) X for the location of the datum in the SW corner.

(b) Individual units within the recovery site.

(c) Size of units.

(d) Codes for each human remains, portion, and disassociated PE recovered.

(e) Quadrants for each item recovered.

(f) Grid coordinates and description of the datum.

(g) Unit conducting recovery.

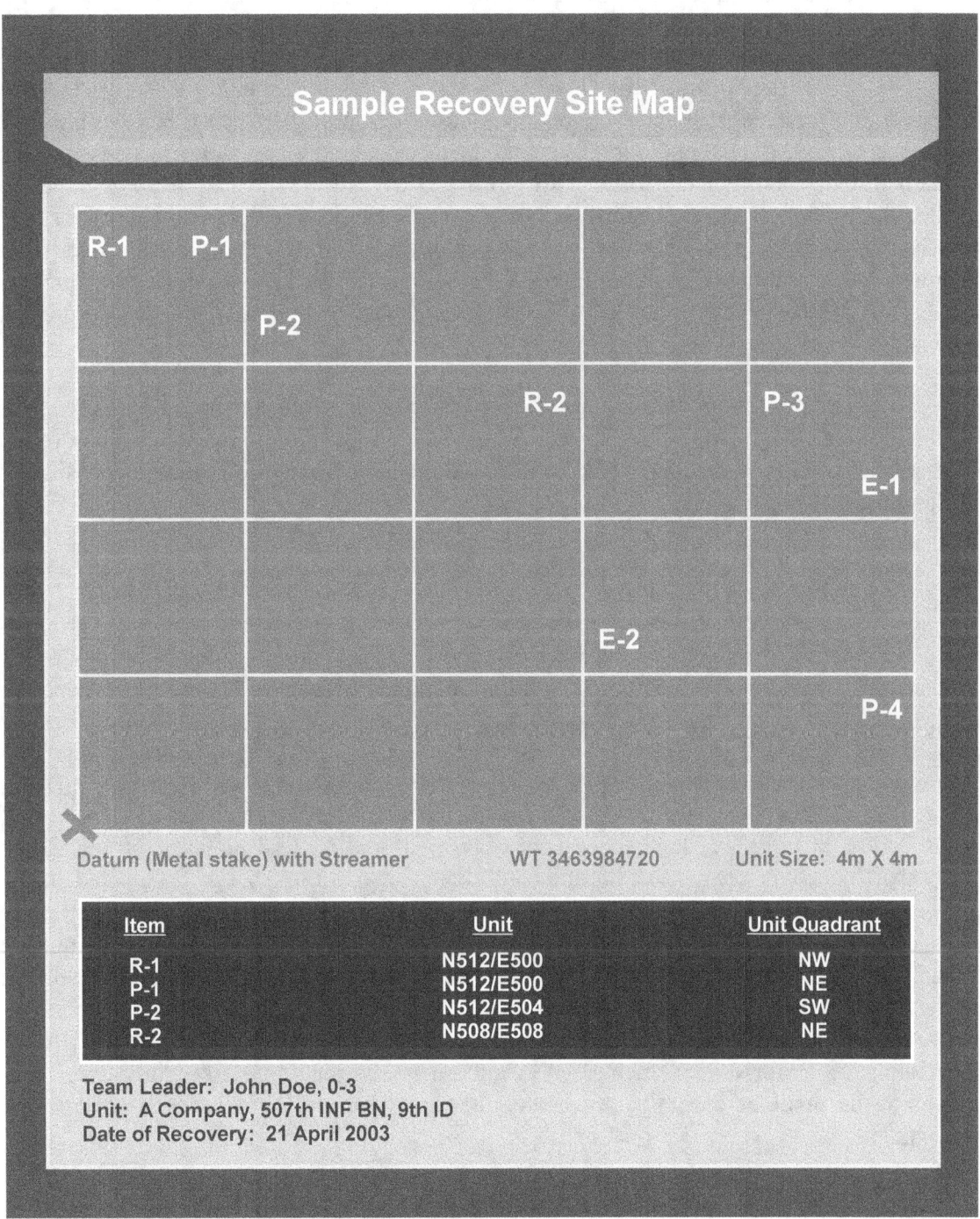

Figure IV-9. Sample Recovery Site Map

        (h) Team leader name and grade.

        (i) Date(s) of recovery operation.

        (j) Vehicle and aircraft ID numbers, if applicable.

      (2) **Field Notebooks.** During recovery operations, the team leader should keep a detailed record of every aspect of the recovery operation in a field notebook. The last page in the notebook should include the team leader's information, dated and signed. This notebook should be forwarded with the human remains to the MA facility.

      (3) **Photographing the Recovery Site.** Digital media is suggested for documenting recoveries. Each recovery site should be photographed on its own memory card(s), each day, and the photographs should be downloaded to a permanent storage outlet in their raw or unadulterated form. Close-ups and overall views of each item should be taken. A description and number of each photograph taken should be recorded in the field notebook or separate photographic log. Each roll of film should be numbered and every roll, memory card, or storage disc of digital media should be forwarded with the human remains to the MACP. (Note: It is important to safeguard this photographic evidence and ensure that no unauthorized photographs are taken.)

      (4) If no human remains are found or if the team must suspend operations for tactical reasons, the team leader will report this information and the extent of the search to higher headquarters. The team leader includes as much detailed information as possible to aid any future S&R missions.

3.   **Mortuary Affairs Collection Point Operations**

     a. The MACP is the basic unit for modern day MA support. Mission planning provides for MACPs to be strategically located throughout the operational area. These MACPs provide DS and/or GS for receiving, refrigeration, processing, tentative ID, and evacuation of human remains and their accompanying PE. When tasked, the MACP conducts or provides personnel to perform or supervise S&R missions. MACPs are mobile, enabling them to support combat maneuver elements, but can remain fixed to support a general area.

      (1) MACPs are established in one of two ways. MACPs designed to provide DS to a combat maneuver element are highly mobile. These points should be located in the forward logistic support area with the combat maneuver element. MACPs designed to provide GS to a given area or major commands are more stationary in their operation and are located at large logistic bases. These points operate in a more traditional manner. In providing GS, these points might be task-organized with increased receiving, processing, refrigeration, and evacuation capacities to serve as a transit or intermediate point for MACPs providing DS to forward elements. While these points are more fixed in nature, they maintain the modular capability to deploy forward with the logistic base or the major command.

      (2) In addition to the MACP's primary mission, the MACP has the secondary mission of conducting or providing personnel to supervise S&R missions when tasked by

higher headquarters. When assigned this mission, the MACP must leave sufficient personnel to maintain and operate the point on a 24-hour basis. Although not a primary mission, an MACP may help conduct or assist in temporary interment operations.

b. **Site Selection**

(1) Site selection for establishing and operating an MACP depends on the support mission. A highly mobile MACP that provides DS to a combat maneuver element should choose a site with considerations for:

(a) Proximity to a main supply route to facilitate delivery and evacuation of human remains.

(b) Accessibility for combat units evacuating human remains as well as being clearly marked so that the unit can recognize the MACP.

(c) Accessibility to mobile refrigeration containers.

(d) Proximity to life support and/or personnel services but out of sight of medical treatment facilities.

(e) Proximity to tactical communications support.

(2) MACPs providing GS to a given area or major command should choose a site based on the following:

(a) Proximity to a main supply route.

(b) Ability to build a road network on site or to use an existing road network.

(c) Ability to build a helipad on site or to use an existing helipad.

(d) Proximity to engineer support for construction and/or maintenance of a road network and helipad.

(e) Proximity to a landing strip or airport.

(f) Proximity to life support and/or personnel services.

(g) Proximity to tactical communications support.

(h) Ability to screen area using natural screening or screening material.

c. **Facility Layout**

(1) MACPs may operate out of a mobile integrated remains collection system (MIRCS), tentage, or a temporary facility (see Figure IV-10).

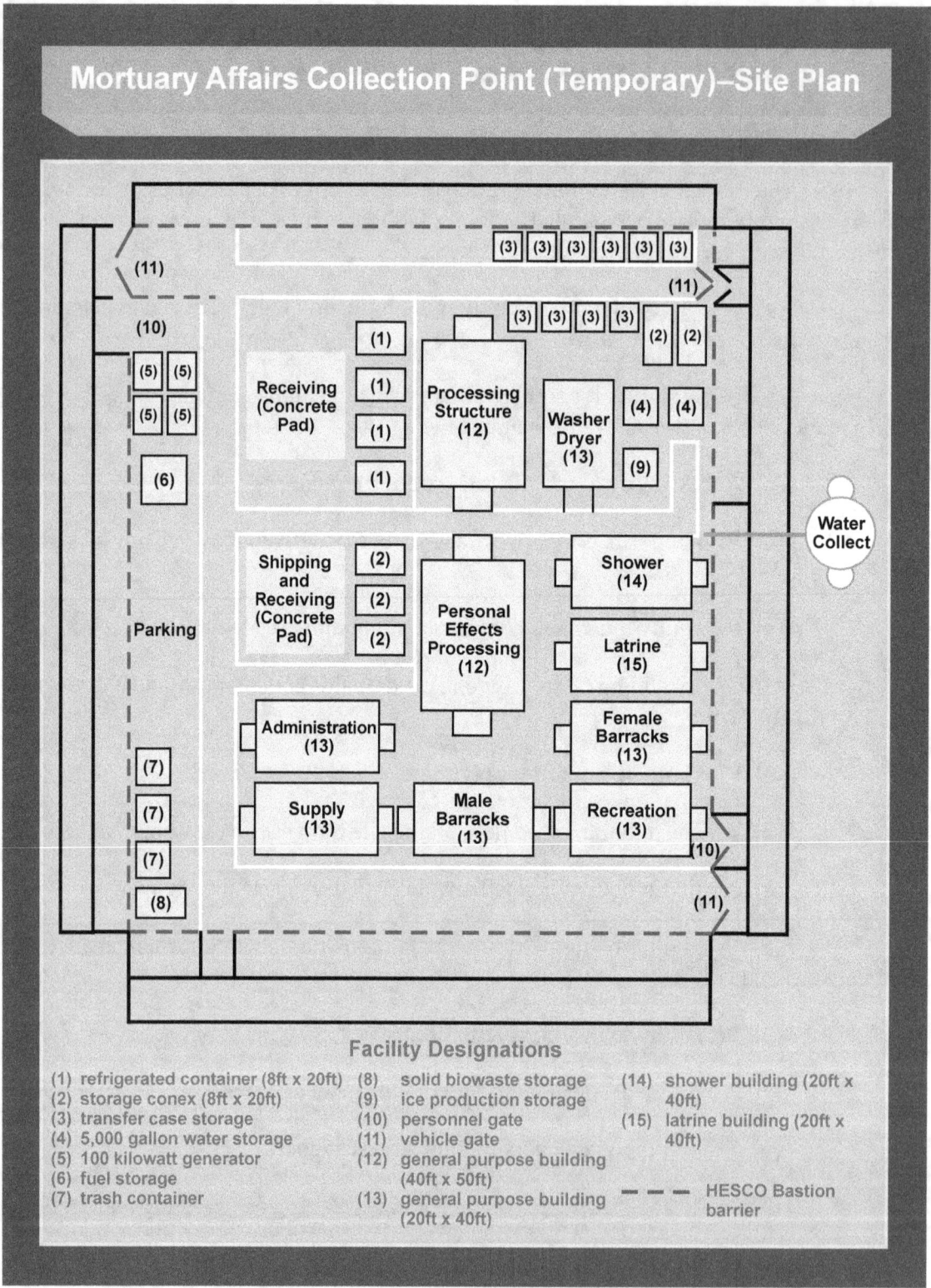

Mortuary Affairs Collection Point (Temporary)–Site Plan

Receiving (Concrete Pad)

Processing Structure (12)

Washer Dryer (13)

Water Collect

Shipping and Receiving (Concrete Pad)

Personal Effects Processing (12)

Shower (14)

Latrine (15)

Administration (13)

Female Barracks (13)

Supply (13)

Male Barracks (13)

Recreation (13)

Parking

Facility Designations

(1) refrigerated container (8ft x 20ft)
(2) storage conex (8ft x 20ft)
(3) transfer case storage
(4) 5,000 gallon water storage
(5) 100 kilowatt generator
(6) fuel storage
(7) trash container

(8) solid biowaste storage
(9) ice production storage
(10) personnel gate
(11) vehicle gate
(12) general purpose building (40ft x 50ft)
(13) general purpose building (20ft x 40ft)

(14) shower building (20ft x 40ft)
(15) latrine building (20ft x 40ft)

- - - HESCO Bastion barrier

Figure IV-10. Mortuary Affairs Collection Plan (Temporary)–Site Plan

(2) An MACP is composed of three basic sections: receiving, processing, and evacuation. The facility layout is based upon the structure and the support mission of the MACP. Highly mobile MACPs might be forced to operate all sections out of the MACP's mobile refrigeration container, from the back of a vehicle, or from a designated area on the ground. These points have the flexibility to tailor their facility layout based on the tactical situation. The ability of these MACPs to establish a temporary facility depends directly on the maneuver scheme of the unit supporting the MACP.

(3) A more stable, better organized MACP should be established in secure areas. The following actions should be taken to ensure successful operation of the MACP: establish a road network with parking areas with directional signs; erect screening material at the earliest possible moment to shield the operations of the MACP from public view from the ground and, if possible, from the air; construct a perimeter to prevent unauthorized personnel and news media from entering the area; coordinate engineering support to construct a helipad near the MACP, if one does not already exist; arrange engineering support to establish or improve a road network and perimeter for the CP; tailor the facility layout to the features of the area to be used. Figure IV-11 is an illustration of a recommended MACP layout.

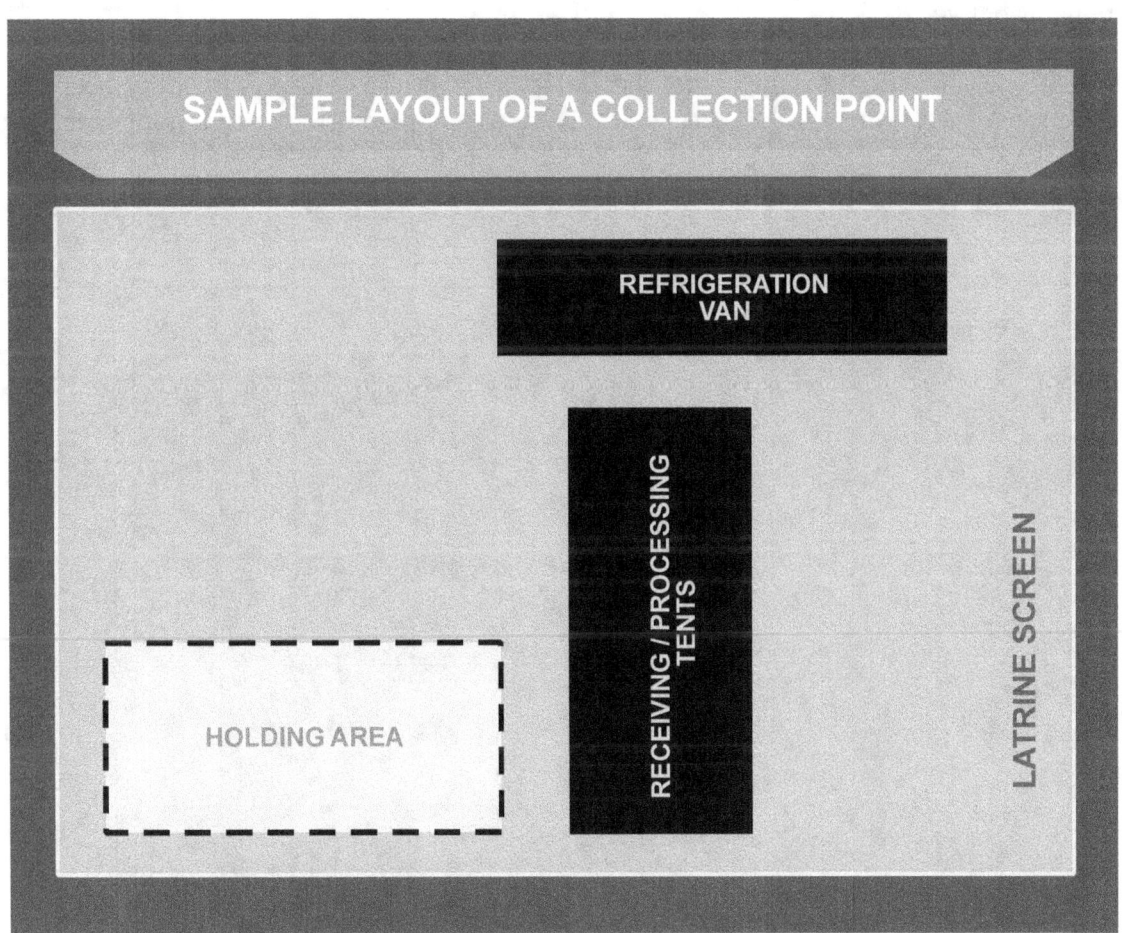

Figure IV-11. Sample Layout of a Collection Point

d. **Operations**

(1) **Receiving Operations**

(a) When possible, x-ray human remains and PE during receiving operations at an MACP for unexploded ordnance (UXO), booby traps, and other hazardous items prior to entering the receiving area. Receiving personnel must verify that this was accomplished. Verification that human remains and PE are clear of UXO may be accomplished via fluoroscope, digital x-ray, or, at a minimum, handheld metal detector. The level of verification will be determined by the GCC based on the level of risk to personnel and strategic airlift assets. If items are found, EOD personnel must be notified at once and processing must cease until items have been cleared for further processing.

(b) Prepare the DD Form 1077 (Collection Point Register of Deceased Personnel). The DD Form 1077 is a daily log of all human remains received at the MACP, whether unidentified, BTB, or portions. Prepare a new register each day the MACP is in operation. The reporting period starts at 0001 and ends at 2400 (local time). Retain a copy of all registers at the MACP for internal records.

(c) Upon arrival of the human remains, MACP personnel record all required information on the DD Form 1077 (Figure IV-12). Confirm the actual number of human remains delivered.

(d) Human remains are checked for recovery tags and any other accompanying paperwork. Recovery tags, if present, are removed and placed in the case folder file, and MACP evacuation tags are placed on the human remains. Do not delay normal processing and evacuation for lack of information. Evacuation number preparation instructions: The

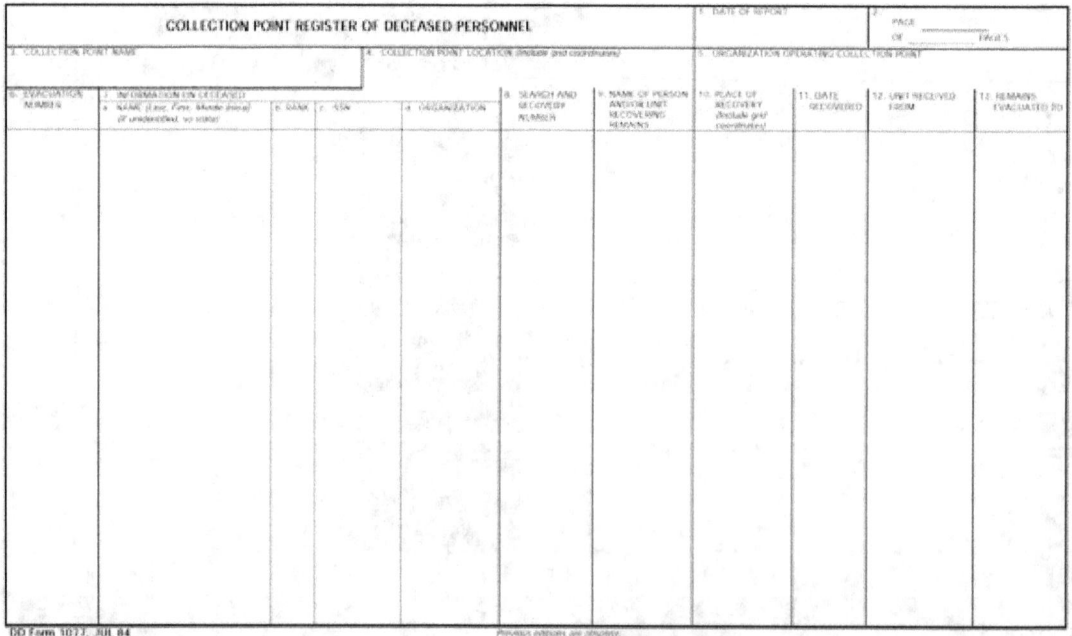

Figure IV-12. DD Form 1077, Collection Point Register of Deceased Personnel

The evacuation number has four parts:

1. A letter code R, P, E, D, T

2. Sequential number and year

3. Branch of Service and unit operating the collection point

4. Collection point identifier (number or location)

Example: EVAC # R11-94/AR54th QM CO/Balad

This EVAC # represents a human remains/the 11th evacuation in 1994 evacuated by the Army 54th Quartermaster Company collection point Balad.

evacuation number consists of a sequential number. A letter is placed in front of the evacuation number to identify what is being evacuated. An "R" can represent a BTB or unidentified human remains. The BTB is one where tentative ID can be obtained from ID media on the human remains. An unidentified is assigned when there is not any ID media to aid in ID in order to assign a BTB identity to the human remains. A "P" represents a portion, an "E" represents PE, a "D" represents disassociated effects, and "T" represents transfer of those items through an additional MACP during the current calendar year. The evacuation number is automatically assigned if the MACP is using MARTS.

(e) Complete two evacuation tags for each human remains. For BTB human remains, record the last name, first name, middle initial, and the last four digits of the Social Security number (SSN) on one side of the tag. For unidentified human remains, write "unidentified" instead. On the reverse side, record the evacuation number issued to each human remains as recorded on DD Form 1077 and seal number used to seal the HRP. One tag is attached to the human remains and the other to the HRP (see Figure IV-13).

(f) When MACP personnel process body portions, the evacuation tag is completed as follows: "PORTIONS" is written on one side of the tag; beneath "PORTIONS" the sequential "P" number of portions is written as shown on Figure IV-14. The reverse side is completed the same as for human remains. When placing several portions into one HRP, recovered from the same general location, the portions will not be individually bagged unless there is a strong presumption that the human remains belong to a distinct BTB or that the place or recovery (provenience) information for each portion is critical to an investigation. When possible, maintain skeletal integrity and keep skeletal remains together. The HRP must have an evacuation tag; on the front, the word "PORTIONS" is written and beneath it the total number of portions contained in the HRP. Portions recovered from geographically or incidentally distinct areas should be bagged separately from one another. When preparing for evacuation, HRPs with portions that have been tagged and sealed may be placed inside a second HRP to consolidate them for transport. This means that there would be an outer HRP which contained separate tagged and sealed HRPs, an inner pouch and an outer pouch. The evacuation tag would be marked on the front "PORTIONS," and beneath it the total number of portions contained in the HRP from both

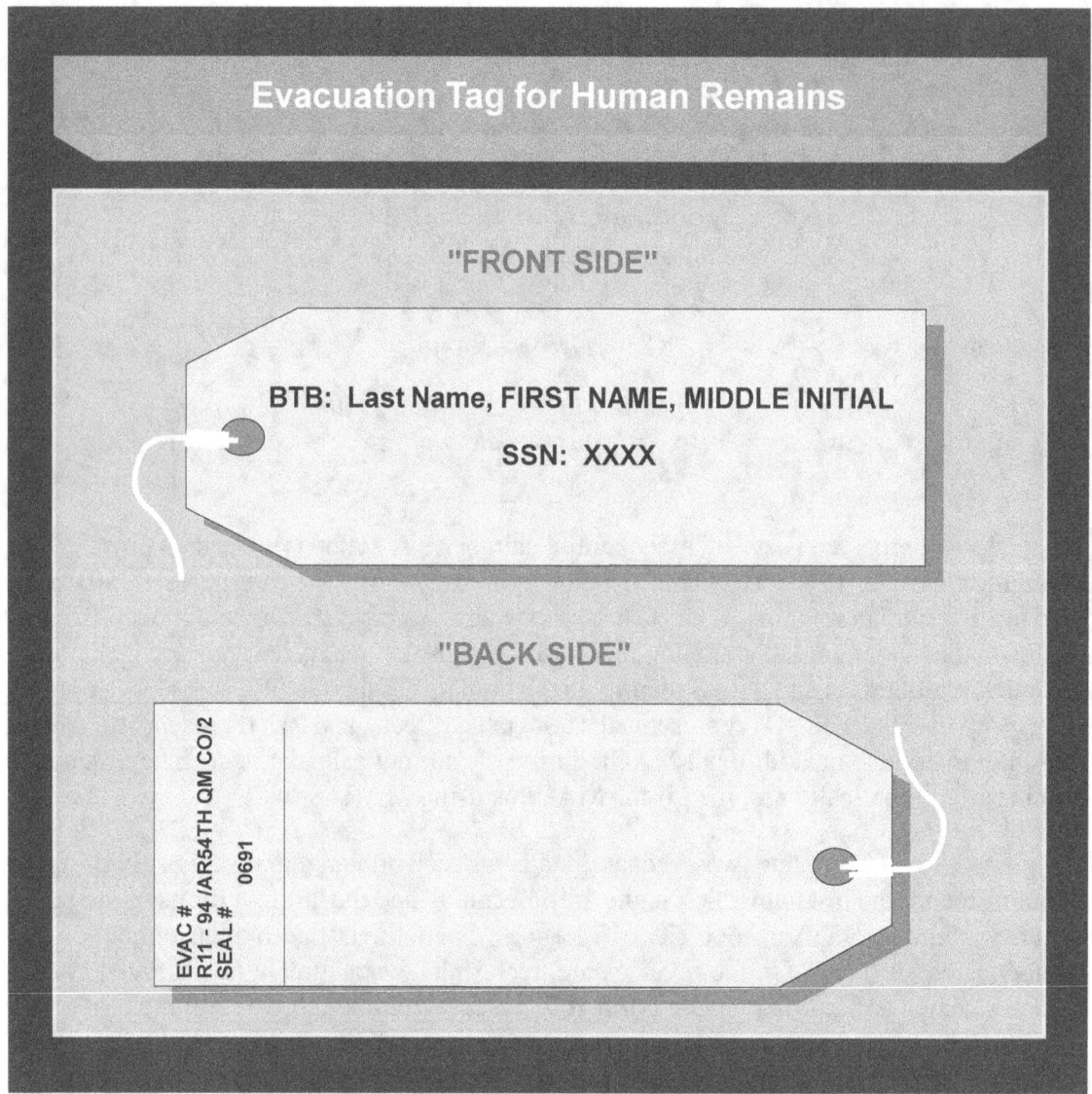

Evacuation Tag for Human Remains

"FRONT SIDE"

BTB: Last Name, FIRST NAME, MIDDLE INITIAL

SSN: XXXX

"BACK SIDE"

EVAC #
R11 - 94 /AR54TH QM CO/2
SEAL #   0691

Figure IV-13. Evacuation Tag for Human Remains

internal pouches. The back of the tag is completed as all others (Figure IV-15). Do not physically associate any portions with other portions or human remains. HRPs will contain unidentified human remains, BTB human remains, or portions of human remains. Commingling of these categories of human remains in a single HRP is not authorized. Note: An "R" number will be assigned to any item found that constitutes more than 50 percent of a human body and includes a majority of the torso. The team leader will make this determination. Items not representing more than 50 percent are classified as a portion and will receive a sequential "P" number. A torso will be marked as human remains. Body regions such as an isolated head or legs, even if attached at the pelvis, will be marked as portions.

(g) Based on the workload, move the human remains to the processing area or keep the human remains at the receiving holding area under refrigeration to wait for further processing.

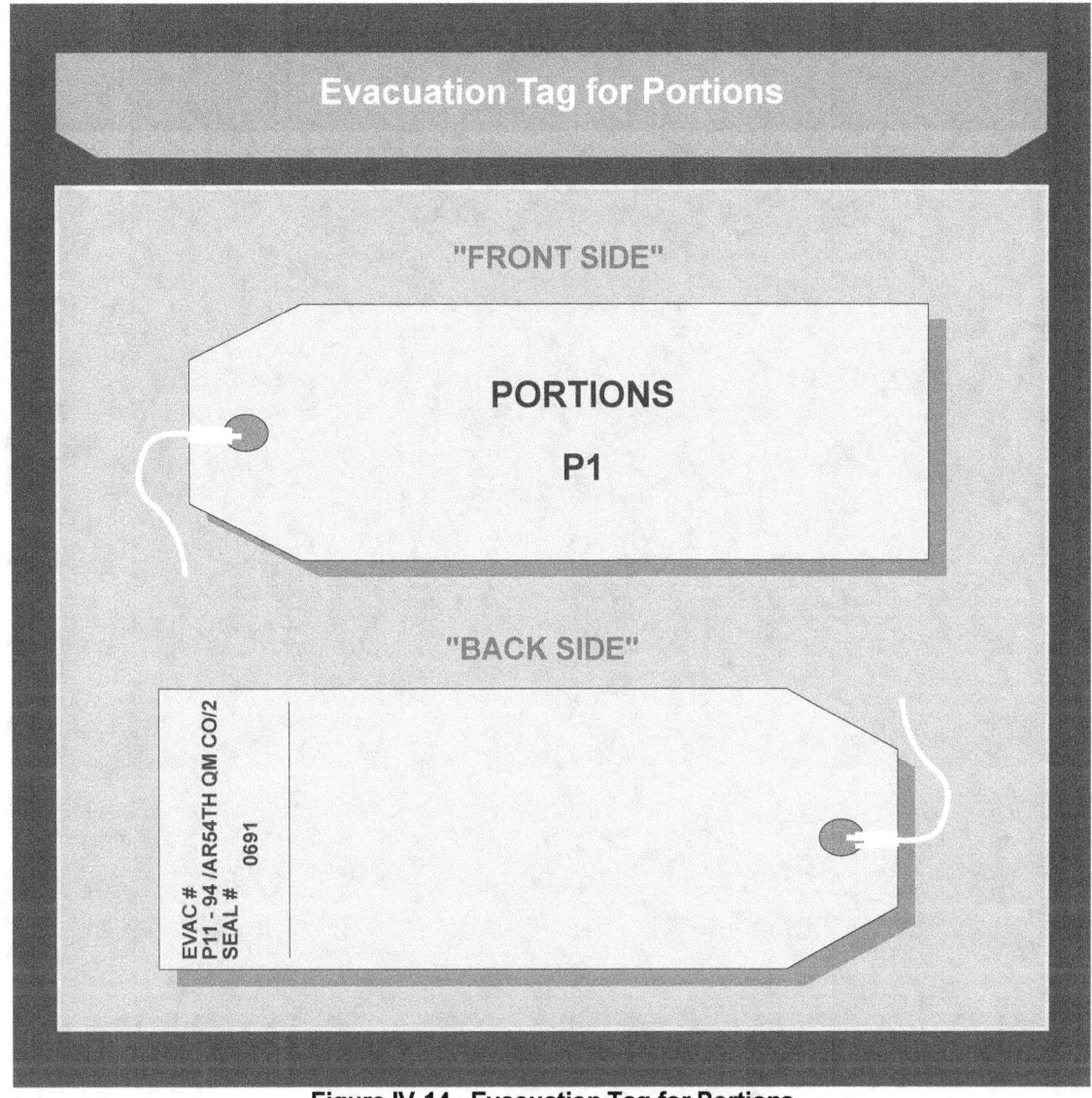

Figure IV-14. Evacuation Tag for Portions

(h) Initiate an original and duplicate individual case file. The top portion of the file should have BTB name, rank, SSN, seal number, and evacuation number. Create an alpha index card containing the following information: BTB name or unidentified, SSN, evacuation number, and other appropriate remarks (Figure IV-16). This file is kept at the MACP as a quick reference for questions about human remains processed through the MACP.

(i) Initiate a case file in MARTS by "accepting" the human remains into the system. Prepare all MA documents in MARTS if available. If MARTS is not operational, follow the guidance for preparation of paper forms.

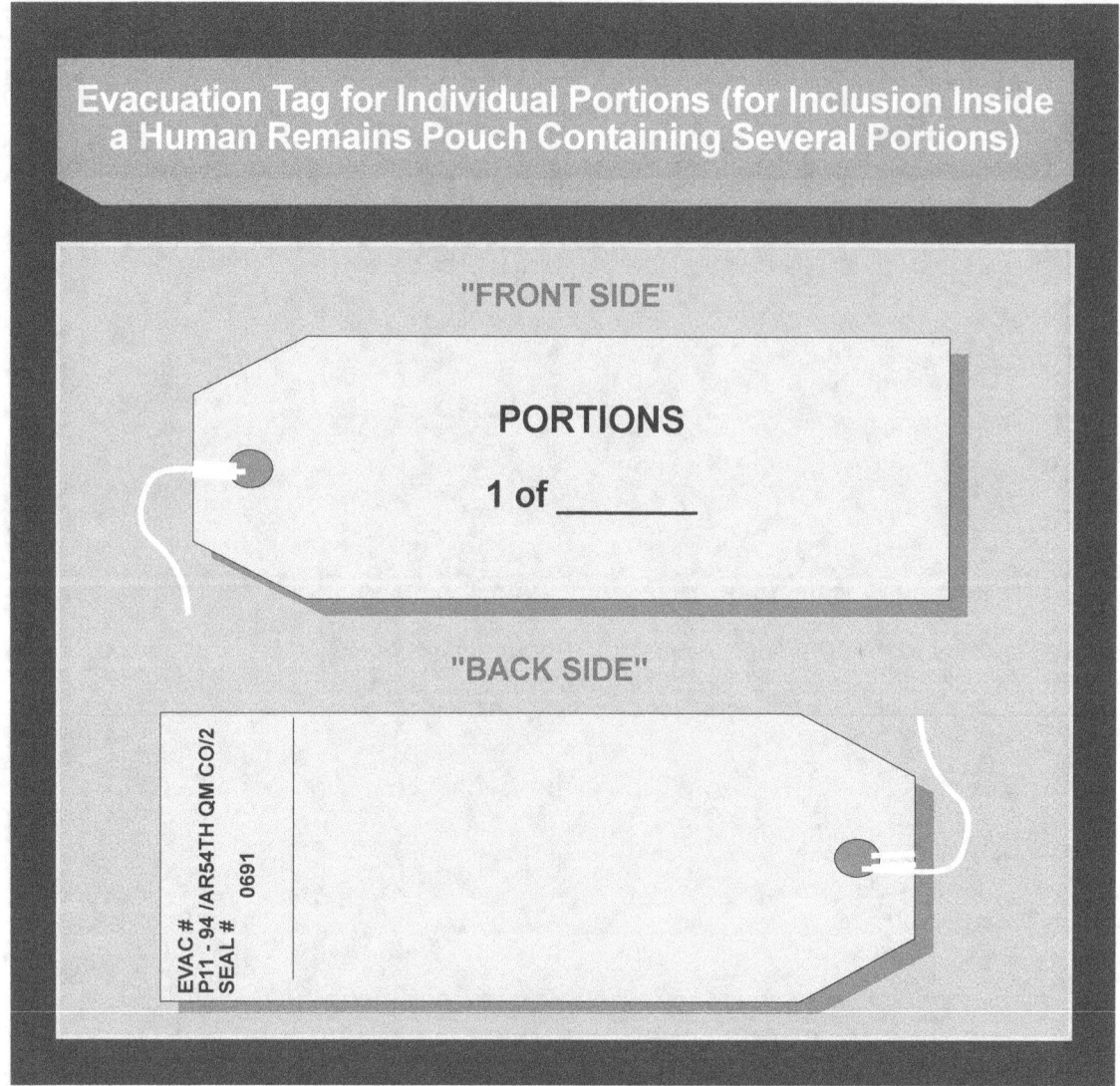

Figure IV-15. Evacuation Tag for Individual Portions (for Inclusion Inside a Human Remains Pouch Containing Several Portions)

(2) **Processing Operations**

(a) The method and extent of processing conducted at the MACP depends on the prevailing operational constraints and local MA procedures. A mobile forward MACP might not have the time or support to conduct full-scale processing operations. When the MACP workload is overwhelming, the MACP OIC/NCOIC may make the decision to follow the minimum hasty processing procedures. The minimum procedures that must be accomplished are: prepare evacuation tags; complete DD Form 1077; remove any ammunition, explosives, weapons, or classified material; place evacuation tag on human remains; and if not already in an HRP, place human remains in an HRP. Put the PE bag in the HRP, then put an evacuation tag on the HRP and seal it. The human remains are then placed in the refrigeration container. A DD Form 1075 (Convoy List of Remains of Deceased Personnel) must be prepared. See Figure IV-17. Finally, load the human remains on the transport vehicle. The driver must sign for the human remains on the DD Form 1075.

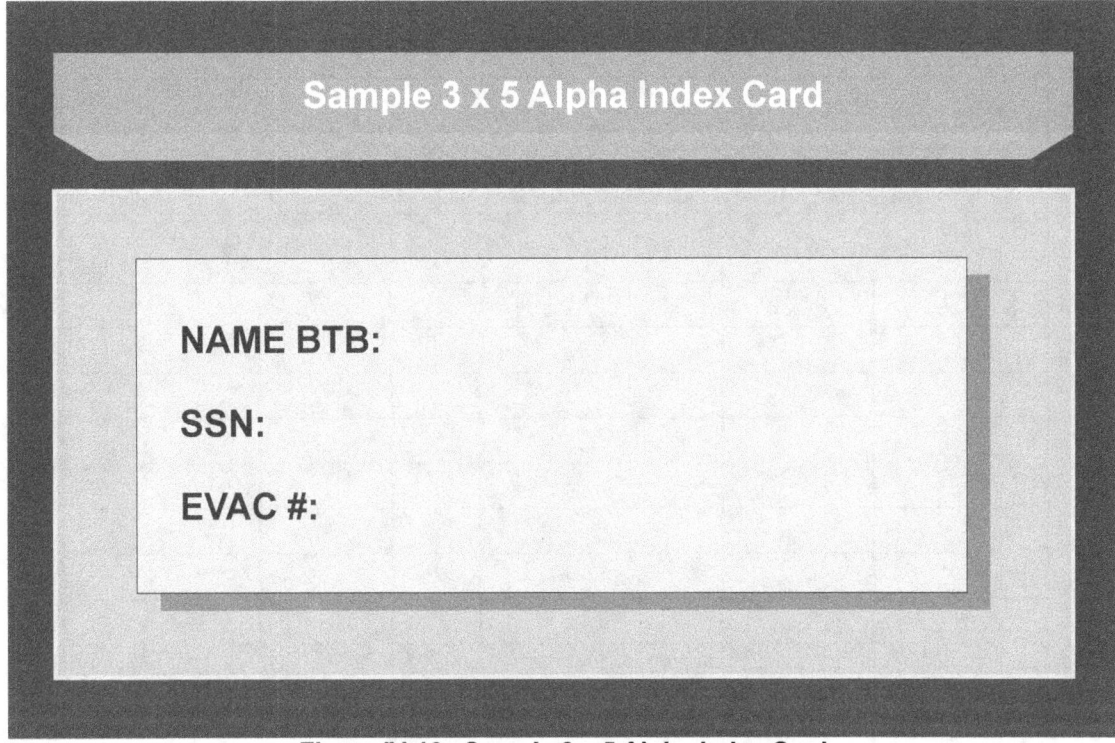

Figure IV-16. Sample 3 x 5 Alpha Index Card

(b) When human remains are taken to the processing area, personnel who operate the processing section examine all documents in the case file and the state of the human remains. Check to see if a DD Form 1380 (US Field Medical Card), Standard Form (SF) 600 (Health Record—Chronological Record of Medical Care), or DD Form 2064 (United States Department of Defense Certificate of Death) is present. See Figure IV-18 and Figure IV-19. Certified medical authority will pronounce death and complete a DD Form 2064 or other appropriate documents for transport of the human remains back to Dover AFB mortuary. On the death certificate, the cause of death will be listed as "Pending AFME determination."

(c) Check the state of the human remains to determine if they are intact. In cases where human remains are missing major portions, check to see if there is any documentation from the unit indicating that a search for missing portions was conducted. If sufficient documentation does not exist, attempt to contact the unit for a report. After all attempts to recover major portions have been exhausted, generate a certificate of non-recoverability of missing major portions. **Do not delay shipment** of the recovered remains in order to search for missing portions. Include this certificate in the case file. If information is received after the human remains have been evacuated, prepare a message stating all pertinent information and forward it through higher headquarters to the JMAO.

CONVOY LIST OF REMAINS OF DECEASED PERSONNEL

PRIVACY ACT STATEMENT

AUTHORITY: 10 USC Sections 1481 through 1488, EO 9397, Nov. 1943 (SSN).

PURPOSE AND USE: This form is used to establish initial identification of deceased personnel.

DISCLOSURE: Personal information provided on this form is given on a voluntary basis. Failure to provide this information, however, may result in improper identification of the deceased person and person making visual identification.

1. FROM	2. TO	3. DATE PREPARED (YYYYMMDD)	4. PAGE OF PAGES

5. VEHICLE/AIRCRAFT ID NUMBER	6. EVACUATION NUMBER	7. TENTATIVELY IDENTIFIED DECEDENT (If unidentified, so state)			
		a. NAME (Last, First, Middle Initial)	b. GRADE	c. SSN	d. ORGANIZATION

8. AIRCRAFT/VEHICLE DEPARTED	9. AIRCRAFT/VEHICLE COMMANDER		
a. TIME	a. NAME (Last, First, Middle Initial)	b. GRADE	c. ORGANIZATION
b. DATE (YYYYMMDD)	d. SIGNATURE		e. DATE SIGNED (YYYYMMDD)
10. AIRCRAFT/VEHICLE ARRIVED	11. RECEIVING OFFICIAL		
a. TIME	a. NAME (Last, First, Middle Initial)	b. GRADE	c. ORGANIZATION
b. DATE (YYYYMMDD)	d. SIGNATURE		e. DATE SIGNED (YYYYMMDD)

DD FORM 1075, JUL 1998 (EG)   PREVIOUS EDITION MAY BE USED.   Designed using Perform Pro, WHS/DIOR, Jul 98

Figure IV-17. DD Form 1075, Convoy List of Remains of Deceased Personnel

1. NAME (Last-First-Middle Initial)/NOM, PRENOMS		2. SERVICE NUMBER/NUMERO MATRICULE	3. GRADE/GRADE	4. NATION/NATION (e.g. Etats Unis)
5. FORCE/ARMEE	6. BRANCH AND TRADE/ARME (e.g. Infanterie)	7. UNIT/UNITE		8. SERVICE (Yrs)/DUREE DES SERVICES (e.g. 2 6/12)
9. AGE/AGE	10. RACE/RACE	11. RELIGION/RELIGION	12 FACILITY WHERE TAGGED/LIEU D'ETABLISSEMENT DE LA FICHE	13. DATE AND HOUR TAGGED/DATE ET HEURE D'ETABLISSEMENT DE LA FICHE

14. DIAGNOSIS (Including cause)/DIAGNOSTIC (Cause comprise)

NATURE OF CASUALTY OR ILLNESS / NATURE DE LA BLESSURE OU MALADIE

18. DATE & HOUR INJURED/DATE ET HEURE DE LA BLESSURE

DISABILITY/INCAPACITE	ENEMY ACTION/ DU FAIT DE L'ENNEMI	
16. INJURY/BLESSURE	☐ YES/OUI	☐ NO/NON
17. SICK/MALADIE	☐ YES/OUI	☐ NO/NON

19. WHAT WAS HE DOING WHEN INJURED/QUE FAISAIT-IL LORSQU'IL FUT BLESSE

15. LINE OF DUTY/EN RELATION AVEC LE SERVICE

20. TREATMENT GIVEN (For antibiotics specify which and give dose, hour and date)/ TRAITEMENT EFFECTUE (Si des antibiotiques ont été donnés, précisez leur nature, la dose, l'heure et la date)

TREATMENT/TRAITEMENT EFFECTUE	a. DOSE/ DOSE	b. HOUR AND DATE/ HEURE - DATE
22. MORPHINE- 1st/MORPHINE- 1ere		
23. MORPHINE- 2nd/MORPHINE- 2eme		
24. MORPHINE- 3rd /MORPHINE- 3eme		
25. TETANUS TOXOID/ VACCIN ANTITETANIQUE		
26. A. T. SERUM/SERUM ANTITETANIQUE		

21.TOURNIQUET (Yes or No; Time & date applied)/ MISE EN PLACE D'UN GARROT (Oui ou Non; heure et date)

27. DISPOSITION-DISPOSAL/DESTINATION DONNEE AU BLESSE	28. HOUR AND DATE/ HEURE ET DATE	29.MEDICAL OFFICER (Signature & Grade)/SIGNATURE ET GRADE DU MEDECIN

DD FORM 1380. 1 JUN 62   U. S. FIELD MEDICAL CARD/FICHE MEDICALE DE L'AVANT ETATS-UNIS

30.	a. ABSOLUTION/CONFESSION	b. HOLY COMMUNION/SAINTE COMMUNION	c. EXTREME UNCTION/EXTREME ONCTION
	d. OTHER MINISTRATIONS/AUTRES MINISTERES	e. CHAPLAIN (Signature)/SIGNATURE DE L'AUMONIER	

31. DIET/REGIME ALIMENTAIRE
☐ REGULAR/NORMAL   ☐ LIQUID/LIQUIDE   ☐ NOTHING BY MOUTH/RIEN PAR VOIE ORALE

32. REMARKS/REMARQUES

☆ U. S. GOVERNMENT PRINTING OFFICE: 1967—173-261

Figure IV-18. DD Form 1380, US Field Medical Card

UNITED STATES DEPARTMENT OF DEFENSE CERTIFICATE OF DEATH

SECTION I - DECEDENT INFORMATION

1. NAME OF DECEASED (Last, First, Middle)	2. GRADE	3. BRANCH AND COMPONENT OF SERVICE	4. SSN

5. ORGANIZATION	6. CITIZENSHIP	8. DATE OF BIRTH	9. GENDER
	7. STATE, NATION OF BIRTH		☐ MALE ☐ FEMALE

10. RACE	11. HISPANIC ORIGIN YES ☐ NO ☐	12. MARITAL STATUS	13. RELIGION

14. NAME OF NEXT OF KIN	15. RELATIONSHIP TO DECEASED

16. STREET ADDRESS OF NEXT OF KIN	17. CITY OR TOWN AND STATE OR COUNTRY

SECTION 2 - MEDICAL STATEMENT

18. DATE OF DEATH	19. TIME OF DEATH	20. PLACE OF DEATH

21. CAUSE OF DEATH	22. INTERVAL BETWEEN ONSET AND DEATH
a. IMMEDIATE CAUSE[1]	
b. DUE TO	
c. DUE TO	
d. OTHER SIGNIFICANT CONDITIONS[2]	

23. AVIATION-RELATED: YES ☐ NO ☐	24. COMBAT-RELATED: YES ☐ NO ☐	25. OTHER (Explain below) ☐

26. CIRCUMSTANCES SURROUNDING DEATH DUE TO EXTERNAL CAUSES

27. MANNER OF DEATH

a. NATURAL ☐	b. ACCIDENT ☐	c. SUICIDE ☐	d. HOMICIDE ☐	e. UNDETERMINED ☐	f. PENDING ☐

g. AUTOPSY PERFORMED: YES ☐ NO ☐	h. DATE OF AUTOPSY	i. PLACE OF AUTOPSY

I HAVE VIEWED THE REMAINS OF THE DECEASED AND DEATH OCCURRED AT THE TIME INDICATED AND FROM THE CAUSES AS STATED ABOVE

28a. CERTIFYING PHYSICIAN NAME	28b. GRADE	28c. TITLE OR DEGREE
28d. CERTIFYING PHYSICIAN SIGNATURE		28e. DATE
29a. PATHOLOGIST NAME	29b. GRADE	29c. TITLE OR DEGREE
29d. PATHOLOGIST SIGNATURE		29e. DATE

SECTION 3 - MORTUARY AFFAIRS

30a. MORTICIAN PREPARING REMAINS	30b. GRADE	30c. LICENSE NUMBER AND STATE
30d. INSTALLATION OR ADDRESS	30e. DATE	30f. SIGNATURE

31. NAME OF CEMETERY OR CREMATORY	32. LOCATION OF CEMETERY OR CREMATORY

33. TYPE OF DISPOSITION	34. DATE OF DISPOSITION

[1] State disease, injury or complication which caused death, but not mechanism of dying such as heart failure, etc.
[2] State conditions contributing to the death, but not related to the disease or condition causing death

DD Form 2064, TEST

Figure IV-19. DD Form 2064, United States Department of Defense Certificate of Death

(3) Chain of custody and inventory integrity for decedent effects (DE) is a primary responsibility of the MA community; two person controls will be maintained while conducting an inventory of DE or PE. Identify, inspect, and record all official military and personal ID media, PE, and personal clothing and equipment using DD Form 890 (Record of Identification Processing [Effects and Physical Data]) (see Figure IV-20) and DD Form 1076/1076C (Record of Personal Property/Personal Effects and Record of Personal Property/Personal Effects Continuation Sheet) (see Figure IV-21 and Figure IV-22). Search all personal equipment, clothing, pockets, and the areas around the neck, wrists, and fingers for PE. (Note: Be particularly careful during processing to avoid contaminating or destroying forensic evidence. Carefully remove the DE from the pockets. Minimize handling to preserve physical and biological forensic evidence. DE should not be removed from the human remains. Record the items and leave in place, annotating their location on a DD Form 1076. Pay particularly close attention to locating the ID tags and the ID card. Leave ID tags/ID card in the location found on the human remains. Use official ID media found as a basis for establishing tentative ID. Leave all ID media, PE, clothing and organizational equipment on the human remains for forensic analysis. Inventory PE and record these items on DD Form 1076. Note: No military clothing or military issued items are annotated on this form. Only PE found on the human remains or in the human remains' clothing or equipment are annotated on this form.

(4) In cases when disassociated effects are received at an MACP, do not attempt to associate them with a particular human remains. Create a file using the DD Form 1076. Generate a disassociated effects tag (Figure IV-23) for the disassociated effects. The tags will have the words "DISASSOCIATED EFFECTS" written on one side. On the reverse side assign a sequential "D" number to each disassociated effect. Record Service letter designator, the unit operating the MACP, and MACP number designator. Place the disassociated effects, with one copy of the DD Form 1076 and the tag, in the slide closure plastic bag and store in one or more PE bag(s) as needed. Place the other tag on the PE bag. Evacuate the loose PE when evacuating human remains as a separate item. Disassociated effects will not be transported in an HRP or placed in a transfer case.

(5) The use of MARTS software at the MACP will facilitate expedient processing and tracking of human remains and PE throughout the process.

(6) Take two sets of pictures for each human remains using a digital camera. Take a full facial picture, complete anterior photo of the body, then gently roll the body over and take a posterior view of the body. The pictures are used to document the state of the human remains at the time the human remains enter the MA system. Pictures should be stored on disk and only released to the AFMES.

(7) Place the original, completed case file in a closed or sealed plastic bag placed inside the HRP. If transporting the human remains inside a transfer case, tape the sealed plastic bag to the transfer case lid. The duplicate case file is kept at the MACP along with a statement as to whether PE were present on the human remains and if they were evacuated

RECORD OF IDENTIFICATION PROCESSING
(Effects and Physical Data)

DATE

LAST NAME - FIRST NAME - MIDDLE INITIAL *(Or unknown number)* | GRADE | SERVICE NO. SSAN | CIL CASE NUMBER *(If applicable)*

NAME OF CEMETERY, EVACUATION NUMBER, OR SEARCH AND RECOVERY NUMBER | PLOT | ROW | GRAVE

RECEIVED FROM

IMPRINT OF IDENTIFICATION TAG

OFFICIAL IDENTIFICATION FOUND WITH REMAINS *(Include personal effects aiding identification)*

ITEMS OF CLOTHING AND EQUIPMENT FOUND WITH REMAINS *(Indicate type, color, size, markings, service, etc. If laundry marks are indistinct, follow procedures outlined in TM 10-286)*

FINGERPRINTS TAKEN ☐ YES ☐ NO | X-RAYS MADE ☐ YES ☐ NO | FLUOROSCOPE STATEMENT ATTACHED ☐ YES ☐ NO

PHOTOGRAPHS TAKEN ☐ YES ☐ NO | ANTHROPOLOGICAL STATEMENT MADE ☐ YES ☐ NO | CHEMICAL STATEMENT ATTACHED ☐ YES ☐ NO

PHYSICAL DESCRIPTION

ESTIMATED HEIGHT | MUSCULARITY | COLOR OF HAIR | RACE OR NATIVITY

TATTOOS, SCARS OR MARKS ON BODY

EVIDENCE OF HEALED FRACTURES AND BONE MALFORMATIONS

WOUNDS OR INJURIES

I HAVE PERSONALLY VIEWED THE REMAINS OF THIS DECEASED AND ALL RESULTING INFORMATION HAS BEEN RECORDED TO THE BEST OF MY KNOWLEDGE.

NAME, GRADE, AND ORGANIZATION | SIGNATURE

DD FORM 890, JAN 58 PREVIOUS EDITION OF THIS FORM IS OBSOLETE.

Figure IV-20. DD Form 890, Record of Identification Processing (Effects and Physical Data)

from the MACP. Additional documentation that could be in the file includes a DD Form 1076, DD Form 2064, SF 600, DD Form 1380, DD Form 565, and photos of the human remains. The HRP is then sealed and stored or evacuated. The seal number should already be recorded on the case file and both evacuation tags.

RECORD OF PERSONAL PROPERTY/PERSONAL EFFECTS

1. DATE (YYYYMMDD)	2. PAGE OF PAGES

PRIVACY ACT STATEMENT

AUTHORITY: 10 USC Sections 1481 through 1488, EO 9397, Nov. 1943 (SSN).

PURPOSE AND USE: This form is used to establish association of personal property/personal effects.

DISCLOSURE: Personal information provided on this form is given on a voluntary basis. Failure to provide this information, however, may result in improper identification of the personal effects/personal belongings.

3. PERSONAL PROPERTY/PERSONAL EFFECTS BELIEVED TO BE OF:

| a. NAME (Last, First, Middle Initial) (or Unidentified) | b. GRADE | c. SSN | d. ORGANIZATION | e. STATUS | f. DATE OF STATUS (YYYYMMDD) |

| 4. PLACE OF RECOVERY (include grid coordinates) | 5. DATE OF RECOVERY (YYYYMMDD) | 6. EVACUATION NUMBER |

7. INVENTORY OF PERSONAL PROPERTY/PERSONAL EFFECTS Use DD Form 1076C for additional entries.

| a. QUANTITY | b. DESCRIPTION | c. RECEIVED | d. CONDITION | e. DISPOSITION |

8. FUNDS/NEGOTIABLE INSTRUMENTS/OTHER HIGH VALUE ITEMS TRANSMITTED WITH EFFECTS Use DD Form 1076C for additional entries.

| a. QUANTITY | b. DESCRIPTION | c. RECEIVED | d. CONDITION | e. DISPOSITION |

9. PREPARING OFFICIAL

I certify that the accuracy and propriety of the above inventory is in accordance with the current DoD directives governing it.

| a. NAME (Last, First, Middle Initial) | b. GRADE | c. ORGANIZATION |
| d. SIGNATURE | e. POSITION | f. DATE SIGNED (YYYYMMDD) |

10. RECEIVING OFFICIALS

I certify that the above listing comprises all the personal property and/or personal effects located in this area. I also certify that all my other responsibilities under current DoD regulations and applicable directives have been read and understood.

a. NAME (Last, First, Middle Initial)	b. GRADE	c. ORGANIZATION
d. SIGNATURE	e. POSITION	f. DATE SIGNED (YYYYMMDD)
a. NAME (Last, First, Middle Initial)	b. GRADE	c. ORGANIZATION
d. SIGNATURE	e. POSITION	f. DATE SIGNED (YYYYMMDD)
a. NAME (Last, First, Middle Initial)	b. GRADE	c. ORGANIZATION
d. SIGNATURE	e. POSITION	f. DATE SIGNED (YYYYMMDD)

11. PERSON ELIGIBLE TO RECEIVE EFFECTS (PERE) PERE determination is the responsibility of an appointed Summary Court Martial Officer.

I understand that delivery of the personal property and/or personal effects to me does not in itself vest title for this property or effects in me. Further, I accept this property effects contingent upon possible disposition to others in accordance with applicable state laws.

| a. NAME (Last, First, Middle Initial) | b. SIGNATURE | c. Were Personal Effects Inventoried before Receipt? (X as appropriate) ☐ YES ☐ NO | d. DATE SIGNED (YYYYMMDD) |

DD FORM 1076, AUG 2005, TEST   PREVIOUS EDITIONS ARE OBSOLETE

Figure IV-21. DD Form 1076, Record of Personal Property/Personal Effects

(8) Storage/Evacuation Operations

(a) Coordinate for transportation to evacuate the human remains. When vehicles are used, they must be covered. Aircraft are the preferred method for evacuating human remains.

RECORD OF PERSONAL PROPERTY/PERSONAL EFFECTS *(Continuation Sheet)* *To be used only in conjunction with a completed DD Form 1076*	1. DATE *(YYYYMMDD)*	2. PAGE OF PAGES

3.   PERSONAL PROPERTY/PERSONAL EFFECTS BELIEVED TO BE OF:

a. NAME *(Last, First, Middle Initial) (or Unidentified)*	b. GRADE	c. SSN	d. ORGANIZATION	e. STATUS	f. DATE OF STATUS *(YYYYMMDD)*

4.   INVENTORY OF PERSONAL PROPERTY/PERSONAL EFFECTS

a. QUANTITY	b. DESCRIPTION	c. RECEIVED	d. CONDITION	e. DISPOSITION

5.   FUNDS/NEGOTIABLE INSTRUMENTS/OTHER HIGH VALUE ITEMS TRANSMITTED WITH EFFECTS

a. QUANTITY	b. DESCRIPTION	c. RECEIVED	d. CONDITION	e. DISPOSITION

6.   RECEIVING OFFICIALS

I certify that the above listing comprises all the personal property and or personal effects located in this area. I also certify that all my other responsibilities under current DoD regulations and applicable directives have been read and understood.

a. NAME *(Last, First, Middle Initial)*	b. GRADE	c. ORGANIZATION	
d. SIGNATURE		e. POSITION	f. DATE SIGNED *(YYYYMMDD)*
a. NAME *(Last, First, Middle Initial)*	b. GRADE	c. ORGANIZATION	
d. SIGNATURE		e. POSITION	f. DATE SIGNED *(YYYYMMDD)*
a. NAME *(Last, First, Middle Initial)*	b. GRADE	c. ORGANIZATION	
d. SIGNATURE		e. POSITION	f. DATE SIGNED *(YYYYMMDD)*

7.   PERSON ELIGIBLE TO RECEIVE EFFECTS (PERE)   PERE determination is the responsibility of an appointed Summary Court Martial Officer.

I understand that delivery of the personal property and or personal effects to me does not in itself vest title for this property or effects in me. Further, I accept this property effects contingent upon possible disposition to others in accordance with applicable state laws.

a. NAME *(Last, First, Middle Initial)*	b. SIGNATURE	c. Were Personal Effects inventoried before Receipt? *(X as appropriate)* ☐ YES ☐ NO	d. DATE SIGNED *(YYYYMMDD)*

DD FORM 1076C, AUG 2005, TEST

Figure IV-22. DD Form 1076C, Record of Personal Property/Personal Effects (Continuation Sheet)

(b) Human remains awaiting evacuation must be kept under refrigeration. The temperature of the refrigeration container is maintained between 34 and 40 degrees Fahrenheit (1.1 and 4.4 degrees Celsius). Holding human remains in a refrigeration container will minimize decomposition. Do not freeze human remains under any circumstances. Ensure that the temperature is checked at periodic intervals. Additionally,

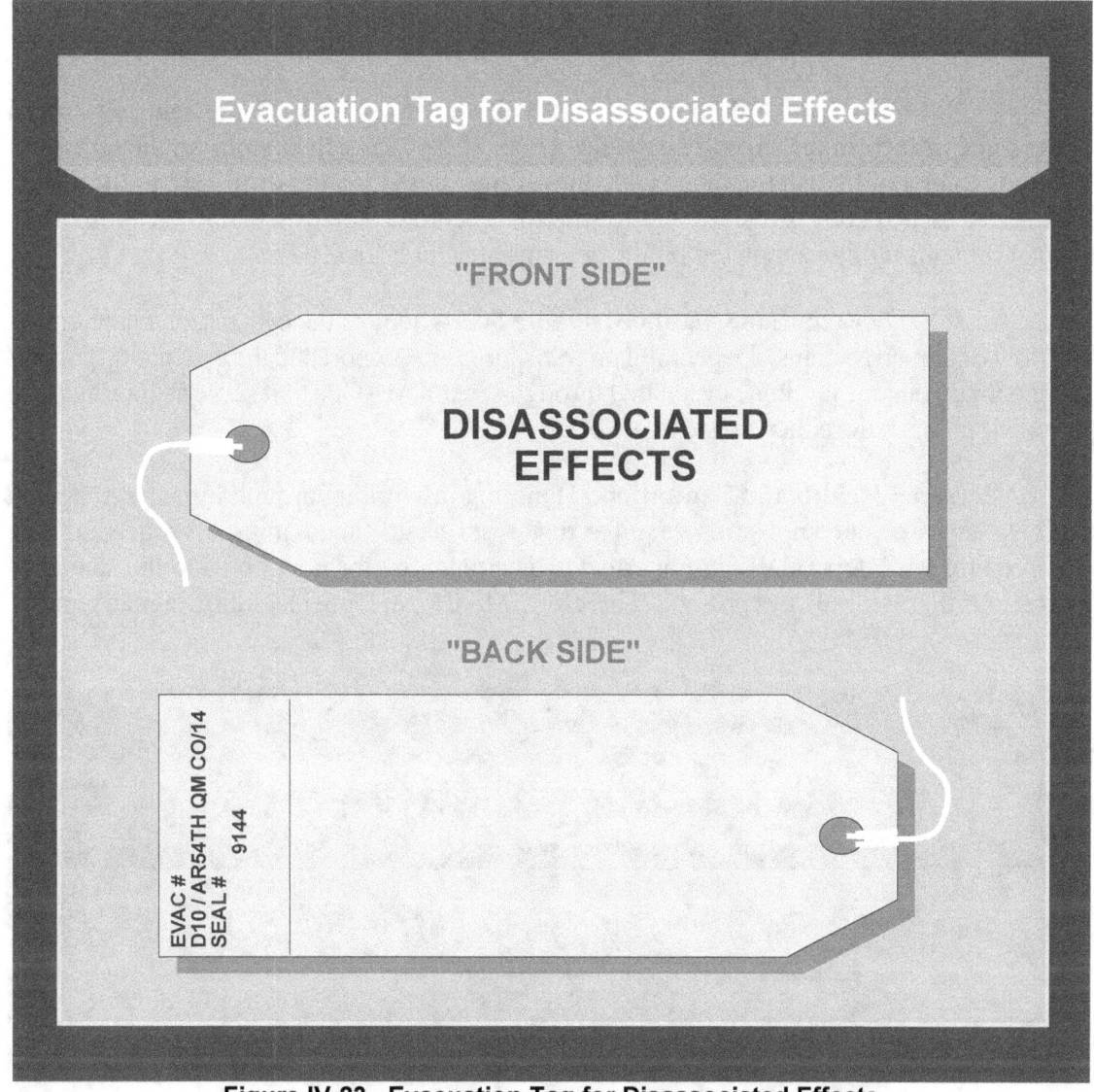

Figure IV-23. Evacuation Tag for Disassociated Effects

ensure that maintenance checks are performed as prescribed in applicable technical manuals on the refrigerator unit and generator.

(c) Upon arrival of transportation, load the human remains on a first received/first evacuated basis. Ensure that the human remains are handled in a respectful and reverent manner. Carry human remains feet first and face up. Position human remains in such a manner that prevents the stacking of human remains. Secure human remains in such a manner that prevents shifting during movement.

(d) Use of radio frequency identification (RFID) tags or current AIT for tracking human remains and PE should be initiated at the MACP whenever possible for better tracking and visibility of human remains and PE. Prior to loading and evacuation of human remains or PE, MA personnel prepare and input required information into MARTS to include tracking information such as barcode tag or RFID tag. MA personnel ensure that the tag is activated prior to shipment.

(e) Initiate a DD Form 1075. List all human remains that are being evacuated at the same time from the MACP on the DD Form 1075. The driver signs on the DD Form 1075 for receipt of human remains. Give the original copy of DD Form 1075 to the driver. Maintain a signed copy at the MACP for internal records. The evacuation location of the human remains will be annotated on the appropriate DD Form 1077.

(f) **Evacuation Channels.** Figure IV-24 depicts the evacuation channels for the flow of human remains. Depending on transportation support and the evacuation support plan, human remains might be evacuated through several MACPs that serve as intermediate or transit points before they arrive at a TMEP.

e. **Personal Health and Sanitation.** Handling or working around human remains in various stages of decomposition requires that strict health and sanitation procedures be enforced for the safety of all those involved. The potential for infection and the spread of contagious disease is always present. Therefore, MACP personnel handling human remains

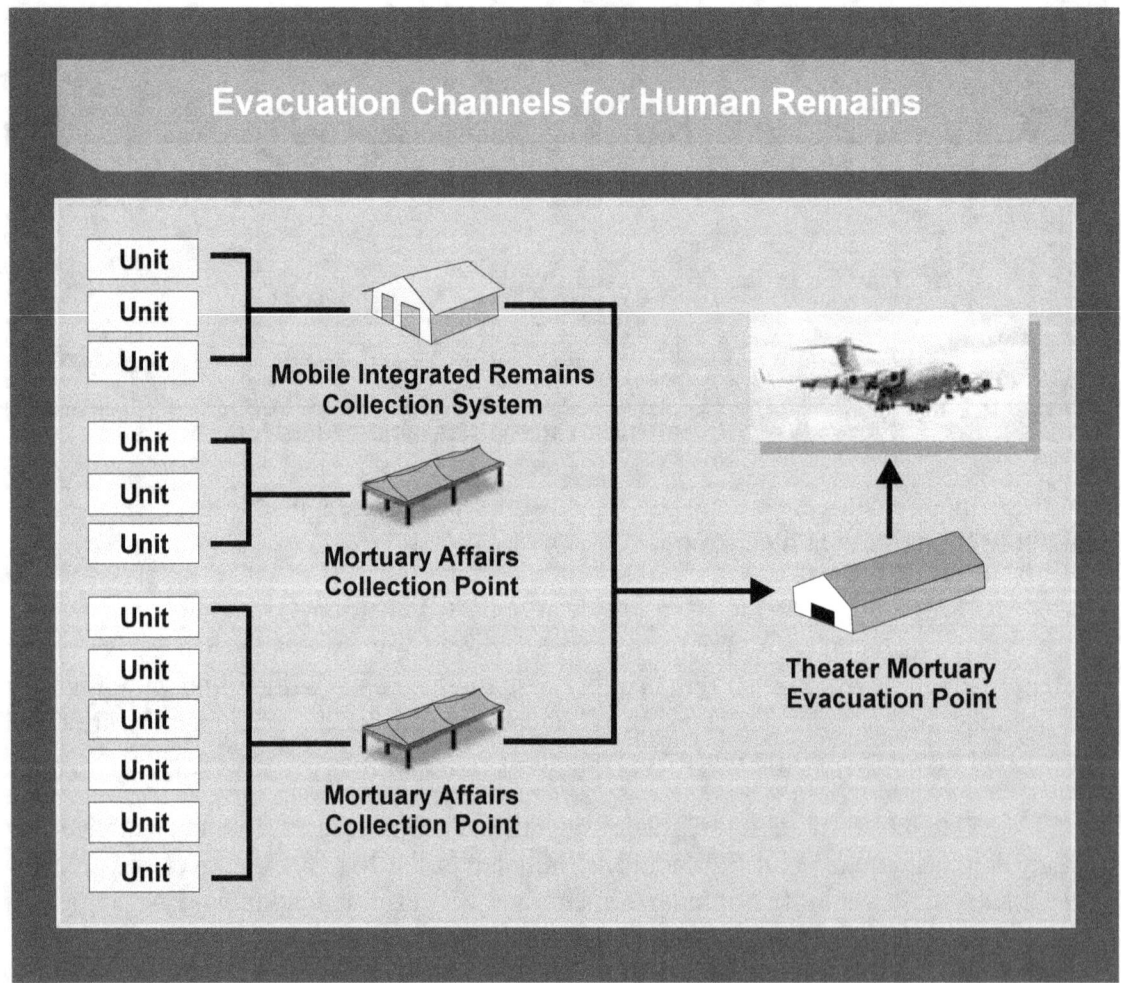

Figure IV-24. Evacuation Channels for Human Remains

or working in the areas where human remains have been should always be conscious of sanitation hazards and keep themselves and their work areas clean. Personnel handling human remains should wear, at a minimum, rubber gloves and surgical masks with eye protection.

f. **Transit Collection Point Operations.** Some operations in a theater require logistic support that spans vast areas to include more than one country. A transit collection point may be utilized. Human remains and DE that arrive at the MACP in transit to the TMEP are assigned a transit number, which is entered on the evacuation tag attached to the HRP or container. The transit number consists of the letter "T," calendar year, MACP branch of Service, MACP unit, and MACP identifier. To complete the DD Form 1077, enter "T" in block 6, enter the evacuation number and seal number in block 7a, and complete block numbers 12 and 13. Normally, there is no need to open the HRP or break the seal. If, however, the JMAO approves removal of the seal, or the seal is broken in transit or at the MACP, the incident must be documented. Record the reason, person responsible, location, and the date/time of the incident on the MA forms accompanying the HRP and in MARTS. Also record any corrective actions taken. Place a new seal on the HRP and record the serial number on the case file, in MARTS, and on the evacuation tags. If PE containers are damaged or seals are broken in transit, the MA personnel will conduct a two-person inventory with the personal effects inventory officer (PEIO) and report any discrepancies to the TMAO and the appropriate investigative agency. If the PEIO is not present, the MA personnel will conduct a two-person inventory and report any discrepancies to the PEIO, TMAO, and appropriate investigative agency. The PE will be packaged, sealed, and marked for onward shipment. MACPs are not staffed to handle PE but can be directed to assist in evacuation to the PE depot. Augmentation may be required to perform this task.

4. **Theater Mortuary Evacuation Point Operations**

a. A TMEP will be established with the primary mission of evacuating all human remains and accompanying PE to a military mortuary. The TMEP is task-organized to provide the following capabilities:

(1) Receive human remains and accompanying PE from any theater location.

(2) Perform quality assurance checks on existing documentation and/or initiate, complete, or obtain required processing documentation. "Receive" human remains in MARTS or initiate documentation in MARTS if a file does not exist.

(3) Prepare human remains for evacuation and/or hold and refrigerate human remains until transportation out of the theater can be arranged.

(4) Coordinate for aircraft and initiate all required shipping and special handling documents.

(5) Load, palletize, and tie down transfer cases and transport pallets to the Air Mobility Command (AMC) cargo special handling area.

b. Locate the TMEP at or adjacent to a major APOE. This arrangement will capitalize on all available aircraft and corresponding logistic support. Additional TMEPs may be established at other APOEs throughout the theater based on the following factors:

(1) The geographical size, population, and location of units in the theater.

(2) The projected number of human remains and the availability of aircraft to evacuate them.

(3) The operational concept and scheme of maneuver for all units in the theater.

c. The TMEP can, when tasked, operate a PE transfer point. When tasked with this secondary mission, the TMEP is organized to:

(1) Receive pre-inventoried and packaged PE from units in theater.

(2) Store and safeguard PE until transportation is coordinated.

(3) Load, palletize, and tie down PE and transport pallets to AMC cargo holding area for shipment to CONUS.

d. **Site Selection**

(1) Location of the TMEP is key to the overall success of its mission. Choose a site based on the following factors:

(a) Quick, easy access to and from all flight lines.

(b) Quick, easy access to AMC operations, transportation, and cargo and/or special handling areas.

(c) Ability to use existing facilities and/or build or install temporary fixed facilities such as trailers, refrigeration vans, and cold storage units.

(d) Ability to use an existing and/or build a road network to handle and regulate large traffic flow.

(e) Ability to use existing and/or install cooling system, ventilation system, electrical lines, phone lines, and water lines.

(2) TMEP personnel must coordinate with the area commander prior to selecting a proposed site to ensure the proposed site will not interfere with any ongoing flight line or base operations.

e. **Organizational and Facility Layout**

(1) When developing a site layout, consider the following:

(a) Vehicle and helicopter traffic flow, to include parking.

(b) Refrigeration containers. The MIRCS has the capability to store 15 remains in individual refrigeration units and may be used to support this requirement. Army MA companies have MIRCS as part of their authorized equipment.

(c) Electrical power source or generators.

(d) Water support.

(e) Communications.

(f) Waste disposal (regular and hazardous).

(g) Supply, equipment, and publication storage.

(h) Laundry and personal hygiene facilities.

(i) Morale and/or welfare recreation facilities.

(2) In establishing the actual layout for the facility, consideration should be given to structuring the facility in a manner that minimizes the manual lifting of human remains. Figure IV-25 illustrates a suggested site layout for a TMEP.

(3) Consider the supplies and services that an HN can provide when establishing and equipping a TMEP. Depending on the operational area and contractual agreements, the HN might be in a better position to provide support. Supplies and services often available through HNS include:

(a) Office, communications, and publication supplies and equipment.

(b) Medical and sanitation supplies and equipment.

(c) Sanitation and waste disposal treatment and removal.

(d) Refrigeration vans or trucks.

(e) Commercial vehicles and materials handling equipment with drivers.

(f) Bagged crushed ice delivery or equipment to produce ice.

(g) Maintenance personnel.

(h) Aircraft cargo loading specialists or laborers.

(4) TMEP personnel must remember the overall sensitivity of their mission when they use HN labor.

(5) A TMEP is structured into four sections. These sections are: receiving, processing, administrative, and evacuation sections.

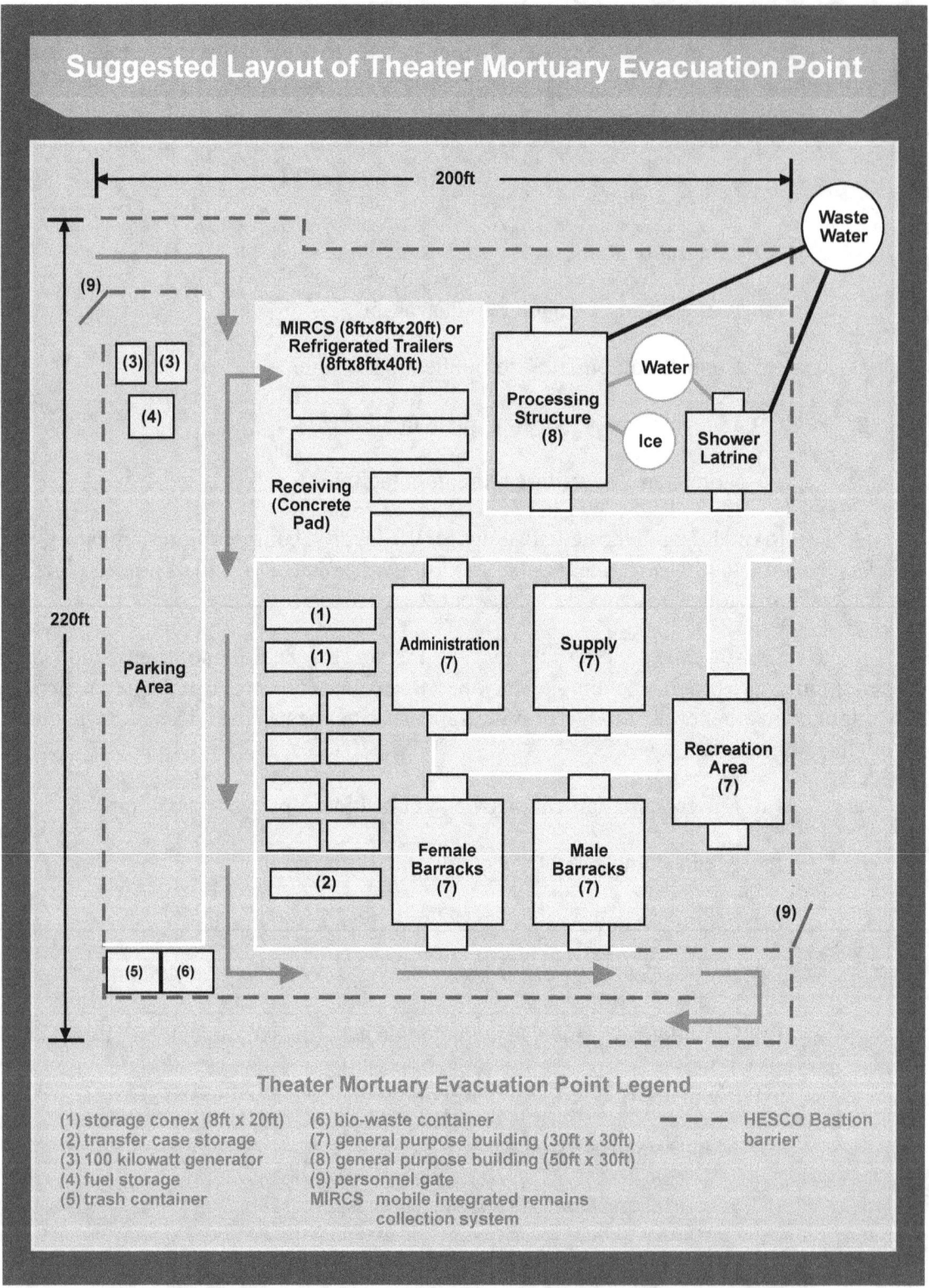

Figure IV-25. Suggested Layout for Theater Mortuary Evacuation Point

(a) **Receiving Section.** Receiving section personnel must meet the driver or persons transporting the human remains, portions, and/or effects. The receiving clerk:

<u>1</u>. Obtains DD Form 1075 from the driver.

<u>2</u>. Checks off human remains on DD Form 1075 as they are offloaded and ensures that the seal number on the HRP matches evacuation tag and case file.

<u>3</u>. Using a detection device, such as a handheld metal detector, digital x-ray, or fluoroscope, conduct a sweep of the HRP for explosive ordnance and UXO. Ensure the human remains, portions, or effects are safe for transport or request EOD support as required to clear the human remains of ordnance for transport. If EOD personnel require breaking of the seal in order to clear ordnance, request permission from the TMAO or JMAO. Follow procedures as outlined in Chapter IV, "Mortuary Affairs Battlefield Operations," paragraph 3f., "Transit Collection Point Operations." Safety of personnel always has priority over procedures. Once the human remains are free of explosive ordnance and UXO, sign for human remains and PE after completing an inventory with the driver.

<u>4</u>. Prepares two TMEP evacuation tags using a TMEP evacuation number, which is the same as an evacuation number with the exception that the MACP number is replaced with TMEP and name.

<u>5</u>. Records entry into the TMEP evacuation log (Figure IV-26) based on convoy list data and enters name data on the TMEP case folder. Note: This log entry is recorded in a standard "RECORD" book in order to have a paper copy on hand.

<u>6</u>. Enters location of human remains (e.g., processing tent, holding tent, or reefer trailer number) onto case folder.

<u>7</u>. Removes MACP evacuation tags, places them in case folder, and secures one TMEP evacuation tag to human remains and one to the HRP.

<u>8</u>. Upon completion of receiving tasks in MARTS or paper copy, gives case folder to processing section.

(b) **Processing Section.** The processing section uses a four station (inspection, processing, fingerprint, and QC) procedure to process the human remains. The processing leader receives the case folder from the receiving section and:

<u>1</u>. Verifies that all paperwork and evacuation tag numbers match human remains.

<u>2</u>. Verifies that DD Form 2064, DD Form 1380, or SF 600 listing a decedent is present. If no form listing a decedent is present, request a certified medical authority from the nearest medical unit examine the human remains and complete a DD Form 2064, DD Form 1380, or SF 600 prior to evacuation from the theater of operation. Cause of death will be "pending AFME determination" when the human remains are under the control of the AFMES.

Suggested Format for Theater Mortuary Evacuation Logbook

LOGBOOK

THEATER MORTUARY EVACUATION POINT LOGBOOK
LOCATION: _____

OPERATING ORGANIZATION MAC/ARTMEP/1

DATE OF REPORT 25 JAN XX

EVAC		DECEASED INFORMATION	EVAC	TRANSFER	MISSION	AIRCRAFT	DEPART	DESTINATION	PROCESSING REMARKS
NO	TIME RECEIVED	NAME, SSN, BRANCH OF SERVICE	DATE	CASE NO	NO	TAIL NO	TIME		
									DELIVERED BY: SSN: UNIT:
									DELIVERED BY: SSN: UNIT:
									DELIVERED BY: SSN: UNIT:
									DELIVERED BY: SSN: UNIT:
									DELIVERED BY: SSN: UNIT:
									DELIVERED BY: SSN: UNIT:
									DELIVERED BY: SSN: UNIT:
									DELIVERED BY: SSN: UNIT:

Figure IV-26. Suggested Format for Theater Mortuary Evacuation Logbook

<u>3</u>. Directs transfer of human remains from storage unit to the processing area.

(c) **Administrative Section.** The administrative section has responsibility for the decedent case file, establishment of the TMEP case file, and performs the following functions:

<u>1</u>. Receives case folder and paperwork from processing section, QC (station 4).

2. Makes alpha card file. For information on the purpose and instructions on creating the alpha card file, refer to paragraph 3d.(1)(h) and Figure IV-16, Sample 3 × 5 Alpha Index Card.

<u>3</u>. Carbon copies, scans/uploads (into MARTS), or photocopies DD Form 2064, DD Form 1380, DD Form 1076, DD Form 565, SF 600 or other records that arrived with human remains. Places forms in TMEP case folder, which has been created for the files.

<u>4</u>. Calls air terminal operations center (ATOC) to determine flight schedules, flight time, and date. Informs them of how many pallets (e.g., 12 deceased to a pallet, 5 pallets to a C-130 aircraft, 18 pallets to a C-17, and 36 pallets to a C-5) are ready for shipment. Human remains should not be held longer than 24 hours. If a longer delay is projected, a flight diversion should be requested.

<u>5</u>. Obtains flight mission number and estimated time of departure from ATOC and informs the shipping section leader.

<u>6</u>. Prepares transportation documents: DD Form 1384 (Transportation Control and Movement Document) (see Figure IV-27), DD Form 1387 (Military Shipment Label) (see Figure IV-28), and DD Form 1387-2 (Special Handling Data/Certification) (see Figure IV-29). Use date human remains will be evacuated on forms.

<u>7</u>. Places transportation documents and original decedent documents (e.g., DD Form 2064, DD Form 565) in the case folder to be evacuated with the human remains. Places photocopies of same in the TMEP case folder.

<u>8</u>. Takes case folder that is to be evacuated with human remains to the evacuation NCOIC.

<u>9</u>. Prepares and inputs required information into MARTS and uses an AIT system for capturing data, such as barcode tags or RFID tags.

<u>10</u>. Transmits data to CONUS using the automated system.

TRANSPORTATION CONTROL AND MOVEMENT DOCUMENT							PAGE NO.
1. DOC ID	2. TRLR CTR	3. CONSIGNOR	4. COMMODITY SPECIAL HANDLING	5. AIR DIM	6. POE		7. POD
8. MODE	9. PACK	10. TRANSPORTATION CONTROL NO.	11. CONSIGNEE	12. PRI	13. RDD	14. PROJ	15. DATE SHPD / 16. ETA / 17. TR ACCT
18. CARRIER	19. FLIGHT-TRUCK-VOY-DOC NO.	20. REF	21. REMARKS			22. PIECES	23. WEIGHT / 24. CUBE

a. Transship Point	b. Date Rec	c. Bay Whse	d. Date Shpd	e. Mode Carrier	f. Flight-Truck-Voy Doc No.	g. Ref	h. Stow Loc	i. Split	j. Cond	k. Signature-Remarks
25.										
26.										
27.										

28. CONSIGNEE	29. DATE RECEIVED/OFFERED *(Sign)*	30. CONDITION	31. REMARKS

32. DOC ID	33. TRAILER - CON-TAINER	34. CONSIGNOR COMM ABBR OTHER	35. COMMODITY SPECIAL HANDLING	36. VOY NO		37. POD	38. MODE	39. TYPE PACK	40. TRANSPORTATION CONTROL NUMBER	41. CONSIGNEE	42. PRI	43. REMARKS AND/OR					44. ADDITIONAL REMARKS OR		
				Air Dim a.	POE b.							RDD a.	Proj b.	Stow Loc Shpd c.	Stow Loc ETA d.	Tac e.	Pieces a.	Weight b.	Cube c.

DD FORM 1384, OCT 2000 PREVIOUS EDITIONS MAY BE USED.

Figure IV-27. DD Form 1384, Transportation Control and Movement Document

MILITARY SHIPMENT LABEL

MILITARY SHIPMENT LABEL	Form Approved, OMB No. 0704-0188
1. TRANSPORTATION CONTROL NUMBER	2. POSTAGE DATA
3. FROM	4. TYPE SERVICE
5. SHIP TO/POE	6. TRANS PRIORITY
7. POD	8. PROJECT
9. ULTIMATE CONSIGNEE OR MARK FOR	10. WT. (This piece) / 11. RDD

DD FORM 1387, JUL 1999   PREVIOUS EDITION IS OBSOLETE

Figure IV-28. DD Form 1387, Military Shipment Label

    <u>11.</u> Dispatches shipping priority message to message center within 2 hours after actual flight departure. Message, at a minimum, must be addressed to: USTRANSCOM, AMC at Scott AFB, Illinois; the destination military mortuary; and the JMAO.

    <u>12.</u> Reviews and completes the TMEP case folder. The case folder is to be filed sequentially using the TMEP evacuation number.

    (d) **Evacuation Section.** The shipping section's primary functions are to prepare human remains for evacuation and transport human remains to the AMC transportation section for evacuation to the designated DOD mortuary. The evacuation section:

SPECIAL HANDLING DATA/CERTIFICATION

1. ITEM NOMENCLATURE	2. NET QUANTITY PER PACKAGE	3. TRANSPORTATION CONTROL NO.
	4. CONSIGNMENT GROSS WEIGHT	5. DESTINATION
6. SUPPLEMENTAL INFORMATION		

This is to certify that the above named materials are properly classified, described, packaged, marked and labeled, and in proper condition for transportation according to the applicable regulations of the Dept of Transportation. THIS IS A U.S. DEPARTMENT OF DEFENSE SHIPMENT! (Complete applicable blocks below)

7. DTR REFERENCE	
8. HANDLING INSTRUCTIONS	
9. ADDRESS OF SHIPPER	10. TYPED NAME, SIGNATURE AND DATE

DD FORM 1387-2, NOV 2004   PREVIOUS EDITION IS OBSOLETE   Form Approved OMB No. 0704-0188

Figure IV-29. DD Form 1387-2, Special Handling Data/Certification

 1. Receives human remains from QC (station 4) or from the refrigeration unit.

 2. Verifies that the case folder paperwork from administration matches human remains and human remains tags.

 3. Places human remains into transfer case ensuring that only one HRP is placed inside the transfer case. There will be no delay in the evacuation of human remains to the port mortuary. If there are insufficient transfer cases, limited airlift, or any other condition that would delay evacuation of human remains, the designated service component commander may waive the time requirement for return of human remains after coordination with the JMAO/TMAO, Air Force Mortuary Affairs Operations, applicable Service casualty office(s) and AFMES.

 4. Gives the transfer case and security serial numbers to the administrative section for completion of transportation documents message/automation entry.

 5. Secures human remains with tie-down straps in the transfer case. Human remains should be secured as indicated in Figure IV-30 so that the human remains will not shift during transport.

 6. Double seals case file in plastic slide closure bag and secures, with duct tape, to the inside top of transfer case, or if using the improved transfer case, places in transfer case document compartment.

 7. Places bagged wet ice (approximately 40 to 80 pounds) in the transfer case but not in direct contact with human remains. Place ice on the outside of the HRP on and around human remains, but never on top of the face. Ice should be placed as indicated in Figure IV-30.

 8. Secures lid to the transfer case and puts on security seals.

 9. Places DD Form 1387 on top of transfer case at the head end approximately 6 inches from the edge (do not cover transfer case number).

 10. Places DD Form 1387-2 (last copy) into plastic packing list and affixes to transfer case as directed by AMC.

 11. Transfer cases may be palletized to utilize limited airlift support for transport. If transfer cases are palletized, then draping the transfer case with the US flag is not authorized. Utilization of US flags for draping of transfer cases in a conflict operation is not recommended. The transfer case will be prepared for dignified transfer upon its arrival in the US prior to being transferred to the port mortuary.

 12. Palletizes transfer cases. (Maximum 12 per pallet. No more than 4 high.)

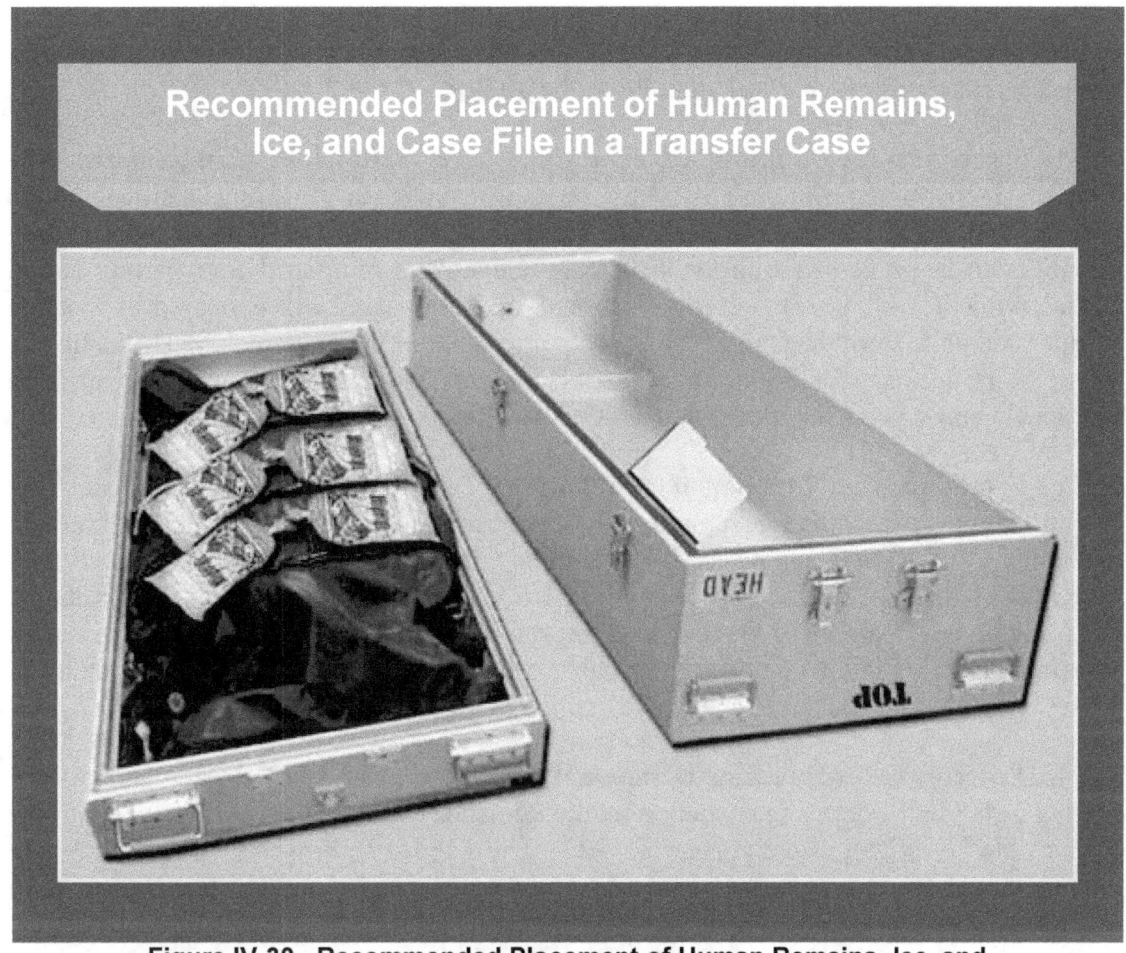

Figure IV-30. Recommended Placement of Human Remains, Ice, and Case File in a Transfer Case

13. Places an RFID tag on each transfer case and if palletizing, places one additional RFID tag securely to the pallet.

14. Places cargo net and tie-down straps on or over cargo.

15. Lifts pallet onto truck.

16. Provides driver with copies of DD Form 1384 (Transportation Control and Movement Document) and DD Form 1387-2 (Special Handling/Data Certification) for each human remains.

17. Delivers human remains to USAF flight line cargo section.

18. Turns over paperwork and human remains to USAF.

19. Ensures that cargo section signs for receipt of human remains.

(6) **PE Operations.** When the TMEP is tasked to handle PE, it processes the PE of deceased or missing personnel. Units are responsible for transporting pre-inventoried (with signed inventory form) and packaged PE to the TMEP.

f. **Procedures for Handling Adversary and Local National Human Remains.** The TMEP will coordinate with the TMAO for the return of adversary and local national human remains and PE to the HN government. Enemy combatants and local national human remains will be processed with the same care and respect afforded US or partner nation human remains. Adversary and local national human remains will be stored in separate refrigerated units from those used for US or partner nation human remains. Utilization of international agencies for the coordination of HN/local national human remains repatriation into local control is encouraged (i.e., Red Crescent/International Red Cross).

g. **Procedures for Handling of Multinational Partner Human Remains.** Handling of multinational partner human remains will be in accordance with established international agreements or STANAGs in place. If no standing agreements or policies are in place, then current US policy and procedures for handling US human remains is in effect. Multinational partner human remains will be accorded the same care and respect given to US human remains. The TMEP will coordinate through the TMAO and embassies for the repatriation of these human remains to the country of origin.

h. **Procedures for Handling Detainee Human Remains.** The US commander of the facility or US unit exercising custody over the human remains shall report the death to the responsible investigative agency and TMAO. The TMAO and investigative agency will contact the AFME to determine whether an autopsy will be performed. The investigative agency representative will accompany the detainee remains to the nearest MACP for transport and evacuation in accordance with GCC policies and procedures. Detainee human remains will not be processed by MA personnel. The detainee remains will be placed in the HRP with minimal handling, and the HRP will be sealed and prepared for shipment. An evacuation number and appropriate shipping documents will be prepared by MA personnel.

For additional guidance on detainee operations, see JP 3-63, Detainee Operations.

CHAPTER V
PERSONAL EFFECTS

"War drew us from our homeland in the sunlit springtime of our youth. Those who did not come back alive remain in perpetual springtime—forever young—and a part of them is with us always."

Author Unknown

1. Introduction

PE include all personal items the individual possesses at the time of death excluding government property. This chapter specifies procedures for unit recovery, collection, inventory, and transfer of PE. It details the procedures for processing PE of all those personnel for which the Armed Forces of the United States are responsible through a PE depot. A subset of PE are those effects that are on the remains; those effects are referred to as DE. In addition to PE, all individual combat clothing and equipment will be recovered and returned with the human remains for examination upon autopsy. Individual combat clothing and equipment integrity studies are conducted by the Services. If the individual combat clothing and equipment is removed for lifesaving procedures, the individual combat clothing and equipment should be transported to the specified mortuary with the name of the BTB decedent, if known. Individual combat clothing and equipment will be inventoried and tracked through MARTS.

2. General Guidance

a. **Procedures.** Disposition of PE includes the collection, receipt, recording, accountability, storage, and disposal of the PE of US military personnel, civilians under US military jurisdiction, and all deceased persons for whom the US provides mortuary services. The handling of PE begins at the time of initial collection by representatives of the Armed Forces of the United States and extends to the time of receipt by the PERE, representatives of the host country or allied nation, or until other disposition is made in accordance with applicable regulations.

b. All efforts are made to safeguard and protect PE from the elements and pilferage during the entire handling and transportation process.

c. PE will be carefully handled and the chain of custody documented at each step in the MA process.

d. PE of military members leaving the theater of operation for noncombat-related medical reasons will be evacuated through normal unit supply channels.

3. Roles and Responsibilities

a. **Geographic Combatant Commander's Responsibilities.** The GCC is responsible for the control and coordination of MA support. This includes PE support for all US military personnel, US civilians and others, multinational partner, local national, and adversary personnel. PE of friendly personnel will be processed in accordance with standing agreements. In the absence of agreements, PE should be processed in the same manner as for US personnel. Processing of PE of deceased adversary detainees should be in accordance with the Geneva Conventions Relative to the Treatment of Prisoners of War. PE of other adversary dead will also be processed in accordance with the Geneva Conventions and should be evacuated to a PE depot. See, for example, Geneva Convention I for the Amelioration of the Condition of the Wounded and Sick in Armed Forces in the Field, Article 16 (Recording and forwarding information). When arrangements are made to transfer PE to the host country or a friendly nation, commanders will maintain accountability records and provide information for all adversary or multinational partner deceased for which they have responsibility.

b. **Theater Mortuary Affairs Officer.** The TMAO is responsible for determining the theater process for handling and evacuation of PE. The theater MA officer will determine if and when a theater personal effects depot (TPED) will be established, and will provide guidance on the flow of PE. The theater MA officer will also coordinate to ensure a smooth flow of PE to a CONUS PE depot.

c. **Mortuary Affairs Collection Point Responsibilities.** The MACP is responsible for inventorying, recording, safeguarding, and evacuating all DE. In addition, the MACP personnel will advise unit personnel on correct handling procedures for inventorying, recording, safeguarding, packaging, and evacuating PE for members of their unit. When required, the MACP will assist the unit in evacuating PE to the TMEP/TPED or CONUS PE depot as appropriate.

d. **Deployed Unit Responsibilities.** Each deployed unit is responsible for the appointment of a PEIO. The unit is responsible for the collection, inventory, safeguarding, packaging, and evacuation of all PE for the unit member. The unit commander is responsible for ensuring all the inventory officer duties are completed. The unit appointed inventory officer in theater will not contact or ship PE directly to the family. It is the unit's responsibility to coordinate final disposition of PE in accordance with applicable Service regulations.

e. **Theater Inventory Officer Responsibilities.** The theater inventory officer is the sole responsible designee that ensures there is a clear chain of custody from the moment of incident to the MACPs. The inventory officer must perform an inventory using two-person control and process PE in accordance with Service policy. For deceased members, annotate "Blue Bark" immediately following the name on the package label. Under no circumstances is the inventory officer to ship PE or organizational clothing and individual equipment to the PERE or to the unit at home station. Inventory officers are not authorized to retain PE. Under no circumstances is the inventory officer to communicate directly with the PERE. Any discrepancies will be reconciled through the CONUS PE depot reconciliation cell.

f. **Theater Personal Effects Depot Responsibilities.** The TPED is responsible for the receipt, safeguard, inventory (when required), storage, palletizing, and evacuation of PE back to the CONUS PE depot. When the TPED is located in the operational area, the depot may process the PE of deceased US military personnel, US civilians and others, multinational partner, local national, and adversary personnel that come into custody of the US military. In the case of multinational partner, third country, local national, and adversary PE, the TPED will work to return those effects back to the originating country representative as promptly as possible.

g. **Theater Mortuary Evacuation Point Responsibilities.** The TMEP may be required to act as an intermediary transfer point between the units in theater and the CONUS PE depot when a TPED is not operational. The TMEP is then responsible for the receipt, storage, palletizing, and evacuation of PE to the CONUS PE depot. If the TMEP receives PE in a damaged container that resulted in unsealed or opened PE, the TMEP will contact the unit to conduct a joint inventory of PE and will assist in the repackaging of the PE prior to shipment.

h. **Continental United States Personal Effects Depot Responsibilities.** The CONUS PE depot is responsible for the receipt, safeguard, inventory, screening, cleaning, packaging, shipment, and maintenance of files and reports, as well as coordination of transfer of effects to the appropriate Service representative for transfer of PE to the PERE.

i. **Service Casualty Office Responsibilities.** Each Service maintains a casualty assistance office as the focal point on all casualty matters. The casualty assistance officer maintains an organizational capability to provide for casualty reporting, recording, notification, and assistance. The Service casualty assistance office will appoint in writing a casualty assistance officer to assist the family in all casualty matters to include the receipt and inventory of PE. The Service casualty assistance office will provide all casualty assistance officers the requisite training.

j. **Medical Treatment Facilities.** Medical treatment facilities procedures safeguard the PE of personnel receiving care. However, it is not their primary concern; their focus is on saving lives. The medical staff will collect, safeguard, and inventory the effects of patients and decedents once the medical care has been completed. The PE of the patient or the decedent should accompany them whenever possible. The unit PEIO officer is responsible for recovering all PE and individual combat clothing and equipment to include PE and individual combat clothing and equipment at medical treatment facilities.

4. Unit Tasks

a. **Unit Commanders.** Will assign in writing a PEIO and ensure the inventory officer receives training required to fulfill the duties. The commander is responsible for ensuring the inventory officer completes all the duties assigned.

b. **Unit Tasks During Military Operations.** PE of persons deceased or missing may be found in unit joint security areas, storage points, medical treatment facilities, and other locations. These effects are collected, safeguarded, inventoried, and evacuated to the PE depot in accordance with the inventory officer guidelines and checklist. Refer to current Service regulations on handling of PE. The inventory will show the status of the individual as deceased, missing, or medical evacuee, or interred as appropriate. The unit is responsible for gathering, inventorying, and evacuating the PE to the depot. The unit PEIO is responsible for the PE and will deliver the PE to the designated MA facility or PE depot where a joint inventory with depot personnel will be conducted if required. In cases when the TMEP serves as an intermediary transfer point between the units in theater and the PE depot, the unit is responsible for collecting, inventorying, and packaging the PE. The unit should package PE in such a manner that the package will pass customs packaging requirements (e.g., no explosives, flammables, or contraband). The unit coordinates for packaging supplies through the appropriate unit supply channels. AIT device, such as barcode label or RFID tag, is placed on the outside of the package. The RFID tag or barcode label will record the appropriate information regarding casualty status, decedent, PE, and organization. Copies of the inventory are placed on the inside and on the outside of the package. Once the PE are packaged, the unit arranges for transportation to the appropriate location, such as the TMEP, TPED, or joint personal effects depot (JPED). However, it is important to note that the unit maintains responsibility for the contents inside all packages, since sealed packages will not be opened for a joint inventory while in transit. If a package is found unsealed, MA personnel and the PEIO will conduct a joint inventory. If unit personnel are not available, then MA personnel will conduct a two-person inventory. Any discrepancies will be noted and rectified if possible. If items have been lost, pilfered or damaged, MA personnel will initiate an investigation by notifying the TMAO, military police, or investigative authorities.

c. **Unit Tasks During Peacetime.** During peacetime, the unit is responsible for collection, inventory, safeguarding, packaging, evacuation, and coordinating final disposition of PE in accordance with applicable Service regulations.

5. **Personal Effects in a Theater of Operations**

The handling of PE in a theater is based on the MA support structure which is in place. In a theater of operations, it is critical to account for all PE. This responsibility falls on the unit commander and the appointed inventory officer. The PEIO's duties do not end once the PE have been collected, inventoried, packaged, sealed, and shipped from the theater. The inventory officer will not be relieved until the CONUS PE depot inventory officer has verified that the PERE has received the PE and all outstanding issues have been resolved. The procedures followed for accounting for and processing PE in a theater of operation are outlined below.

a. **Mortuary Affairs Collection Point.** When human remains arrive at the MACP, personnel will conduct an inventory of all DE and organizational equipment that may be on the human remains. With as little handling as possible and extreme care not to damage any forensic evidence, inventory but do not remove DE from the body. Sentimental DE (e.g., rings, jewelry, religious medals) and other high-value PE shall be inventoried and will remain with the human remains. Only the AFME is qualified to determine if DE are or are not needed for ID. Unnecessary removal of DE may cause loss of forensic evidence. Do not remove organizational and government equipment from the human remains. Individual combat clothing and equipment should not be removed from the human remains, but may be shifted to search for explosive ordnance, UXO, weapons, and classified materials. All individual combat clothing and equipment will be left on the human remains for evacuation.

Remove all classified material, explosive ordnance, UXO, and weapons. Weapons are returned to the unit or turned in through normal supply procedures. Do not remove the ID tags and ID cards under any conditions. Keep them in the original location on the human remains where they were found at the time of recovery if there is no risk that they will become unsecured or lost. DE are inventoried and left in the original location on human remains for evacuation to the servicing mortuary.

b. **Theater Mortuary Evacuation Point.** The TMEP's role in handling PE in a theater of operations should be limited to DE whenever possible. The TMEP is not adequately staffed to function as both a TMEP and a TPED. The TMEP will have the primary responsibility for accounting for DE in a theater of operation. The TMEP will ensure that all DE are accounted for and properly stored for shipment to reduce damage. Any discrepancies in DE records will be investigated and accounted for by the TMEP. The seal should never be broken just to re-inventory DE. However, when the JMAO/TMAO has authorized the breaking of the HRP seal, the DE will be re-inventoried to ensure that all DE are accounted for. The human remains will not be delayed in transit to rectify DE discrepancies.

(1) When the TMEP is tasked to handle PE as an in-transit transfer point, it processes it in the following manner. Upon arrival, TMEP personnel verify that packages are sealed and properly labeled. An RFID tag, barcode tag, or package label is placed on the outside of the PE container. The tag or label will record the appropriate information regarding casualty status, decedent, PE, and organization. Personnel verify that the name on the package label matches the name of the signed inventory sheet and annotate on the inventory sheet that the package was sealed at arrival. The signing of the inventory sheet only certifies liability for the actual sealed package and not the contents inside the package.

(2) Establish a case file for each package of PE received. Assign an evacuation number for all packages pertaining to a particular individual. The evacuation number consists of three parts: a numerically sequential case number, the location of the TMEP, and the number of packages containing PE for the particular individual. Record the evacuation number on the case file and on all applicable inventory sheets and/or DD Form 1076 inside the file. Prepare and secure an evacuation tag to each package pertaining to a particular individual. Place a plastic packing list envelope on each package and place a copy of the inventory sheet for that package inside the envelope.

6. **Theater Personal Effects Depot Operations**

a. **Introduction.** When a PE depot is established, the need for a Service to handle the disposition of PE is eliminated. The primary mission of the TPED is to receive, safeguard, inventory, store, process, and evacuate PE for deceased and missing personnel to the CONUS PE depot. When the PE depot is located in the operational area, the depot may process the PE of deceased US military personnel, US civilians and others, multinational partner, local national, and adversary personnel that come into custody of the US military.

b. **Theater Personal Effects Depot Functional Sections**

(1) The TPED is structured into four main sections: receiving, processing, storage and shipping, and administrative sections. The primary functions of each section are as follows: See Figure V-1.

(a) Receiving Section. Receive, account for, and store all PE.

(b) Processing Section. Screen, inventory, and package PE.

(c) Storage and Shipping Section. Initiate required shipping documents, coordinate for transportation, ensure tracking device is activated, and consolidate packages for shipment.

(d) Administrative Section. Prepare and maintain all required reports and case files and provide administrative assistance to the inventory officer.

(2) **Receiving Section.** When the PE depot is located in the operational area, personnel who operate the receiving section accomplish the following tasks:

(a) Meet with organizational representatives.

(b) Log the case in the PE depot logbook (see Figure V-2). Assign a case number for each case. The case number consists of a sequential number and the current year. Record the case number and PE depot name and location on all processing documentation.

(c) Obtain all inventory sheets or DD Form 1076 from the unit representative.

(d) Establish a paper case file for each individual and an automated case file in MARTS.

(e) Record the name, rank, SSN, and branch of Service of the individual on the top of the case file.

(f) Conduct a joint inventory to verify and account for all items on the inventory sheets or DD Forms 1076 when the containers are damaged or when seals or locks are broken.

(g) Record any discrepancies on the inventory sheet or DD Form 1076 and initiate an investigation, if necessary.

(h) If the discrepancy cannot be resolved internally, turn the case over to the appropriate criminal investigation agency and continue to monitor progress of the investigation.

(i) Obtain the correct casualty status of the individual for each package of PE.

(j) Process the PE of deceased personnel for shipment to the CONUS PE depot. Ensure all data is properly entered into MARTS.

(k) Secure and store PE until they are shipped to the CONUS PE depot.

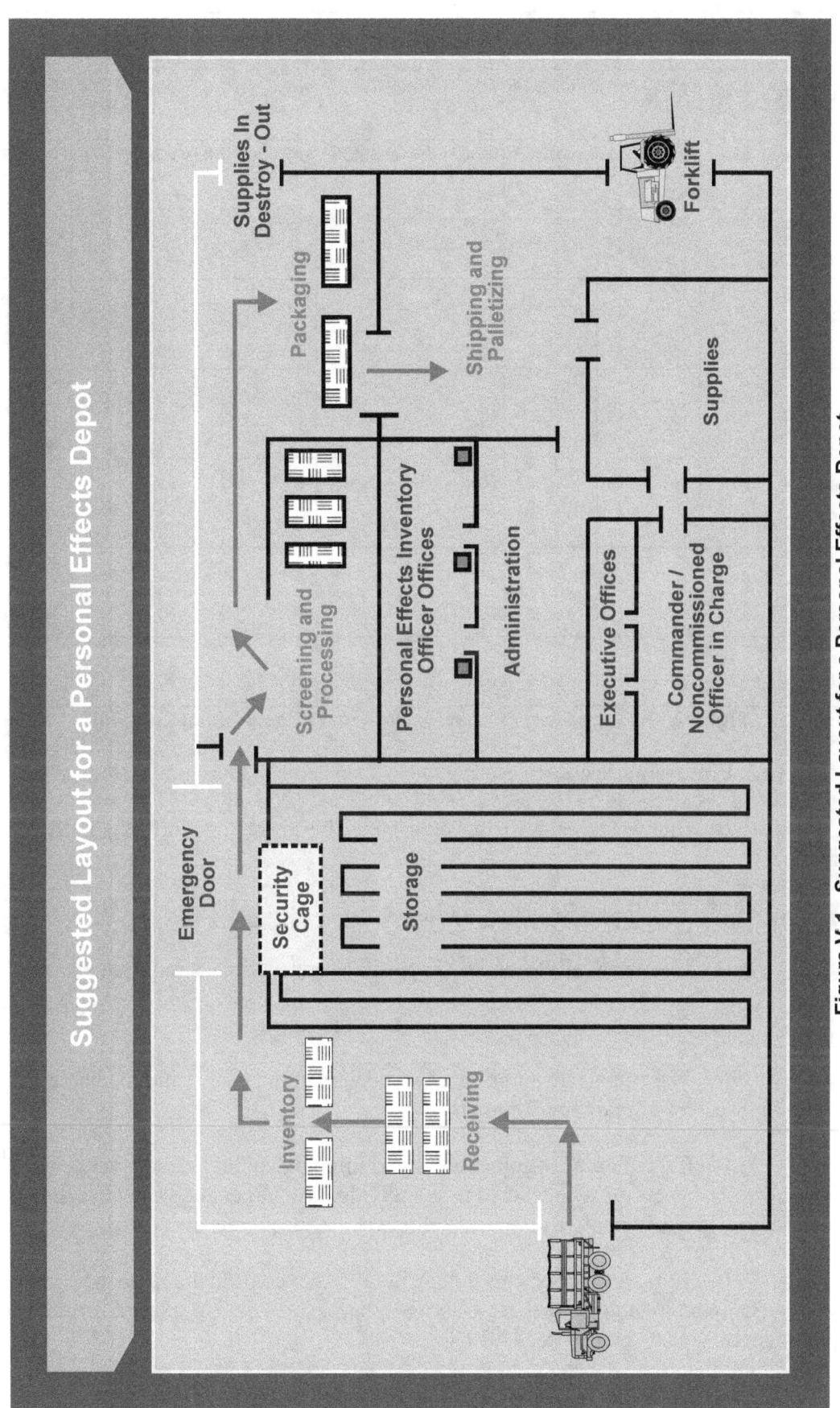

Figure V-1. Suggested Layout for a Personal Effects Depot

SUGGESTED FORMAT FOR PERSONAL EFFECTS DEPOT LOGBOOK									
OPERATING ORGANIZATION MAC/ARTMEP/1	PERSONAL EFFECTS DEPOT LOGBOOK #1 LOCATION:							DATE OF REPORT 25 JAN XX	
EVAC	TIME	DECEASED INFORMA- TION	EVAC	TRANSFER	MISSION	AIRCRAFT	DEPART	DESTIN- ATION	PROCESSING REMARKS
NO.	RECEIVED	NAME, SSN, BRANCH OF SERVICE	DATE	CASE NO.	NO.	TAIL NO.	TIME		
									DELIVERED BY: SSN: UNIT:
									DELIVERED BY: SSN: UNIT:
									DELIVERED BY: SSN: UNIT:
									DELIVERED BY: SSN: UNIT:
									DELIVERED BY: SSN:

Figure V-2. Suggested Format for Personal Effects Depot Logbook

(3) **Processing Section**

(a) Check the case file to determine the exact location of all PE for the individual.

(b) Screen and inventory all items.

(c) Document all PE on DD Form 1076 and 1076C as required.

(d) Place the inventory documents in the case file.

(e) Place items inventoried into a container and take it and the documents to the shipping section or into secure storage.

(f) If the PE are not going directly to shipping, all high-dollar-value items and official personal papers must be secured in an individual container and stored in a safe or in a locked security cage. Annotate on the case file where those items are stored.

(g) Complete documents for any items removed from the PE that are not being shipped. (Only remove items that are classified, hazardous, or that did not meet customs requirements.) Update entries in MARTS.

(4) **Storage and Shipping Section**

(a) Prepare the PE for shipment by completing the following:

1. Select proper size containers for shipment.

2. Line all containers with packing material.

3. Coordinate for a customs inspection to coincide with the actual packing of PE.

4. Wrap all items that may become damaged in shipment.

5. Place items in the container in reverse order from that appearing on the inventory to allow for the unpacking of the items in the order shown on the inventory.

6. Place a copy of the inventory inside on the top of the PE prior to closing the container.

7. Close and seal the container for shipment.

8. Write data to the AIT device, such as RFID tags. Ensure RFID data is entered into MARTS.

9. Activate tracking device and request quality assurance NCOIC verify procedures have been followed.

(b) After the containers are closed and sealed, label the containers with an AIT device or label. The AIT device or label will record the appropriate information regarding casualty status, decedent, PE, and organization. Verify that the status on the container matches the status shown on the inventory documents. Attach a plastic packing list envelope to the outside of each container.

(c) The quality assurance NCOIC of the packing and shipment operations verifies:

1. The contents packed against the inventory sheet for accuracy.

2. That all items are packed in a professional manner according to current directives and guidance.

3. That containers are securely sealed and in good working order upon completion of packing.

4. That proper labels and shipping documents are placed on the container.

5. That the items are shipped to the correct address—CONUS PE depot or as directed for non-US personnel.

<u>6.</u> That the containers are shipped on a government bill of lading or by registered or insured mail.

<u>7.</u> That disposition instructions are requested and implemented for oversized items.

<u>8.</u> That data is correctly written to the AIT device (RFID tag) and the data on the RFID tag is correctly associated and visible in the radio frequency in-transit visibility server.

(d) Complete the required shipping documents based on previous coordination with AMC transportation personnel and coordinate for an aircraft. Palletize the containers and arrange to transport the pallets to the AMC cargo section. Send a representative with the pallets to the AMC cargo area. Upon delivery of the pallets, have the representative obtain a signature on the Air Force Form 127 (Traffic Transfer Receipt) from the AMC cargo representative.

(e) PE must be stored in a secure location with controlled access. Items should be individually sealed once inventory has been completed. Access is granted maintaining two-person control. High-value items need to be given another level of security—locked in a safe or a cage—again maintaining two-person control.

(5) **Administrative Section**

(a) Provide administrative assistance to the inventory officer at the PE depot.

(b) Prepare and maintain the original case files.

(c) Prepare and maintain an internal copy of each case file to document all events pertaining to the case.

(d) Monitor the status of the PE.

(e) In cases of missing PE, initiate and conduct appropriate inquiry to determine loss or theft. Report suspected thefts of PE to appropriate law enforcement agencies. Report loss of PE via chain of command for appropriate disciplinary action.

(f) Request disposition instructions for oversized items of PE.

(g) Coordinate the return of any multinational and adversary PE that may be in the custody of the TPED through command channels to the appropriate government or representative.

c. **Accountability**

A two-person inventory will be conducted by the person delivering and receiving a deceased person's PE when the containers are damaged or when seals or locks are broken. If no inventory is required, chain of custody receipt will reflect secured PE containers only. A receipt will be provided to any person delivering PE to the TPED. The receipt provides a chain of custody, establishes an inventory of items, and documents the acceptance and release of responsibility for PE. When possible, digital photographs of high-dollar-value items will be taken and forwarded as part of the documentation with the PE shipment. Copies will be retained at the TPED.

d. **Theater Personal Effects Depot. A TPED may not always be established in a theater of operations.** A TPED may be established to facilitate the transport of PE from the theater to the JPED. In an immature theater, a TPED assists unit personnel with inventory and packaging of decedent and missing in action PE for shipment as well as coordinating evacuation. Establishment of a TPED allows for consolidation of assets to support this mission. MACPs are not staffed to provide this support. The following planning factors should be considered when determining if and where a TPED will be established.

(1) The amount of PE to be processed and evacuated out of the AOR as well as the assets and personnel required to establish a TPED.

(2) Availability of air transport is a key factor along with facility requirements. Site selection, development, and sustainment are major factors in determining the value of a TPED.

(3) The following guidance is provided in selecting a site and developing a site layout:

(a) Ability to establish separate areas for each section with sufficient space to accomplish its designed function.

(b) Ability to establish controlled receiving and shipping points.

(c) Ability to build or emplace storage bins or shelves.

(d) Ability to secure high-dollar-value items.

(e) Ability to store oversized or bulky items.

(f) Ability to locate close to air evacuation channels and TMEP.

(g) Ability to write data to RFID tags or other approved AIT devices.

7. **Joint Personal Effects Depot Operations in the Continental United States**

The JPED operates under the auspices of the Army's Human Resources Command (HRC). HRC's Human Resources Center of Excellence at Fort Knox, Kentucky, and the Casualty and Mortuary Affairs Operations Center (CMAOC) maintains a JPED as required to support DOD operations around the world. CMAOC oversees the JPED, providing guidance, direction, and human resource support. Policy changes and guidelines are made available through Service-specific publications.

a. **Facility Layout.** A JPED is structured into five main sections: receiving, administration, processing, inventory officer final inventory, and shipping sections. The primary functions for these sections are as follows:

(1) Receiving Section. Properly receive, account for, visually inventory, categorize, and scan for explosive ordnance, UXO, weapons, and classified materials on all incoming PE in preparation for the processing section.

(2) Administrative Section. Prepare and maintain all required reports and case files and provide administrative assistance to the casualty assistance officer or inventory officer.

(3) Processing Section. Inventory, screen, launder/clean, and photograph.

(4) Inventory Officer/Final Inventory Section. Verify inventory and shipping documents and pack and prepare packages for shipment. Store packaged items in a secure area until shipment. Place destruction document for each item destroyed in the case file. See Figure V-3.

(5) Shipment Section. Properly ship all PE to the assigned casualty assistance officer assigned to the PERE. Verify PERE and casualty assistance officer. Verify receipt of shipment.

b. **Joint Personal Effects Depot Operations**

(1) PE can be received from a theater of operation or from a mortuary. Mortuaries that receive deceased personnel and their accompanying DE examine the effects for ID value. After examining the effects, the mortuary forwards the effects and accompanying inventory documents to the PE depot.

(2) Upon receipt of effects, the receiving section will complete the following tasks:

(a) Photograph the containers to document their external condition as they were received at the PE depot. Then open the containers and remove RFID tag and paperwork. RFID tags are inactivated and returned to Dover AFB. Sort PE containers by BTB name. Photograph footlockers/containers to document their external condition as they were received at the PE depot.

(b) Scan PE containers using an x-ray machine for UXO.

(c) PE are separated and secured in the receiving holding area according to status, including, but not limited to deceased, very seriously injured, seriously injured, not seriously injured, medically evacuated, and other.

(d) Assign a PE depot ID number to shipment case and input data into the PE depot database. Affix an ID slip to each container for ID and preparation for processing.

(e) Store containers until the processing section is prepared to receive them.

SUGGESTED FORMAT FOR CERTIFICATE OF DESTRUCTION						
Evacuation number/case number E101-94/ARMY 54THQMCO/TMEP1 Date 10/02/03						
THE FOLLOWING ITEMS OF PERSONAL EFFECTS/PROPERTY HAVE BEEN DESTROYED FOR THE REASON(S) INDICATED.						
Name of Deceased Last, First, MI	Grade/Rank	SSN	DATE & PLACE OF DEATH			
Pilot, Pat D.	O5	440-44-2581	Riyadh, Saudi Arabia			
ITEMS	CONTAMINATED	BURNED	SOILED	UNSANITARY	DAMAGED	REMARKS
Jacket, Desert Camou	X		X	X		Bloody
Trousers, Desert Camou	X		X	X		Bloody
Boots, Tropical	X		X	X	X	Bloody
Helmet, Kevlar	X				X	Crushed
Undergarment (shorts)			X	X		Bloody
Undergarment (T-shirt)			X	X		Bloody
WITNESS: Cassandra A. Gunter Cassandra A. Gunter			DESTROYING OFFICER: Robert D. Hood LTC Robert D. Hood			

Figure V-3. Suggested Format for Certificate of Destruction

(3) Processing Section

(a) Receive one shipment case from the receiving section as identified by date received to process. Check the shipment number. Deceased have priority by date, and wounded follow. PE are processed on a first in, first out basis.

(b) Conduct the pre-inventory. Annotate any discrepancies for missing or extra items not on the theater inventory.

(c) Conduct a full detailed inventory, in accordance with Service regulations and current CONUS PE depot guidance.

(d) Photograph all items in the inventory even if they are government property or are identified for destruction. Exception is that **no typed or written classified** documents will be photographed. Classified digital media (e.g., compact discs, thumb drives, computers) will be photographed in accordance with current guidance.

(e) Secure the PE and paperwork until it can be reviewed by the administrative/reconciliation section.

(f) Contained in the processing section are subsections to include: supply section, destruction section, photo lab, laundry section, safe room, and media/forensic center. Each of these sections assist in the processing procedures.

(4) **Administrative/Reconciliation Section**

(a) Receive documentation from processing line.

(b) Validate documentation against the database.

(c) Prepare correspondence for theater PEIO as required; function as an intermediary with the theater PEIO as required.

(d) Scan documentation into the database.

(e) Create discrepancy file for QC as required.

(f) Create and maintain updated reports as required.

(5) **PEIO/Final Inventory Section**

(a) Conduct final inventory of the PE.

(b) Validate the processing of all inventory, military clothing, and equipment records. Ensure items for reintegration into the supply system are sent to the appropriate management and control system.

(c) Provide accountability for all sensitive items, classified material, biohazard/contaminated PE, and items of high value. Ensure the final inventory and signed documentation are complete for all PE that are shipped for final disposition.

(d) Conduct briefs on the final inventory process as required.

(e) Fold, pack, seal, prepare packing slips, store, or move PE to the shipping area for final disposition.

(6) **Storage and Shipping Section**

(a) **Organizational Equipment.** All organizational clothing, equipment, and other government property are returned through the unit supply chain once they have been released by the AFME. Once returned, it is a supply function to account for the organizational equipment.

(b) Verify the PERE and the casualty assistance officer using Defense Casualty Information Processing System.

(c) Obtain the casualty assistance officer mailing address and inform him when a shipment has been made. PE are shipped to the casualty assistance officer, not the PERE.

(d) Coordinate for transportation.

Intentionally Blank

CHAPTER VI
MORTUARY OPERATIONS

1. Overview

a. DOD installations provide mortuary services for authorized personnel through contract with local commercial vendors. When commercial mortuary services are not available or are cost prohibitive, DOD or the Services may establish regional mortuaries. The Army and the Navy currently operate mortuary facilities outside of the US to provide mortuary services for eligible deceased personnel. Establishment or disestablishment of overseas Service mortuary facilities is coordinated with the affected Service components and the GCC's staff up to the departmental level.

b. The US Army HRC develops policies and standards for the Casualty and Mortuary Affairs Open Allotment, mortuary services contracts, and mortuary supplies. Further, HRC ensures compliance with established mortuary policies and procedures, conducts biennial reviews, together with the Departments of the Navy and Air Force, and periodic internal reviews to determine adequacy of interment allowances.

c. The Air Force established and maintains the port mortuary at Dover AFB for the Armed Forces of the United States. In accordance with DOD MA policy, the Secretary of the Air Force can also be tasked by DOD to establish additional port-of-entry mortuaries in support of all the Services.

2. Port Mortuary

a. The port mortuary's mission is to fulfill the US commitment of ensuring dignity, honor, and respect to our fallen and provide care, service, and support to their families. The port mortuary is where the AFME's office often determines cause and manner of death and obtains positive ID of deceased personnel. The AFME determines which remains must be evacuated to the port mortuary, such as is often the case for deaths resulting from current operations, suspicious deaths, and homicides.

b. The port mortuary is manned and equipped to provide for or coordinate the full spectrum of mortuary services. The port mortuary is comprised of three distinct branches: the administrative branch, mortuary branch, and operations branch.

(1) The administrative branch is responsible for dual case file management for every human remains processed through the port mortuary from arrival to departure. The administrative branch uses the Mortuary Operations Management System, tracking cost data associated with care and disposition, affecting final disposition, and receiving and processing personnel casualty reports. Administrative personnel coordinate transportation and escort for deceased personnel. Transportation can be through contract military airlift (MILAIR), or MILAIR, unless the PADD directs alternative transportation (i.e., scheduled commercial air).

(2) The mortuary branch is responsible for the supervision and oversight of mortuary functions to include embalming, cosmetics, anatomical restoration, dressing, casketing, and shipping operations. The branch manages all mortuary specialists, autopsy/embalming technicians, and military personnel assigned to augment the mission. The mortuary branch director coordinates with the AFME, administrative branch, and branch of Service liaisons to expedite final disposition.

(3) The operations branch manages dignified transfer arrivals and departures, receiving and tracking, and deployed personnel. The branch coordinates with the AFME and section leaders on the schedule and start/termination times of processing.

3. Department of Defense Regional Mortuaries

Regional mortuaries are strategically placed to support overseas installations and operations and provide the full spectrum of mortuary services for a geographical region to all personnel who are authorized DOD mortuary services. Regional mortuaries provide services to active duty Service members, retirees, dependents, DOD civilians, and other personnel upon special request of DOS or other USG departments or agencies. Services for non-DOD cases are normally provided on a reimbursable basis. Mortuary services include embalming, contracting for cremation, casketing, and shipment of remains to worldwide destinations for final disposition. Overseas mortuaries maintain uniforms and supplies and provide commands the ability to dress, casket, and ship human remains from overseas mortuaries on commercial or military flights to receiving funeral homes or to the Air Force Mortuary at Dover AFB as requested by the supporting Service or the PADD. When staffed with a regional medical examiner falling under the AFME or augmented by the AFMES, a regional mortuary will provide positive ID of all deceased personnel. The regional mortuary is staffed and equipped to provide for or coordinate the full spectrum of mortuary services. Assigned mortuary officers and MA specialists provide invaluable tools to the overseas commands as a forward presence in support of mortuary operations in the AOR. The US Navy will transport deceased personnel from a ship to the closest regional mortuary or port mortuary for processing and disposition.

4. Installation Mortuary Support

a. In the US, installation mortuary support is handled in accordance with Service and installation regulations and guidance. Installations establish contracts for mortuary services. Often these contracts are administered by the installation casualty office, which also provides casualty services.

b. Installations with concurrent jurisdiction with other state or local governments should establish formal agreements with the local ME/C and appropriate state, local, or tribal agencies in order to facilitate mortuary operations should they ever be needed. These agreements are of paramount importance and should be considered the foundation of any MA effort. All agreements must be undertaken in consultation with the Office of the Armed Forces Medical Examiner (OAFME). The largest part of the MA burden will be handled at the local level. Under concurrent or proprietary jurisdiction, where the local ME/C retains jurisdiction, the local ME/C:

(1) Retains all decision-making authority when managing mass fatalities.

(2) Signs all death certificates for the cause and manner of death.

(3) Identifies assets required to process remains.

(4) Coordinates, integrates, and manages arriving assets.

c. For DOD installations with exclusive federal jurisdiction, the OAFME has primary jurisdiction under Title 10, USC, Section 1471.

Intentionally Blank

CHAPTER VII
HOMELAND DEFENSE AND DEFENSE SUPPORT OF CIVIL AUTHORITIES

1. Introduction

In addition to managing the MA program in a theater of operations, DOD may be required to provide DSCA for domestic incidents as directed by the President or when consistent with military readiness and appropriate under the circumstances and the law as per Homeland Security Presidential Directive-5, *Management of Domestic Incidents,* and DODD 3025.18, *Defense Support of Civil Authorities (DSCA),* to support civilian entities following the occurrence of a natural, man-made, or terrorist incident.

a. The US military support to civil authorities is not new, as the military has responded to civil emergencies and natural disasters since the Truman era. With the increase in terrorist acts, and natural and man-made disasters, it is likely that Title 10, USC, forces could be called upon to assist in mitigating the effects of future disaster events.

b. When employing DOD assets to a civil disaster event, DOD directives clearly stipulate DOD be considered a "resource of last resort" providing capabilities only when local, state, tribal, and/or other federal assets have been exhausted or when a military-unique capability is required. When military assets are deployed, they will support the lead federal agency while maintaining C2 of their forces.

For additional details related to the initiation of DSCA, see JP 3-28, Defense Support of Civil Authorities.

2. Roles and Responsibilities

a. The National Response Framework (NRF) provides affected jurisdictions access to several federal assets relating to MA as listed:

(1) Department of Homeland Security (DHS) establishes federal response operations structures in Presidential declared disasters/emergencies including: the deployment of emergency response teams, establishment of joint field office (JFO), coordination of overall incident, provision of funds and issuance of mission assignments to include those assigned for the MA mission.

(2) Federal Emergency Management Agency (FEMA) leads DHS preparedness efforts for all hazards, and manages federal response and recovery efforts following any national incident. FEMA also initiates proactive mitigation activities and trains first responders.

(3) DHHS provides oversight of Emergency Support Function (ESF) #8, the ESF applicable to mass fatality management, and is responsible for assisting the ME/C office in coordinating response activities. DHHS deploys the appropriate personnel to meet the requirement. DHHS works with the funeral directors, and ME/Cs to call upon these organizations to provide additional personnel surge capacity if requested.

(4) A disaster mortuary operational response team (DMORT) from DHHS's National Disaster Medical System provides local ME/Cs with MA-specific support. A DMORT can provide a disaster portable morgue unit; assistance with obtaining decedent ID by gathering fingerprints, forensic dental and samples for pathology, histology, or other laboratory analysis; and conducting anthropological review. They are capable of gathering antemortem data and can track decedent and related case data when the decedent is under the DMORT's responsibility.

(5) The FBI is the lead investigative agency for terrorism and certain other types of mass casualty crimes. The FBI has investigative, forensic, and victim assistance responsibilities and the capabilities to carry out these responsibilities. The FBI is mandated by law to identify victims of federal crimes, establish contact information for NOK, and provide rights, information, and assistance services to them. The FBI has units specifically trained to work these areas. The Evidence Response Team Unit is responsible for evidence collection. The Disaster Squad's mission is to assist in ID of victims at major disasters and criminal scenes through prints; it deploys with remote Integrated Automated Fingerprint Identification System workstations. The Office of Victim Assistance coordinates the overall victim assistance program.

(6) National Transportation Safety Board (NTSB) has a legislated responsibility to provide family assistance coordination and facilitation of victim ID following major aviation, highway, marine, pipeline, and passenger rail accidents. The NTSB has a standing memorandum of agreement with the AFMES, whereby the AFMES provides ID and anthropological support on a reimbursable basis.

(7) The role of the National Cemetery Administration of the Department of Veterans Affairs under ESF #8 is to inter and memorialize eligible veterans and advise on methods of interment.

(8) FEMA urban search and rescue team may be able to provide consultation or support to recover decedents. During the performance of their mission, they may come into contact with decedents, which need to be handed off to local ME/C.

(9) DOS provides assistance when decedents include foreign nationals to include obtaining relevant information to support the ID of potential foreign nationals and coordination to return foreign national decedents.

(10) American Red Cross (ARC). The ARC is an NGO recognized in the NRF, and identified as a support agency under ESF #8. ARC often supports decedent family care in creating lists of decedents and gathering contact information.

b. Within DOD, MA capabilities exist at the Service level that can be called upon to support a DSCA MA mission assignment. DOD Title 10, USC, assets that have a primary or secondary MA capability include the Marine Corps, with S&R and MA capabilities; the Navy, which has an embalming capability; the Air Force with S&R and MA augmentation capabilities; and the Army, with both reserve and active duty units, capable of providing S&R, collection, processing, and evacuation support.

c. The National Guard (NG) also contains MA assets to include Air National Guard (ANG) aircraft; S&R teams; chemical, biological, radiological, nuclear, and high-yield explosives (CBRNE); fatality search and recovery teams (FSRTs). The National Guard Bureau (NGB), a joint activity of DOD, facilitates the interstate support of NG units, to include FSRTs, while under state control, and coordinates with state adjutants general to federalize such units as may be needed to support federal military response requirements.

d. Figure VII-1 identifies the most typical deployable MA assets for each tier of the response—local, state, and federal—and depicts the general timeframe as to when each asset is most likely to engage in a response effort. All MA assets are not automatically deployed for each mass fatality incident, but are deployed based on the magnitude of the event, the asset capability, and the needs of the local jurisdiction.

3. National Response Framework

a. According to the NRF, the responsibility for responding to disaster incidents begins at the local level, specifically the local government affected by the disaster. The NRF, however, plays a key role in helping community leaders mitigate the effects of the disaster event by facilitating the involvement of state, federal, and private sector assets prepared to aid the local response effort. This is primarily accomplished by providing a framework to effectively organize a multi-agency response and assets to backfill the local response.

b. When an incident exceeds local, tribal, or state resources, the federal government provides necessary coordination, leadership, and resources to efficiently mitigate large-scale or catastrophic events. To achieve this end, the President appoints a principal federal official, the Secretary of Homeland Security (SECHS), to assume overall federal incident management.

c. Such coordination is needed under one of three conditions.

(1) Whenever a federal department or agency acting under its own authority requests DHS assistance;

(2) When local, tribal, or state authorities request federal assistance; and

(3) When more than one federal agency or department has become involved in the response, or when the President directs SECHS to assume incident management activities.

d. Each ESF identifies a coordinator and primary and supporting agencies. MA activities are included within ESF #8—Public Health and Medical Services.

e. The ESF coordinator and primary agency for ESF #8 is DHHS and is supported by many agencies, one of which is DOD. ESF #8 addresses a broad range of public health and medical services including MA, which is identified as mass fatality management, victim ID, and decontaminating remains.

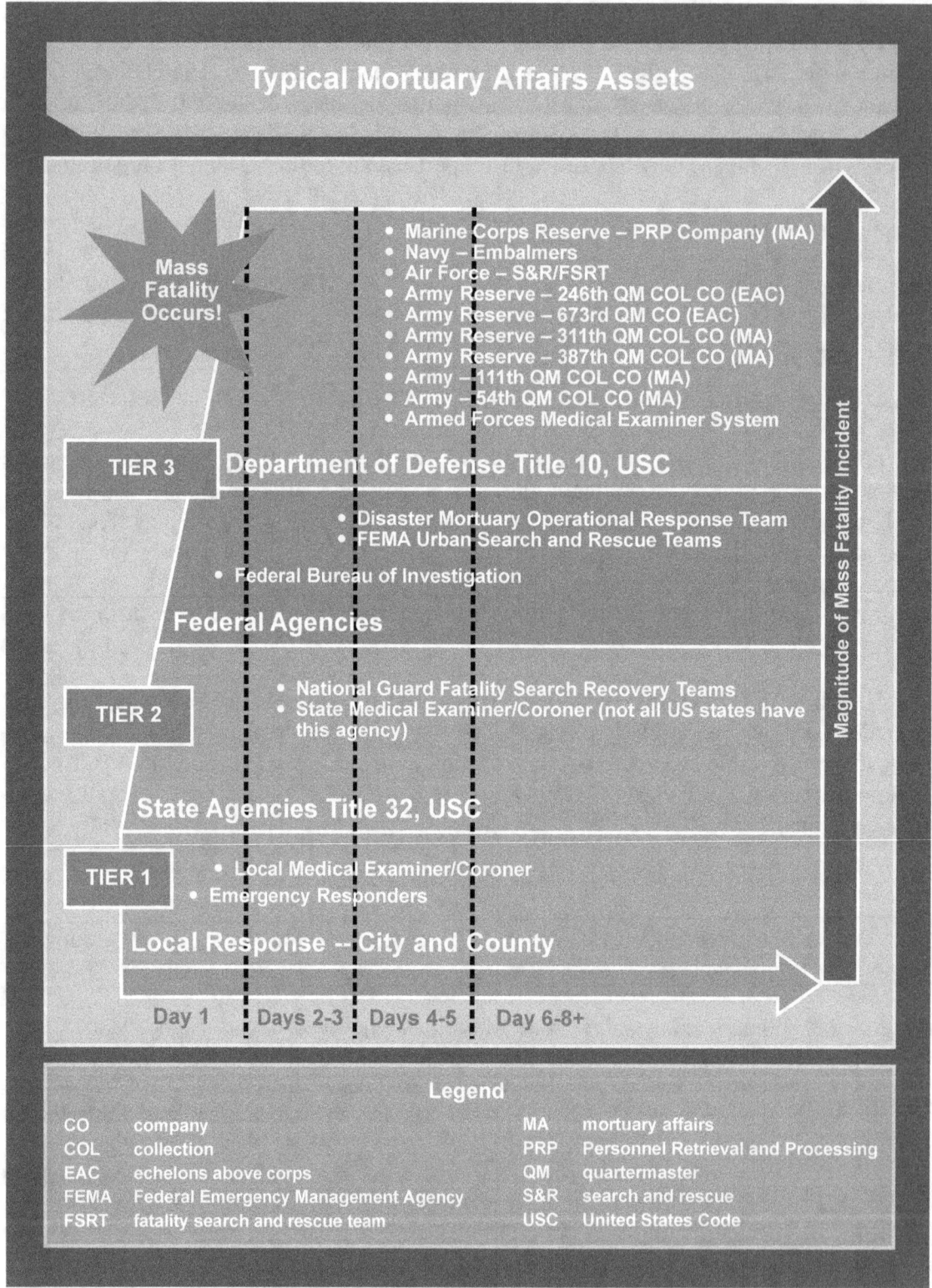

Figure VII-1. Typical Mortuary Affairs Assets

f. Under the NRF, DOD could be asked to provide capabilities that other agencies do not possess or that have been exhausted or overwhelmed. Support is provided with the provision that it does not conflict with DOD's mission or its ability to respond to military operational contingencies.

4. **Defense Support to Civil Authorities**

a. United States Northern Command (USNORTHCOM) and USPACOM provide DSCA as directed by the President or SecDef, which is typically after local, state, tribal, and other federal resources are overwhelmed and civil authorities have requested DOD assistance. USNORTHCOM and USPACOM deploy a defense coordinating officer (DCO), who serves as DOD's single POC in the JFO (with the exception of US Special Operations Command and US Army Corps of Engineers assets) and validates requests for assistance. Supporting the DCO is a defense coordinating element consisting of staff and military LNOs who facilitate DOD coordination in support of all activated ESFs. Emergency preparedness LNOs are senior reserve officers who represent their Service at the appropriate JFO conducting planning and coordination responsibilities in support of civil authorities.

b. A state governor will designate a state coordinating officer (SCO) upon requesting federal assistance (Stafford Act declaration). The SCO works directly with the federal coordinating officer (FCO) and DCO in the JFO, the primary federal incident management field structure. The SCO coordinates with the FCO to determine state requirements. If DOD resources are required the FCO provides an RFA to the DCO who will validate and forward the request for SecDef approval.

c. The SCO, FCO, and DCO operate from an established JFO facility that provides telephone and full media support to effect multiagency coordination. A unified coordination group meets within the JFO to identify gaps and review local, tribal, or state government RFAs.

d. For disaster events involving a large geographic area, multiple SCOs, FCOs, DCOs or JFOs may be established.

e. Concurrent to DHS activities, USNORTHCOM, the principal GCC responsible for coordinating military assistance, alerts its subordinate organizations to prepare to provide disaster response support. Initially, a USNORTHCOM situational awareness team will stand up to determine the required type of force package to deploy. Following these initial assessments, USNORTHCOM will delegate C2 to the joint force land component commander as the command element for all deployed Title 10, USC, military forces. NG forces in state active duty or Title 32, USC, status remain under the C2 of the adjutant general in each affected state.

f. Only under the following conditions are DOD assets deployed to support a civilian response effort:

(1) Commander, USNORTHCOM, implements a DSCA execute order, which allows Title 10, USC, forces to be deployed without a Presidential disaster declaration.

(2) Local, tribal, and state governments officially submit an RFA through their emergency operations centers to obtain resources not available through the local, state or federal government. Note: To obtain DOD assets, the DCO must validate the request and obtain approval from SecDef to ensure the military's primary mission to protect and defend the US and our allies against all enemies is not hindered.

(3) Immediate Response Authority. Immediate response authority is any form of immediate action taken by a DOD component or military commander, under the direction of DOD directives and any supplemental guidance, to assist civil authorities to save lives, prevent human suffering, or mitigate great property damage under imminently serious conditions. When such conditions exist, commanders and responsible officials are authorized to take necessary action to respond to requests from civil authorities consistent with applicable laws and regulations.

For further guidance, refer to JP 3-28, Defense Support of Civil Authorities, *and DODD 3025.18,* Defense Support of Civil Authorities (DSCA).

g. When DOD assets are used, the President and SecDef establish priorities and determine what DOD resources will be made available for DSCA mission assignments, applying the following principles:

(1) Civilian resources are applied first in meeting civilian RFA(s). Faith-based organizations and community-based organizations have a long tradition of helping Americans in need and have a long tradition of aiding victims of disasters.

(2) DOD resources are provided only when necessary to provide capabilities unique to the military or to augment the capabilities of civilian authorities.

(3) Title 10, USC, military forces work in support of the appropriate local, tribal, state, or federal jurisdiction but will retain C2 of DOD assets at all times.

5. **National Mass-Fatality Management Framework**

a. Once assets are deployed, DOD units must interface with civilian entities in accordance with the National Incident Management System (NIMS) incident command system (ICS). Normally a unified command structure is established versus an ICS when DOD assets are involved to ensure an integrated response for all agencies involved. Figure VII-2 identifies a typical ICS.

b. DOD assets will interface with civilian response units within the ICS. MA units will operate within the operations section, as part of a fatality management branch and under the DOD chain of command at all times. In most instances, the local ME/C will staff this position.

c. Fatality management operations are not always conducted within the fatality management branch, as each jurisdiction may apply the ICS differently. Often MA operations not performed at the disaster site, such as decedent investigations, will occur at a separate location, having its own command structure, which may or may not be

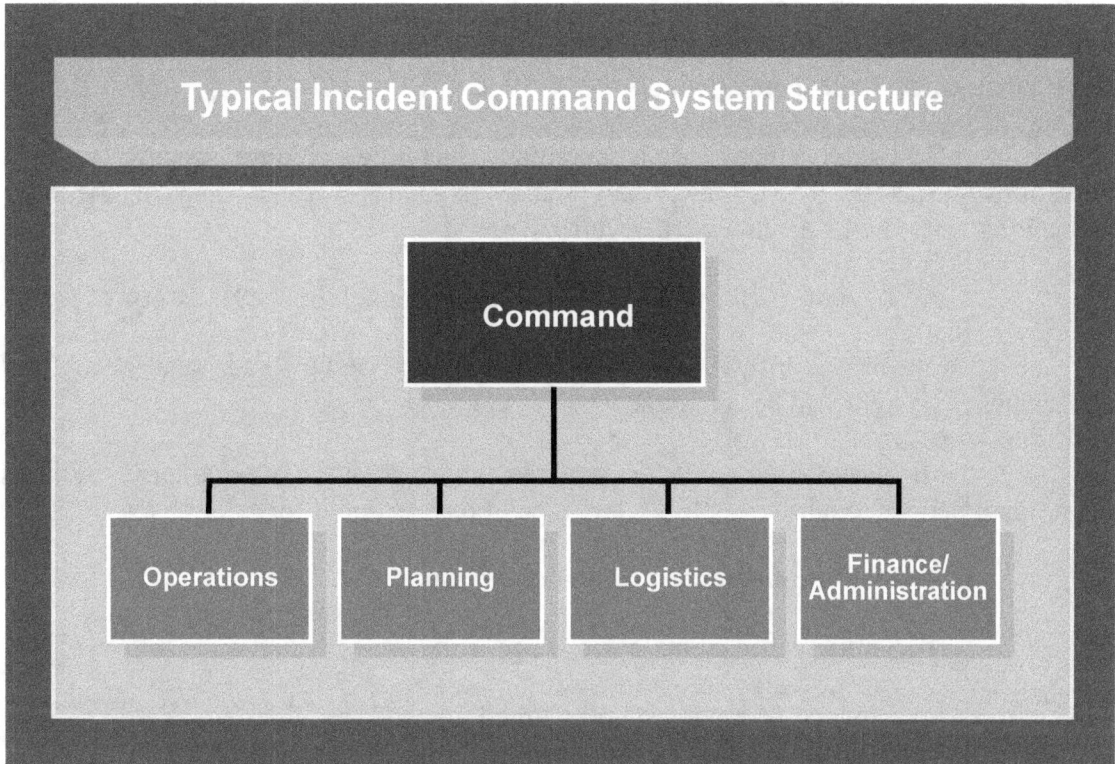

Figure VII-2. Typical Incident Command System Structure

linked to the jurisdictional ICS for the disaster site. MA operations typically occurring at separate locations include conducting antemortem data collection, postmortem data collection, decedent external/internal exams, as well as decedent storage and preparation for final disposition. It is likely each of these locations will operate in accordance with the ICS, by appointing a leader and dividing the labor into groups and teams, with whom DOD assets can interface.

d. Special Considerations

(1) MA Support Requests. When providing MA support to civilian authorities, DOD will tailor the response based on the RFA. Requests may include: reception, advisor support, photography operations, administrative and logistic support, DNA sample collection, recovery, transportation, human remains storage (refrigerated), and interim disposition operations. In addition, DOD may also be asked to provide support for agent detection and decontamination of human remains.

(2) ME/C Jurisdiction. MA leadership will identify or confirm the entity that has jurisdictional authority over decedents. In most instances, it is the local or state ME/C, but in some instances an interim ME/C representative may be designated. DOD personnel should note that ME/Cs have jurisdictional authority over the decedent only and work closely with law enforcement agencies having jurisdictional authority over the crime scene, if applicable.

(3) Local ME/C Coordination. MA mission assignments will identify a civilian POC with whom military commanders can interface. Coordination between the military and civilian counterpart should include:

(a) Establishment of a common operating picture specific to MA operations. Specifically, DOD-civilian entities should review a map of the area, identifying where MA operations are occurring.

(b) Review of all MA goals and objectives involving DOD assets.

(c) Review of MA operations involving DOD assets and how local government oversight will be achieved.

(d) Identification of communication format, expectations, defined operational periods requiring briefings, and type of data required for briefings.

(e) Identification of and resolution of issues.

(f) Safety requirements.

(g) Review of operational instructions and requirements (e.g., use of specific tools or documentation of decedent information).

(h) Appropriate interface with public media elements.

(i) Establishment of DOD MA asset end points.

(4) DOD Personnel Management. To accomplish the wide variety of potential assignments, DOD may deploy both skilled and non-skilled MA personnel. The civilian sector is responsible for providing just-in-time training to DOD personnel on proper techniques, safety precautions, and handling of decedents in accordance with civilian procedures and standards. Both skilled and non-skilled personnel should expect to receive some just-in-time training. Trained MA personnel may be paired with non-trained MA personnel to provide technical assistance and supervision.

(5) Posse Comitatus. DOD MA personnel must be mindful of acting independently of civilian ME/C personnel when performing tasks. Due to constraints placed on Title 10, USC, forces, DOD personnel must obtain appropriate authorization to perform MA-related tasks and the appropriate civilian oversight. For example, DOD MA personnel cannot perform decedent recovery tasks that entail entering civilian homes without the presence of local law enforcement or ME/C personnel. Unilateral action by DOD personnel in these circumstances would result in a violation of the Posse Comitatus Act (Federal law Title 18, USC, Section 1385). State Title 32, USC, MA assets, such as the ANG FSRTs, are able to perform decedent recovery tasks, when directed.

(6) Terrorist Act. The FBI has jurisdiction in events involving weapons of mass destruction (WMD), terrorist events, or suspected terrorist events. Consequently, DOD

MA assets may need to interact with the FBI in addition to the ME/C and adhere to FBI protocols regarding the collection of evidence.

(7) Decedent Identification. Decedent ID is an ME/C responsibility. DOD MA assets support the ID process through forensic recovery and preservation of decedent ID material.

6. Chemical, Biological, Radiological, and Nuclear Consequence Management

a. An incident involving CBRN agents or materials may require a DOD response in support of USG efforts. During such catastrophic incidents, SECHS will notify the President and implement the NRF Catastrophic Incident Supplement to expedite relief efforts.

b. During CBRN events that go beyond the ability of a state to respond, USNORTHCOM or USPACOM will activate and deploy CBRN response forces tailored to the scale and scope of the incident. DOD CBRN response forces have unique skill sets and equipment that can be deployed in support of civilian CBRN response assets. CBRN incidents may cause mass fatalities. When authorized by SecDef, DOD MA assets can help mitigate the potential health risks posed by mass fatalities and assist in incident response and recovery operations.

c. In an incident involving CBRN agents or materials, the NGB notifies the adjutant general for the 50 states and territories to place their weapons of mass destruction–civil support teams (WMD-CSTs), chemical, biological, radiological, nuclear, and high-yield explosives enhanced response force package (CERFP), FSRTs, and homeland response forces (HRFs) on alert for deployment. WMD-CSTs are able to deploy rapidly to a CBRNE incident, assist local first-responders in determining the nature of the attack, provide medical and technical advice, and pave the way for the identification and arrival of follow-on state and federal military assets. When the incident exceeds the capability of the regional CERFP, the regional HRF will be generated. NG WMD-CSTs and CERFPs normally will deploy under state control. The NGB will coordinate such interstate support and will facilitate any necessary federalization of NG forces.

For more information on CBRN response, see JP 3-41, Chemical, Biological, Radiological, and Nuclear Consequence Management.

7. Homeland Defense

GCCs are responsible for coordinating DOD MA operations within their AORs. In DSCA incidents, local, tribal, or state ME/Cs will usually maintain jurisdiction over both military and civilian fatalities, including decedents from mass fatality incidents. Jurisdiction varies depending on geographic area and is dependent on federal, state, or local laws. In concurrent jurisdiction, the local ME/C has primary authority to conduct the medicolegal death investigation, including the autopsy, but may waive jurisdiction to the military or request AFMES assistance. In proprietary jurisdiction, the local ME/C has sole authority to perform the autopsy. Deaths in areas of exclusive federal jurisdiction are the responsibility of the AFME regardless of the military affiliation, or lack thereof, of the individual. Active duty military deaths usually are determined to be under either exclusive federal or concurrent jurisdiction. Military installations are not necessarily under exclusive federal jurisdiction; the installation SJA should identify the base's jurisdiction before an incident or be consulted during early stages of the response phase. In accordance with Title 10, USC, Section 1471, the AFME may conduct its own forensic pathology investigation to determine the cause or manner of death if such an investigation is determined to be justified. However, this activity may or may not occur in conjunction with local medicolegal authorities' investigation. If the AFME believes the local ME/C's medicolegal investigation did not meet the needs of DOD, the AFME may exercise secondary jurisdiction and complete an independent autopsy. The remains may therefore be transferred to the AFMES before being released to the PADD. Federal law provides exclusive jurisdiction to the AFME in the event of the death of the President, a member of the President's direct staff, and other key elected officials in the USG.

For more information, see JP 3-27, Homeland Defense.

CHAPTER VIII
CONTAMINATED HUMAN REMAINS AND PERSONAL EFFECTS

1. Introduction

This chapter outlines MA operations in a CBRN environment to include roles and responsibilities, planning factors, and personnel, equipment, and support requirements. It does not provide TTP. For detailed guidance on TTP, contact the JMAC. Refer to Appendix G, "Key Points of Contact," for contact information.

2. Overview of Department of Defense Operations in a Contaminated Environment

The US military trains for and remains prepared to conduct the full range of military operations throughout the operational environment undeterred by the threat of CBRN attacks. CBRN consequence management (CBRN CM) is a USG-level responsibility to which DOD will provide support as directed to DHS, DOS, or other appropriate agencies, in the conduct of CBRN response. However, during combat operations or in specific instances on DOD installations and facilities overseas where HN agreements give DOD primary CBRN CM responsibility, DOD may be tasked with leading the USG CBRN CM effort. All DOD installations develop and exercise CBRN response plans, which outline operations and give tasks to staff functions such as public health and medical services, public affairs, legal counsel, and MA.

See JP 3-11, Operations in Chemical, Biological, Radiological, and Nuclear (CBRN) Environments; *JP 3-40,* Combating Weapons of Mass Destruction; *and JP 3-41,* Chemical, Biological, Radiological, and Nuclear Consequence Management, *for more information.*

3. Mortuary Affairs Operations in a Contaminated Environment

a. **Mission.** The primary MA mission in a CBRN environment is the establishment and operation of a MACRMS to complete MA ID tasks and contamination mitigation.

b. **Goal.** Conduct MA tasks safely to support AFMES positive ID of human remains. Return all human remains to the US or location designated by the PADD for final disposition.

c. Commercial off-the-shelf (COTS) equipment is employed at the MACRMS. Establishing and operating a MACRMS is a theater-level MA mission, requiring specialized personnel and resources. **Safety, not speed, is paramount.** When refrigerated storage is available, recovered human remains should be stored at a temperature range of between 34 and 40 degrees Fahrenheit (1.1 and 4.4 degrees Celsius).

d. Planning considerations for the operation and support of the MACRMS include but are not limited to:

(1) **Capabilities.** Five to 10 human remains processed in a 12-hour period for each MACRMS established.

(2) **Baseline Planning Figures.** Although the MACRMS equipment consists of most items required to safely receive and handle contaminated human remains, certain items of specialized equipment may have to be procured in order to fully process contaminated decedents. Supplies and equipment needs are based on the type and level of contamination hazard present on the human remains. The COTS equipment contains most expendable supplies for personnel to process approximately 50 human remains. Additional personnel and equipment would be required for 24-hour operations.

(3) **Supplies and Equipment.** The MA operational commander is responsible for resupplying the MACRMS. The concept used at a MACRMS is to employ multiple forms of protection, such as specialized tents, monitors, and individual protective equipment. MACRMS personnel will wear the appropriate level of PPE for the hazard. CBRN specialists will assist MA personnel in devising an incident-specific process to manage contaminated human remains that exceed the MA capability.

d. **Unit-Level Operations in a CBRN Environment**

(1) Unit personnel, wearing appropriate mission-oriented protective posture (MOPP) gear, are responsible for the recovery of deceased unit members while evacuating the area. The level and type of contamination should be verified at this time by trained CBRN personnel in order to determine the proper evacuation channels. If no contamination is detected, human remains should be evacuated according to the existing MA procedures in effect. If CBRN personnel are not able to verify the type and amount of contamination, but unit personnel believe contamination may be present, human remains will be treated as if they are contaminated. The area should be marked with appropriate CBRN markings, and appropriate security measures established.

(2) The unit will establish a CP. The CP will receive and triage casualties to include deceased personnel. The unit will transport the human remains to either the CP or to the MACRMS as directed. At the CP, place the human remains in two HRPs or the contaminated human remains pouch (CHRP). The human remains will be stored and prepared for shipment to either the MACP or the MACRMS. The external surface of the HRP or CHRP will be decontaminated and the CBRN personnel will determine if the human remains meet the guidelines for transport to the MACP or MACRMS or if they will be stored at the CP until further guidance is received.

e. **Operational-Level Operations in a CBRN Environment**

(1) **Search and Recovery.** When the unit is unable to recover human remains from the incident site, an S&R team is required to conduct the recovery. Units request S&R teams through their chain of command to the JMAO. This team will work closely with the CBRN personnel to determine routes into and out of the incident site, level of PPE required, as well as when access to the incident site will be granted. The ANG

FSRTs are trained and equipped to operate in CBRN environments and are available for worldwide deployment.

(2) **MACP.** During operations when the scale of contaminated human remains does not warrant the employment of a MACRMS, personnel from the nearest MACP will process and evacuate contaminated human remains. The MACP processing team reports to the tasking POC and follows the required procedures for handling contaminated human remains.

f. Theater-Level Operations in a CBRN Environment

(1) **JMAO.** The JMAO acts as the theater central point of coordination for MA in a CBRN environment. The JMAO will determine when to establish a MACRMS and the location. The JMAO determines how many equipment sets are required to support operations and requests immediate movement of the pre-positioned sets to the operational area. The JMAO also coordinates with DOD entities to obtain specialized personnel and equipment (such as medical or safety personnel and monitoring equipment). Typically, these types of capabilities are required to safely operate and monitor MACRMS operations, equipment, and personnel.

(2) **US Army.** The Army, in coordination with the JMAO, authorizes and arranges for movement of the MACRMS. The systems are moved to a predetermined location near the contaminated area, but outside of any area posing a contamination hazard to the personnel operating the MACRMS. CBRN personnel will designate routes to be used to evacuate human remains from both the contaminated area and from the CP once a route survey is completed. In addition, the Army as EA for theater MA support, in coordination with the JMAO, develops a plan to establish the necessary task force to:

(a) Support the MACRMS.

(b) Position the required equipment.

(c) Provide additional guidance and support for contamination mitigation operations.

4. Mortuary Affairs Contaminated Human Remains Mitigation Site

The MACRMS is an established location utilizing specialized equipment where MA personnel safely handle contaminated human remains and perform the MA tasks. MA personnel attempt to reduce contamination hazards on the human remains for transport through normal MA evacuation channels.

a. **Site Selection.** MACRMS equipment may be pre-positioned to support an operational sector in anticipation of the need to process contaminated human remains or deployed to support a known contaminated area. Proximity to the contaminated area or the sector to be supported is the primary factor for site location, followed by environmental and terrain considerations. The MACRMS should be situated in close proximity to both a medical treatment facility supporting patient decontamination and treatment, and a thorough decontamination site where both troop and equipment decontamination is taking place. The MACRMS site should be located upwind of the contaminated area. CBRN staff should be consulted in picking a MACRMS location, as they can advise on the expected flow of contamination.

(1) **Environmental Considerations**. Factors to be considered are the runoff of contaminated water and the proximity to populated areas. Restoration of a MACRMS site is not an MA concern with the exception of hazardous waste disposal (see paragraph 4e(3), "Hazardous Waste Disposal"); detailed MACRMS site clearance may have to be accomplished by CBRN units. CBRN staff and local governments will have to decide when to declare an area safe for reentry.

(2) **Terrain Considerations.** Due to the large footprint of the MACRMS, the site selected should be relatively flat and accessible by vehicles arriving from the CP or contaminated area via a designated route. Ideally, existing roads should be used by transports arriving from the "warm or hot" zone to the MACRMS receiving point. An additional requirement is a route leading away from the MACRMS release station toward the clean or "cold" zone for human remains evacuation. The area selected should be a minimum of 100 m in length by 75 m in width. A larger area would provide better vehicular traffic flow and refrigerated storage capability. Vehicular access to the MACRMS contaminated waste storage areas and liquid waste sump must be considered during site selection. The inability to provide safe and timely waste removal will result in the MACRMS ceasing operations due to its limited solid and liquid contaminated waste storage capability.

b. **Facility Layout.** The MACRMS is determined by the type of contamination; there are three recommended configurations for the system. There is a recommended configuration for chemical agents, biological agents, and one for radiological agents, each configuration is established based on the stations required to mitigate that hazard. The site should be protected by security personnel with access at the dismount and release points. CBRN markers are emplaced around the entire MACRMS perimeter. Figure VIII-1 shows one of the suggested layouts of the MACRMS. The release station should be upwind of the receiving station to reduce the hazard of contamination.

(1) The suggested MACRMS stations pictured in Figure VIII-1 allow MA personnel to perform the following major tasks:

(a) Receiving and sorting.

(b) External assessment.

(c) Wash/rinse.

(d) ID material/specimens.

(e) CHRP decontamination.

(f) Low-level detection.

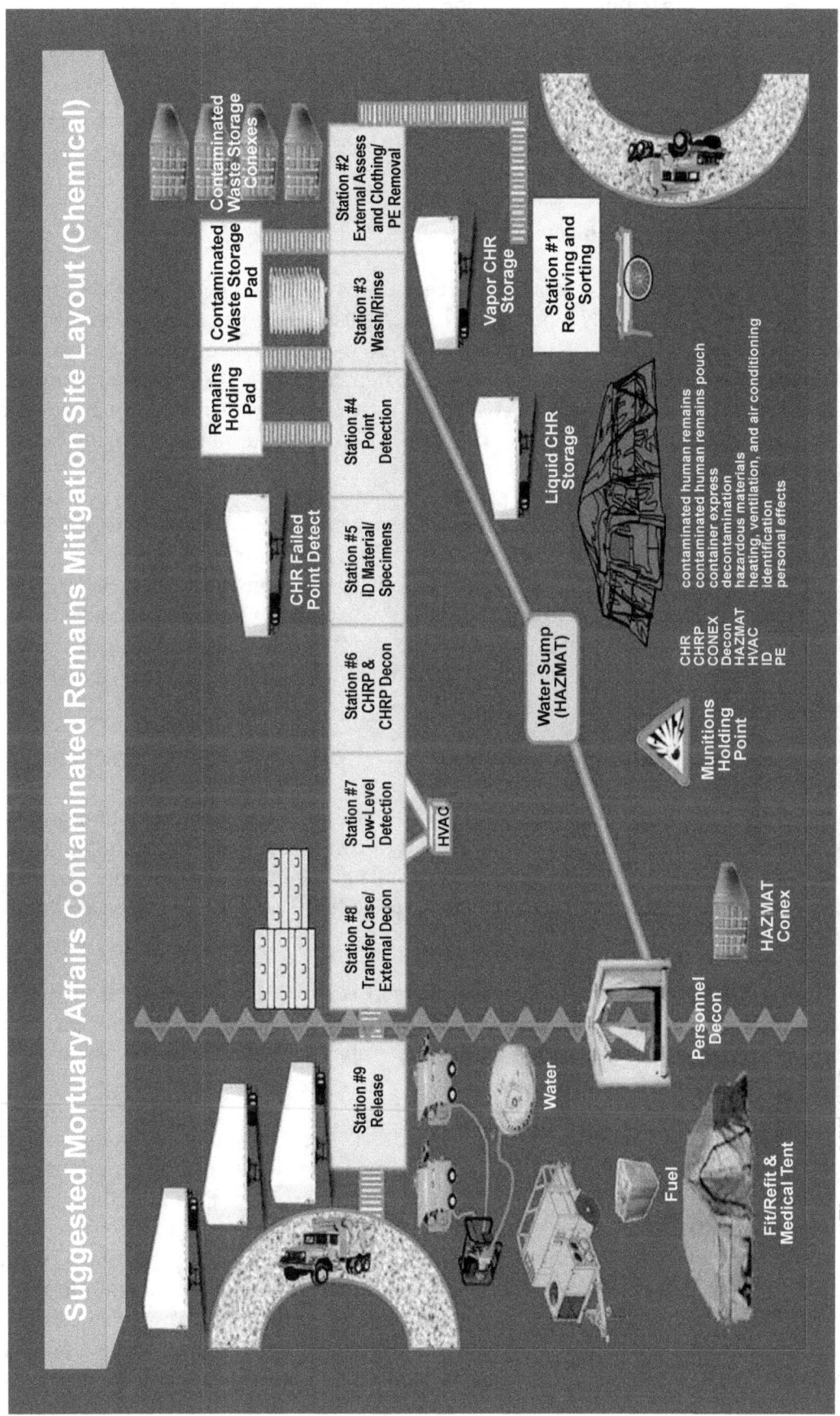

Figure VIII-1. Suggested Mortuary Affairs Contaminated Remains Mitigation Site Layout (Chemical)

(g) Preparation for evacuation or temporary storage.

(h) Release.

(2) Although not part of the human remains processing stations, the MACRMS also requires an environmentally controlled fit/refit and medical area as well as a personnel decontamination system.

(3) **Personnel Requirements**

(a) **Personnel.** Personnel required to operate the MACRMS must be thoroughly trained in CBRN operations and the use of PPE measures. Due to the complexity of MACRMS processes, the specialized training and equipment requirements, and familiarity with MACRMS operations, only trained MACRMS personnel from Army MA units should be tasked for the MACRMS mission. However, additional personnel may be tasked as augmentees for the MACRMS to assist with human remains handling and other necessary MACRMS functions.

(b) **Staffing.** Special personnel requirements exist for the operation of the MACRMS. The MACRMS is task-organized. In addition to organic MA and CBRN personnel, the MACRMS requires augmentation for positions such as CBRN experts, safety officers, medical staff, and logistics staff. MACRMS operation requires 32 to 39 MACRMS trained MA specialists to operate the site for each 12-hour shift. The range in personnel reflects changes in the number of stations within the MACRMS based on the hazard.

c. **External Support Requirements**

(1) **Transportation.** Planners should consider using dedicated transportation assets to reduce confusion and avoid the spread of contamination. Transportation assets will utilize CBRN directed routes to evacuate human remains to and from the MACRMS location. Human remains will not be evacuated until CBRN personnel clear them for transport.

(2) **Engineer Support.** Engineer support is required to prepare the MACRMS, which requires a dug-in, lined, and bermed liquid waste sump, munitions pit, and a suitable road network. Coordination for this support should begin as soon as the MACRMS mission is assigned.

(3) **Internal Communications.** MACRMS personnel will communicate intra-station, as well as throughout, using voice-activated radios capable of operating in conjunction with both standard-issue MOPP or any other issued PPE regardless of level of protection. MACRMS requires internal communication between all stations as well as to outside organizations as required. MACRMS receiving point personnel require effective communication with personnel delivering human remains to obtain information regarding recovery location, unit, contaminant, and information that may assist in ID. MACRMS personnel require information regarding the contaminant to determine the appropriate PPE to safely handle contaminated human remains. Wireless technology will

also be employed in order to transmit photos, digital fingerprints, and other information to the appropriate station for inclusion in the automated MACRMS case file.

(4) **Personnel Decontamination.** MACRMS personnel are capable of performing detailed troop decontamination (DTD) using the personnel decontamination system which is part of the MACRMS. DTD takes approximately 15 minutes per individual. The MACRMS will require complete detailed equipment decontamination.

(5) **Security.** Plan for security personnel to protect against adversary action and/or to prevent unauthorized personnel from entering the MACRMS operational area.

(6) **Medical Support.** Medical support is necessary for MACRMS personnel to treat injuries resulting from work, environmental, or occupational health hazards. Medical personnel will be assigned to the MACRMS fit/refit area to provide medical support.

(7) **Maintenance.** A small engine and an air conditioning/refrigeration mechanic should be assigned to the MACRMS to perform routine, operational, and repair maintenance on all power equipment. Factory trained, bench-level certified repairers are required to maintain and repair specialized COTS equipment. Major repairs should be provided by nearby DS or GS maintenance units.

(8) **EOD Support.** MACRMS receiving point personnel will inspect all human remains for explosive ordnance and UXO. The removal and disposal of explosive ordnance and UXO is the responsibility of EOD. Explosive ordnance and UXO will be placed in a munitions pit until removed or disposed of by EOD personnel. Coordination for EOD support will occur upon the establishment of a MACRMS.

(9) **Life Support and/or Personnel Services.** MACRMS personnel should be supported by the nearest unit for subsistence, laundry, bath, and billeting.

d. **Overview of Contamination Processing.** Three distinct operations have been developed to handle different types of hazards. The three types of processing operations are: chemical processing, biological processing, and radiological processing. The TTP are contained in the MA unit SOP. The JMAC will provide the most current TTP to the MA units as the TTP need to be updated frequently based on current science and technology (S&T) and research and development (R&D). Additionally, supervisors should establish rotational work teams (with work/rest–cool down cycles) to minimize the work load and mitigate heat stress risk.

(1) **Chemically Contaminated Human Remains Processing.** If the cause of death is suspected to have resulted from exposure to a chemical agent, MACRMS personnel will process human remains in accordance with the chemical human remains processing procedures outlined in the unit SOP. The overarching goal to perform the MA tasks and reduce, remove, and contain chemical contamination to allow for storage and transport may not be possible in all cases. Higher headquarters is responsible for creating and implementing an incident-specific plan whenever a hazard cannot be safely handled at the MACRMS. For additional support, contact the Chemical Casualty Care Division

consultation service, US Army Medical Research Institute of Chemical Defense. Contact information is provided in Appendix G, "Key Points of Contact."

(2) **Biologically Contaminated Human Remains Processing.** If the cause of death is suspected to be a biological agent, MACRMS personnel will process human remains in accordance with the biological human remains processing procedures outlined in the unit SOP. CBRN and infectious disease control personnel should be consulted as to the efficacy of MACRMS PPE and adjust posture accordingly. The overarching goal is to perform the MA tasks and reduce, remove, and contain biological contamination to allow for storage and transport. Higher headquarters is responsible for creating and implementing an incident-specific plan whenever a hazard cannot be safely handled at the MACRMS.

For additional support, contact the US Army Medical Research Institute of Infectious Diseases. Contact information is provided in Appendix G, "Key Points of Contact."

(3) **Radiological Contaminated Human Remains Processing.** If the human remains are suspected to be contaminated with a radiological agent, MACRMS personnel will process human remains in accordance with the radiological human remains processing procedures outlined in the unit SOP. The overarching goal is to perform the MA tasks and reduce, remove, and contain radiological contamination to allow for storage and transport. Higher headquarters is responsible for creating and implementing an incident-specific plan whenever a hazard cannot be safely handled at the MACRMS. Monitors and detectors, such as a personal dosimeter, will be used during radiological contamination processing procedures by all MACRMS personnel. For additional support, contact the Armed Forces Radiobiology Research Institute. Contact information is provided in Appendix G, "Key Points of Contact."

e. **Safety and Sanitation.** Safety is a major concern in all operations, and all necessary precautions should be taken in order to protect MACRMS personnel from exposure to chemicals, radioactivity, biological pathogens, as well as other natural and man-made hazards. Leaders must be aware of safety-related factors not only involving contamination, but also in the wear of MOPP overgarments and lifting requirements. Sanitation of the site and personnel is another major concern. MACRMS personnel are working in contaminated areas and are exposed to human remains and are subject to all of the health-related problems associated with this type of environment. A safety officer is needed to implement and monitor compliance with work–rest cycles and safe practices.

(1) **Heat Stress.** Heat stress is a constant threat when working under conditions found at a MACRMS and may result in heat-related injuries, such as heat cramps, heat exhaustion, or, in extreme cases, heat stroke, if not carefully monitored. Supervisors must watch for heat-related symptoms. A medical noncommissioned officer is assigned to the MACRMS to monitor personnel closely for signs of heat injury and to provide first aid. The medic needs to be well versed in the treatment of heat injuries. This medic is stationed in the fit/refit and medical area located on the clean side, and will treat all illness and injuries to MACRMS personnel after removal from their respective

workstation by other station personnel and movement through the personnel decontamination point.

(2) **Work and Rest Cycles.** Information on work and rest cycles may be found in Field Manual (FM) 3-11.4, Marine Corps Warfighting Publication (MCWP) 3-37.2, Navy Tactics, Techniques, and Procedures (NTTP) 3-11.27, Air Force Tactics, Techniques, and Procedures (Instruction) (AFTTP[I]) 3-2.46, *Multi-Service Tactics, Techniques, and Procedures for Nuclear, Biological, and Chemical (NBC) Protection*; FM 4-02.7, Marine Corps Reference Publication (MCRP) 4-11.1F, NTTP 4-02.7, AFTTP 3-42.3 *Multi-Service Tactics, Techniques, and Procedures for Health Service Support in a Chemical, Biological, Radiological, and Nuclear Environment;* and FM 3-11.5, MCWP 3-37.3, NTTP 3-11.26, AFTTP(I) 3-2.60, *Multi-Service Tactics, Techniques, and Procedures for Chemical, Biological, Radiological, and Nuclear Decontamination.* When operating in temperatures above 75 degrees Fahrenheit, leaders must consider the ability of personnel to accomplish the mission. Once personnel reach their maximum work load for heat stress, they cannot recover quickly enough to accomplish the MACRMS mission. Establish rotational work teams to minimize work load against heat stress injuries.

(3) **Hazardous Waste Disposal.** Disposal of contaminated waste is a major concern for the MACRMS. All uniforms, equipment, PE, overgarments, and bandages should be considered contaminated. The MACRMS personnel must dispose of this waste properly. The MACRMS personnel, with proper CBRN support, must close-out operations and complete a thorough decontamination as specified in CBRN decontamination manuals, just as any other unit operating in a contaminated environment would.

For further guidance on waste disposal, refer to JP 3-41, Chemical, Biological, Radiological, and Nuclear Consequence Management, *and FM 3-11.21, MCRP 3-37.2C, NTTP 3-11.24, AFTTP(I) 3-2.37,* Multi-Service Tactics, Techniques, and Procedures for CBRN Consequence Management Operations.

5. **Temporary Storage of Contaminated Human Remains**

Hold contaminated human remains in refrigerated storage (maintaining a temperature range between 34 and 40 degrees Fahrenheit (1.1 and 4.4 degrees Celsius) to preserve the human remains until they can be processed. The storage facility will be monitored for levels of contamination within and around the container or facility. Positive control must be maintained at all times on the storage container/facility and its contents. Security measures should be established to prevent unauthorized access to the container/facility, and the appropriate CBRN markings should be placed on the external surfaces of the container/facility.

Note: Personnel who enter the storage container or who are in the vicinity must wear the appropriate level of PPE to account for concentrated levels of agent in the container or facility.

6. Temporary Interment of Contaminated Human Remains

Temporary interment of contaminated human remains poses a much larger problem than interment of non-contaminated human remains. Interment does not necessarily kill all biological, chemical, or radiological agents; some remain resistant or dormant underground. Temporary interment may be considered for operational requirements, to prevent contamination from spreading, or to support decontamination through natural chemical or biological decomposition. Human remains should be temporarily interred if the contaminant cannot be mitigated for transport through MA channels. If temporary interment is required, contaminated human remains will be processed in accordance with the following guidelines:

a. Follow Appendix B, "Mass Interment," guidelines for interment site selection, construction, and procedures for interment operations. The following additional information specific to contaminated human remains interment is provided.

b. ID of human remains will be made prior to interment. ID will be conducted in accordance with AFMES guidance.

c. Contaminated human remains will be interred in separate rows for each category of CBRN hazard. For example, human remains contaminated with chemical agents will not be commingled with human remains contaminated with biological agents. The contaminated interment site will be a minimum of 100 yards from non-contaminated interment sites.

d. Interment sites will be clearly marked using NATO standard CBRN signage. Security will be posted as required.

e. Security and interment site personnel will wear appropriate PPE in accordance with medical and CBRN guidelines. Medical and CBRN personnel will monitor personnel CBRN exposure levels using approved monitoring devices.

f. Photographs should be taken of all human remains and portions prior to interment.

7. Theater Mortuary Evacuation Point Operations

The TMEP will receive all human remains processed and cleared for evacuation from the MA processing point for contaminated human remains. The TMEP will not process these human remains but rather act as a transfer point. The TMEP will verify that all seals, documentation, special permits, and shipping and warning labels are in place. The TMEP will coordinate transfer back to the US or servicing mortuary or to the HN in accordance with current transportation and international agreements and regulations. The TMEP will coordinate for a special assignment air mission through USTRANSCOM for all human remains with CBRN labels in accordance with current guidelines. The TMEP will verify that the human remains are entered into the database and tracking system as well as notify the CONUS mortuary that human remains with CBRN labels are in transit. When required, a technical escort will be requested and coordinated through higher headquarters. A technical escort is a unique, immediate response capability for chemical and biological warfare material. The technical escort missions include worldwide response for escorting, rendering safe, disposing, sampling verification, mitigating hazards, and identifying weaponized and non-weaponized chemical, biological, and hazardous materials. The Technical Escort Unit is a member of the Army Chemical/Biological Rapid Response Team.

8. Port Mortuary

The port mortuary will receive the human remains from the TMEP and store them until coordination for final disposition can be made. The AFME will determine the handling procedures for human remains marked with CBRN labels on a case-by-case basis, based on contaminant and exposure levels. The port mortuary will determine final disposition requirements and procedures.

9. Final Disposition

Final disposition of human remains will be in accordance with the directions of the PADD, national regulations, and AFME directives. The USACHPPM guidelines have been published to aid in determining the best method for final disposition whether that is interment or cremation.

10. Mortuary Affairs Contaminated Remains Mitigation Site Records

MA personnel must be able to enter vital data into MARTS while working in a contaminated area. The time required to process contaminated human remains is a key planning factor. MA operations and planning must address the procedures and equipment required to allow for transmission of information from the warm zone to the cool zone. This plan should account for communication equipment outages. Interment records will be delivered by escort to the JMAO/TMAO. A copy of all interment records will be sent to the JMAC. See Appendix G, "Key Points of Contact," for mailing address.

Intentionally Blank

APPENDIX A
SAMPLE FORMAT FOR MORTUARY AFFAIRS APPENDIX TO AN OPERATION PLAN

1. Introduction

a. During any military operation, MA must be planned in detail, from the joint force to the lowest level, and included in appropriate plans, orders, and SOPs. MA planning should include procedures for employing, shifting, and resourcing MA personnel and equipment throughout the AOR. Including MA issues in a staff's detailed logistic estimate will provide an overview of support requirements impacting a proposed COA and will help prepare the staff for the anticipated fatalities. MA staff planners must be able to react and respond to any staff or command concern. Not every theater is identical; each has its unique aspects. MA staff planners must create a base plan and modify it for different areas where the command may operate. From the base plan, the staff planner can tailor the plans and annexes to meet the needs of a specific mission. No one plan fits all situations. The J-4 is primarily responsible for the MA appendix, although each staff function will contribute. Subordinate commands will also develop supplements to the OPLAN. Lack of MA support during the initial stage of an operation will cause confusion and failure to recover deceased personnel in a timely manner.

b. The purpose of this annex is to provide a generic format for the MA appendix to the appropriate plan or OPORD annex. Its purpose is to set policies, assign responsibilities, and provide guidance for the MA plans to support combat operations under all conditions. Reference: CJCSM 3122.03, *Joint Operation Planning and Execution System (JOPES), Volume II, Planning Formats.*

2. Sample Mortuary Affairs Appendix to Operation Plan

(CLASSIFICATION)

APPENDIX 3 (MORTUARY AFFAIRS) to ANNEX L (LOGISTICS)

to OPLAN _____ ( )

( ) References: Cite CJCS Memorandum of Policy 16; JP 4-06; Service regulations; support agreements; and other documents necessary for a complete understanding of this appendix.

1. ( ) **Situation.** Identify any significant factors that may influence MA activities in support of the OPLAN. Use the following subparagraphs to the extent necessary.

a. ( ) Adversary. Refer to Annex B, Intelligence. Assess the effect of adversary capabilities and probable COAs on MA activities.

b. ( ) Friendly. Include any non-US military forces and US civilian agencies that will support assigned forces in accomplishing MA activities (e.g., available civilian mortuary services).

2. ( ) **Execution**

a. ( ) Concept of Operations. State the general concept of MA support for the forces assigned for implementation of the OPLAN and comment on MA facilities, interment, and evacuation policies existing at the onset of hostilities and at the time when additional forces and resources may become available. Project when the theater interment and evacuation policy may change. Comment on MC/FI policy and the processing of contaminated human remains.

b. ( ) Tasks. In separate numbered subparagraphs for each applicable component, identify specific responsibilities for MA activities. Indicate, by component, responsibility for as many of the following as applicable.

(1) ( ) MA support of forces of each US Service.

(2) ( ) Establishment and operation of CPs, field processing centers, PE depots, and US cemeteries in the theater.

(3) ( ) Establishment, operation, and maintenance of mortuary facilities.

(4) ( ) POE holding facilities and surface and aerial evacuation of human remains.

(5) ( ) Activation and staffing of the JMAO and the establishment of subarea JMAOs, as needed.

(6) ( ) Designate theater lead Service.

c. ( ) Coordinating Instructions. Include general instructions applicable to two or more components. Include, if applicable, items such as:

(1) ( ) Arrangements concerning MA support of US forces under OPCON of other than a US command.

(2) ( ) Agreements with multinational partners, USG, and NGOs for MA support of multinational partners and civilians in areas where US forces are operating.

(3) ( ) Advisory services to support allied or HN MA activities.

(4) ( ) Approving authority for use of temporary interments to include mass burial techniques and temporary graves.

(5) ( ) Providing J-1 information for joint casualty reporting. Establish JMAO reporting requirements.

(6) ( ) Special instructions for operations involving special operations forces.

(7) ( ) AFMES support.

d. ( ) Special Guidance. Include guidance and policy, not discussed elsewhere, concerning the search, recovery, tentative ID, collection and preservation of biological and physical evidence, religious and cultural considerations, and temporary interment of US military, multinational partner, adversary, and civilian dead under the jurisdiction of the Armed Forces of the United States. Specifically address coordination with the AFMES with respect to preservation of medicolegal findings and evidence. Also discuss the recovery and handling of PE and the establishment, operation, and maintenance of appropriate records and reports. If applicable, include the following:

(1) ( ) Uniform procedures for maintaining continuous accountability of all deceased US military personnel and detainees.

(2) ( ) Evacuation of human remains, both intratheater and intertheater.

(3) ( ) Establishment of permanent cemeteries and temporary interment sites.

(4) ( ) Possible transfer of human remains and PE of multinational partners, adversary personnel, local nationals, and third country nationals to representatives of the country concerned.

(5) ( ) Identity of specific collection locations where non-US fatalities will be delivered.

(6) ( ) Procedures for using DOD mortuary personnel, facilities, and supplies in the operational area.

3. ( ) **Administration and Logistics.** Provides a concept for furnishing logistic and administrative support for MA activities and, as appropriate, includes guidance on the following:

a. ( ) Accounting for and disposition of PE, including those not found on the person of the deceased.

b. ( ) Use of multinational partners and indigenous morticians, mortuaries, and interment facilities, including local procurement of these services to care for deceased HN, multinational partner, and adversary personnel. Only US personnel will process US human remains; however, use of locally procured facilities and equipment is authorized.

c. ( ) Identification of MA theater stocks, to include transfer cases, HRPs, and PPE.

d. ( ) Identification of contracting requirements for such items as facilities, refrigerated storage, ice, and cadaver dogs. For small operations or exercises, this may also include contract shipping and use of HN mortuary facilities.

4. ( ) **Communications Systems.** Summarize special communications system and command procedures required to conduct MA.

Intentionally Blank

APPENDIX B
MASS INTERMENT

1. Introduction

a. Natural disasters, terrorist attacks, and accidents such as plane crashes have the potential to produce catastrophic numbers of fatalities. The earthquake in Haiti in 2010 produced over 230,000 fatalities, the crash of a Polish Air Force Tu-154 in 2010 produced 96 fatalities, and the United Kingdom pandemic in 2008 produced over 3,000 fatalities, all of which resulted in a mass interment of victims.

b. Attacks using WMD have the potential to create extraordinary numbers of fatalities similar to those seen in large accidents and natural disasters. The problem of MC/FIs is significantly compounded if human remains are contaminated. If decontamination of human remains is necessary, MACRMS operations may not be able to keep up with requirements. Decontamination of survivors is the first priority. During wartime, decontamination of essential equipment, facilities, and areas will usually come before the decontamination of human remains.

c. These catastrophes are normally characterized by confusion and chaos due to multiple deaths, dismemberment, commingling of human remains, post-incident fire, and extreme emotional distress for the survivors. Since disasters cannot be predicted, it is imperative to establish a strategy designed to minimize confusion and establish an orderly and timely process for returning human remains to the PADD. An MC/FI is one of the most trying and emotional human experiences, and human remains must be handled with the utmost care, professionalism, and dignity.

2. Guidance

a. There are many factors that can influence the final disposition of human remains. The expedient and respectful repatriation of deceased personnel to their PADD is the top priority of the joint MA program. However, during extreme situations when tactical, logistic, safety, sanitation, or moral considerations leave no alternatives, temporary interments may be authorized.

b. Any event involving MC/FIs will have major environmental, legal, political, and/or religious consequences. The decision on the manner in which the human remains will be handled will most likely be made at the very highest levels of government.

c. Regardless of the circumstances, every effort must be made to positively identify the decedents prior to interment. Meticulous data collection and records management must be undertaken to ensure the ability to locate specific human remains at a future date for repatriation.

3. Mass Casualty/Fatality Incidents During War

a. During combat operations, MC/FIs may be a result of intense combat, disease, environmental conditions, or attacks using CBRN weapons. The decision to temporarily inter may be required for the safety of the forces, or lack of transportation. More significantly, the decision to temporarily inter may be necessary when the fatalities are a result of a CBRN attack or incident. Temporary interment may be the best option when the ability to mitigate the hazard for transportation cannot be achieved and long-term refrigerated storage is not an option.

b. Temporary interment can consist of individual graves, burial by rows, or even as a last resort, mass burials. The Geneva Conventions require parties to a conflict to search for the dead and to prevent their bodies and human remains from being despoiled. For every deceased person who falls into the hands of an adverse party, the adverse party must record, prepare, and forward all ID information, death certificates, and PE to the appropriate parties. Parties to a conflict must also ensure that deceased persons are buried with dignity and with respect to the cultural and spiritual mores of their country. Bodies should not be cremated except for hygiene reasons or for the religious customs of the deceased. Cremation is not authorized for cases under the jurisdiction of the AFMES without prior approval. Interment will be carried out in an honorable fashion, according to the religious rites of the deceased. Reference: Appendix E, "Religious Support to Mortuary Affairs." Temporarily interred human remains should be grouped by nationality, and their graves marked and maintained so they can be easily found.

4. **Mass Casualty/Fatality Incidents in the United States**

a. A terrorist event in an urban location could produce a significant number of fatalities, especially if combined with CBRN effects. Local communities, individual states, and even the USG could be easily overwhelmed by large numbers of casualties. Local ME/Cs, morgues, and funeral homes most likely will not be able to absorb the surge. Some morticians and funeral directors may be reluctant to receive contaminated human remains. Additionally, morticians and funeral directors may be reluctant to receive human remains that were decontaminated unless certified as safe (clean) by some regulatory agency. Issues involved with fatality management interment operations include the following:

(1) **Infection Control**

(a) Enforce the same personal protection precautions required when handling human remains.

(b) Survivability of all pathogens in human remains is not fully understood.

For additional guidance, contact Public Health Command; contact information is provided in Appendix G, "Key Points of Contact."

(2) **Victim Identification and Tracking**

(a) Even in an MC/FI, legal, moral, ethical, psychological, and religious reasons exist to identify the deceased prior to interment.

(b) Release of human remains for interment, cremation, or committal at sea will be delayed unless positive ID occurs or, at a minimum, enough evidence is collected (e.g., dental radiographs, fingerprints, photographs, or potential DNA samples) for determination later.

Note: Positive IDs are never made based on visual recognition.

(3) Establishment of Temporary Morgues

(a) In the event of MC/FIs, the ability of hospitals and ME/C medical treatment facilities to hold all human remains is doubtful. The establishment of temporary morgues may be required in order to account for, identify, prepare, and store human remains prior to interment operations.

(b) Contingency plans must be in place to augment the existing ME/C and funeral home system through the use of temporary morgues to assist in human remains storage and interment operations.

(c) Temporary morgues require temperature and biohazard control, adequate water, lighting, rest facilities for staff, and viewing areas and the capability to communicate with patient tracking sites, interment sites, and the emergency operations center. If a viewing area is to be utilized, a physical barrier (such as a window) needs to be present to prevent the observer from handling or coming in contact with the human remains. A better option is to establish a remote viewing location linked via live video feed to the decedent.

(d) Security must be established for the site.

(4) **Final Disposition or Release of Human Remains.** Many moral, cultural, and religious issues are involved with the disposition of the deceased. Although the President and governors have extraordinary powers under a declared disaster, at some point a decision must be made concerning the release of human remains to families for interment, cremation, committal at sea, or to the state for state-sponsored disposition.

(5) Legal issues may include:

(a) Security at temporary morgues and contamination mitigation facilities.

(b) Evidence collection, storage, and turnover to appropriate authorities.

(c) Release to the PADD.

(d) PE.

(6) Cleanup of the temporary morgues and contamination mitigation facilities needs to be thorough.

b. The military's role in support of the JTF-Civil Support in domestic emergencies is well defined and, under the Posse Comitatus law, is limited in scope and duration. Military resources may temporarily support and augment, but cannot replace local, tribal, state, and federal civilian agencies that have the primary authority and responsibility for domestic disaster assistance. The domestic employment of military forces has myriad legal considerations.

See JP 3-28, Defense Support of Civil Authorities, *for more information.*

c. The military may be asked for personnel support, to help with areas such as assisting with CBRN mitigation, S&R, security, MA, and providing rations and water. The military may also be asked to provide equipment support in the form of vehicles, helicopters, refrigeration units, communications, HRPs, floodlights, and generators.

5. Mass Casualty/Fatality Incidents Outside the United States

For foreign operations, DOS and the US ambassador coordinate US activities through the country team, with US representation as required for the situation. The military chain of command from the President to the JFC remains in effect, even though a non-DOD agency (e.g., DOS) may have overall lead responsibility. The AFMES has a memorandum of agreement with the DOS for forensic examination and ID of American citizens who die outside the US.

6. Mass Interment

The GCC may authorize temporary interments only when operational constraints prevent the evacuation of US/multinational partner human remains out of the AOR or it is deemed prudent for the protection of health and welfare of US/multinational forces. Adversary human remains are accorded the same measures. Each Service component commander must provide or arrange support for its, or attached multinational, deceased personnel subject to GCC's directives and/or mutual support agreements with another Service, provide its own MA support. This includes the proper interment of adversary human remains. When requirements exceed a Service's organic capabilities, the Army component will provide backup GS, when requested.

a. The primary objectives of these operations are to maintain morale and field sanitation and to comply with the rules of law of war, international law, and international agreements. However, human remains are to be evacuated as long as the operational situation permits. The exception to this is the evacuation of adversary human remains, which will be interred unless they are turned over to the HN or the Red Cross/Red Crescent. If they are interred, the site must be noted on accountability records as an interment site.

b. When individual graves cannot be accommodated, mass graves should be constructed consisting of straight rows. The burial site may consist of any number of rows. Each row holds 10 human remains, head to foot, lengthwise (see Figure B-1). The rows are approximately 70 feet long, 3 feet deep, as wide as the earth-moving equipment blade (minimum of 2.5 feet) and at least 7 feet apart (minimum of 2 feet wider than the

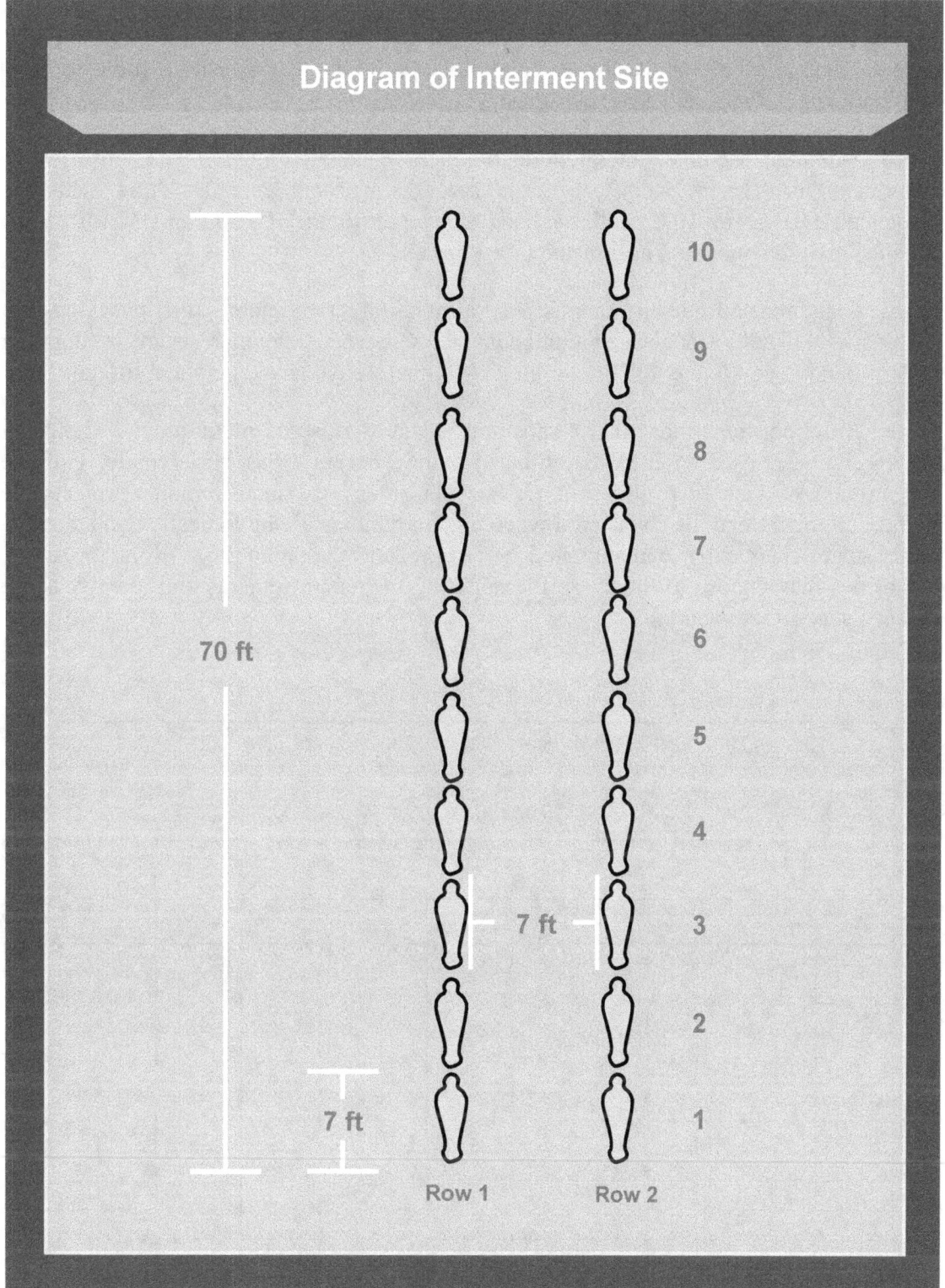

Figure B-1. Diagram of Interment Site

outside track of the earth-moving equipment). Earth-moving equipment should be used if possible, as it can open all types of soil with relative ease. Ideally, rows should be side by side, but may not be if terrain conditions prohibit. Use separate rows for US, multinational partners, and adversary dead.

c. Maintain accurate interment/disinterment records utilizing DD Form 1079 (Interment/Disinterment Register). Interment/disinterment records along with the associated DD Form 1079 will be hand delivered to the TMAO or JMAO at the conclusion of the operation as directed (see Figure B-2).

d. Contaminated human remains pose a much larger problem. Interment does not necessarily kill all pathogens or contaminants; some can remain resistant or dormant underground. See Chapter 8, "Contaminated Human Remains and Personal Effects."

e. An option regarding final disposition is state-sponsored mass burial. Though it has rarely been used in the US, authorities may accept mass burial under extreme circumstances. One such circumstance is when interring human remains protects the living. Interment may be considered when human remains are biologically contaminated rather than chemically contaminated. To prevent contamination from spreading, authorities may choose to minimize the handling of human remains and identify a site that can support mass burial.

INTERMENT/DISINTERMENT REGISTER						1. DATE (YYYYMMDD)	2. PAGE OF PAGES

PRIVACY ACT STATEMENT

AUTHORITY: 10 USC Sections 1481 through 1488, EO 9397, Nov 1943 (SSN).
PURPOSE AND USE: This form is used to establish initial identification of deceased personnel.
DISCLOSURE: Personal information provided on this form is given on a voluntary basis. Failure to provide this information, however, may result in improper identification of the deceased person and person making visual identification.

3. UNIT OPERATING INTERMENT/DISINTERMENT SITE					4. LOCATION OF INTERMENT/DISINTERMENT SITE (include grid coordinates)				
5. PROCESSING NUMBER	6. TENTATIVELY IDENTIFIED DECEDENT (if unidentified, so state)					7. UNIT DELIVERING REMAINS	8. DATE RECEIVED (YYYYMMDD)	9. DATE OF INTERMENT/ DISINTERMENT (YYYYMMDD)	10. INTER/DISINTER LOCATION
	a. NAME (Last, First, Middle Initial)	b. GRADE	c. SSN	d. BRANCH OF SERVICE	e. ORGANIZATION				a. ROW / b. SPACE

DD FORM 1079, JUL 1998 (EG)   PREVIOUS EDITION MAY BE USED.   Designed using Perform Pro, WHS/DIOR, Jun 96

Figure B-2. DD Form 1079, Interment/Disinterment Register

f. The state may be more inclined to accept state-sponsored mass burial if human remains are placed in individual caskets, are located in an area that is protected, and the site is commemorated.

7. Interment Site Selection

When interment is necessary, the burial site should be on high ground with good drainage. Avoid areas that have high water tables or that can flood easily. During the survey of the site, ensure that pilot holes are dug to check for underlying rock formations and ease in digging. Use of preexisting sites is recommended when available.

8. Interment Procedures

When human remains are received, all documentation and information is turned over to interment site personnel. If a list of human remains is present, it will be verified as human remains before being offloaded. Upon verification, MA personnel sign for the human remains.

a. Assign each human remains an interment processing number by using the next available sequential number from DD Form 1079. Use one page of DD Form 1079 for each row of 10 human remains. The number consists of a cumulative number and the current calendar year (e.g., 00024-02).

b. Disassociated portions recovered from the same general location should not be individually bagged, unless there is a strong presumption that the human remains belong to a distinct BTB individual or that the provenience information for where each portion was recovered is critical to an investigation. Portions recovered from geographically and/or incidentally distinct areas should be bagged separately from one another. Multiple S&R numbers may be interred in the same HRP, but it is critical that they are correctly labeled with the applicable location of recovery information within the HRP. Assign each HRP interred with an interment processing number by using the next available sequential number from DD Form 1079.

c. Prepare two metal interment tags (Figure B-3). Mark the processing number on each tag and attach one to the human remains. Attach the other tag to the HRP or burial shroud. Finally, initiate a case file for each human remains, labeling the file with the interment processing number and the name, rank, and branch of Service for each human remains. Include any documentation generated at the MACP as part of the interment case file and in MARTS.

d. Verify that DE and ID media are present and complete blocks 6 through 9 of DD Form 1079. Use "unidentified" if tentative ID cannot be established. Verify or complete DD Form 1076 (Record of Personal Property/Personal Effects), time permitting. Inventory any DE found and leave on the human remains or place in a plastic bag and attach the bag to the human remains for interment. Securely seal the bag. Do not remove ID tags or ID card from human remains.

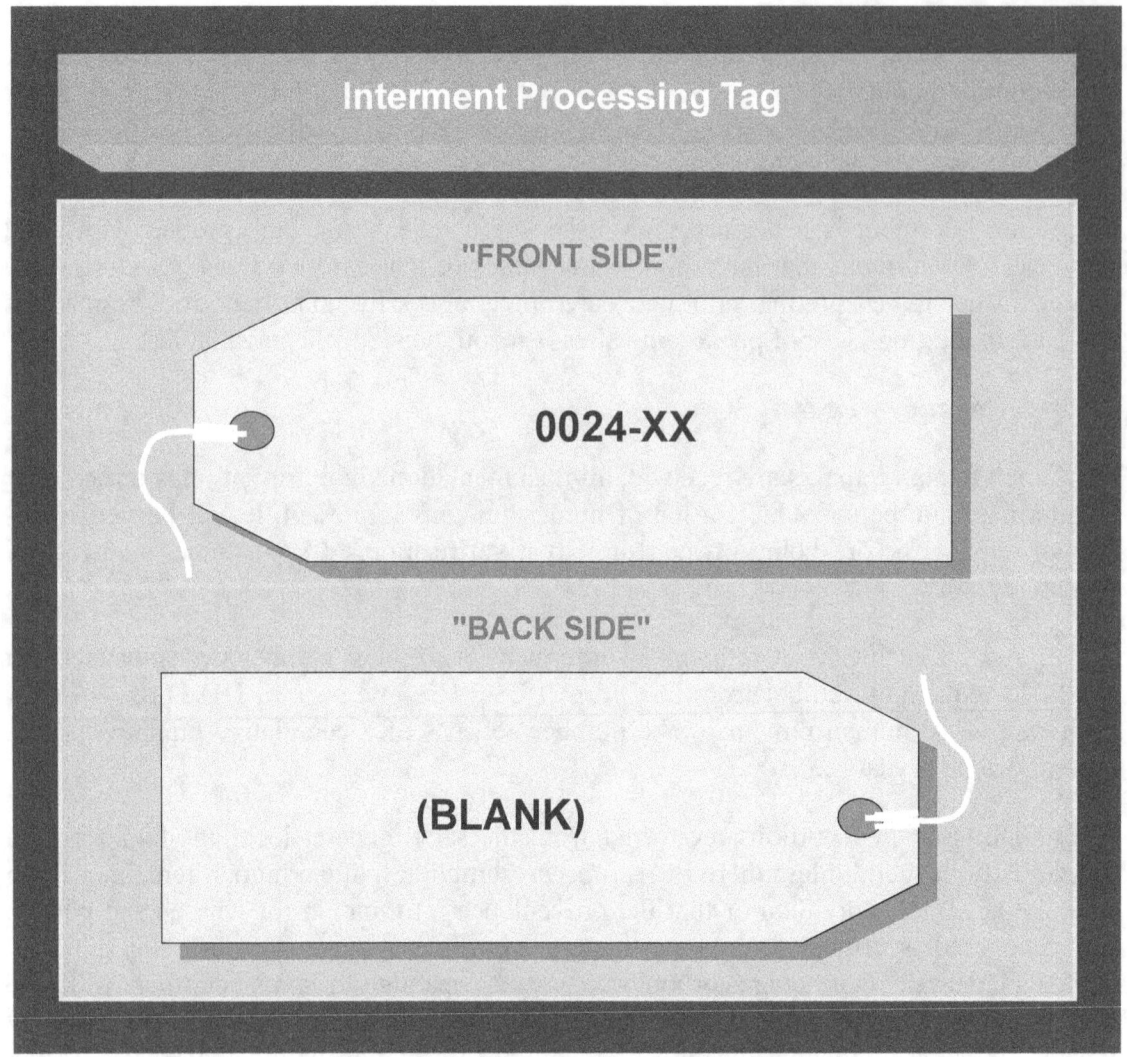

Figure B-3. Interment Processing Tag

e. Verify completion of the DD Form 894 (Record of Identification Processing Fingerprint Chart), printing all available fingers under the direction of DOD or FBI investigative agencies and/or the AFMES. Latent prints may be used if provided by these investigative agencies or AFMES. Ensure that the DD Form 894 or latent prints are placed in the case file and in MARTS.

f. Place the human remains in an HRP or wrap with shrouding material. Attach one metal interment tag to the outside of the HRP or shroud.

g. The assignment of the actual row and space number to the human remains should not take place until the human remains is at the interment site. Then assign the next available interment site row and space number (e.g., row 10, space 6), on DD Form 1079, blocks 11 a. and b. Adversary, multinational, and US human remains should be interred in separate rows to aid in disinterment operations.

h. Enter the row and space number on the top right-hand corner of DD Form 894 and DD Form 1076. Place the human remains in the assigned row and space, in a head-to-foot relationship to other human remains. Place all completed forms in the case folder. Write the name and SSN of the human remains on the folder label, along with the processing number.

9. Closing the Site

a. When all burials have been completed in each row, the row may be refilled. A bucket loader-type vehicle should be used for refill. Care should be taken not to drive over the rows, even after they have been refilled.

b. Mark the beginning and end of each row with a metal stake. The stake should extend into the ground at least 2 feet, and 2 feet should be left above ground. Securely affix a metal tag to each stake indicating the row number. Use a GPS device (if available) to determine the location of each row, and record it on DD Form 1079, block 2. All forms and records will be sent by special courier to the JMAO or TMAO. The JMAO/TMAO will provide one copy of all records of HN or adversary interments to the HN government. The JMAO/TMAO will send the original records for all interments conducted by US forces to the JMAC for archive. The JMAC is required as part of Army EA responsibilities to collect and maintain complete MA records as required.

10. Trench Disinterment Procedures

The following is guidance for the disinterment of human remains temporarily interred in an operational area. Whenever possible, a forensic anthropologist should be present during disinterment activities to verify chain of custody, minimize postmortem damage, and mitigate commingling of human remains.

a. The GCC is responsible for temporary interment/disinterment operations for US human remains and for the return of the human remains to the US or servicing mortuary for disposition. This responsibility is carried out by the JMAO/TMAO. In the event that the human remains of multinational partner personnel are present at the interment site, it should be maintained if operationally feasible until custody of the site can be transferred to the appropriate government. The JMAO/TMAO is responsible for monitoring, coordinating, and providing special guidance during disinterment operations.

b. The MA lead Service and other Service component commanders have the responsibility to coordinate and supervise disinterment operations within their operational area. The MA lead Service normally provides specialized equipment, personnel, and other support as necessary to accomplish the mission. Each individual component commander's MA office coordinates with the JMAO/TMAO and obtains records and reports of burials that will be necessary during the disinterment.

c. Whenever personnel are conducting disinterment operations, they should wear N95 (HEPA) respirators, gloves, aprons, and other types of protective clothing in accordance with component Service health and safety guidance.

For further guidance on the handling of potentially infectious human remains, see USACHPPM Technical Guide 195, Safety and Health Guidance for Mortuary Affairs Operations: Infectious Materials and CBRN Handling.

d. Once in the general area of the temporary interment site, a GPS device, in conjunction with maps, may be used to determine the exact location of each row.

e. A chaplain, if present, may offer a prayer or other appropriate RS. If a chaplain is not available, the senior military person may lead those present in 60 seconds of silence, with bowed heads, as a memorial.

f. Rows may be opened from either end. Using a backhoe and digging with care, the operator should dig down approximately 3 feet. Multiple rows may be opened simultaneously depending on the availability of equipment. Dig the remaining depth with hand tools so as to minimize damage and commingling of the human remains.

g. Remove the dirt from all sides of the human remains carefully. Look for the metal tag that was pinned to the outside of the HRP or shroud. Match the number on the tag to the DD Form 1079 processing number recorded during interment operations.

h. Complete the DD Form 1079 and prepare processing tag in the same manner as in interment operations. Attach this tag to the HRP or shroud.

i. If the HRP or shroud is not intact, the soil in the immediate area should be sifted for skeletal anatomy and PE. Place human remains and HRP on a litter and remove them from the row or interment site.

j. Human remains are processed at an MACP adjacent to the disinterment site. After all rows have been opened and human remains removed, refill all rows and return the area as closely as possible to the original condition. Report through command channels to the JMAO/TMAO when all human remains have been disinterred from the interment site. Include the condition of the restored land being vacated in this site closure report. Once a site has been evacuated, the JMAO/TMAO is responsible for turning the land back to the appropriate HN government agency. If the human remains of deceased adversary or multinational partner personnel are still interred at the site, maintain the site if operationally feasible or until custody of the site can be turned over to the appropriate government.

APPENDIX C
FOREIGN HUMANITARIAN ASSISTANCE

1. Introduction

Upon notification of a foreign humanitarian assistance (FHA) mission, the responsible GCC should task the CCMD staff to conduct a mission analysis and provide planning guidance, to include MA operations. When requested, the JMAC is able to provide subject matter experts (SMEs)/LNOs assistance in coordinating at the interagency/intergovernmental level and SME support to the CCMDs in planning and operations. During the analysis phase, the staff officer should contact the J-4 of the Joint Staff to determine if any cooperation agreements exist between the supported foreign governments or between multinational partners. During this phase, logistic planners should coordinate with subordinate and supporting commands to determine their MA force structure and capabilities. Use of contract support for MA should be considered for equipment and supporting tasks such as refrigeration, cadaver dog, engineer support, and additional transportation assets. Contracting MA processes out to a private company restricts the flexibility and control of the CCDR in directing MA. Only US MA personnel will process US human remains. In addition, if DOD is responsible for the recovery effort, then DOD must ensure proper procedures are followed to the level expected by the American public.

a. FHA missions will vary, each in its own unique way. Upon approval of the OPLAN, the GCC may assign a staff officer as the joint MA officer.

b. Upon deployment of the JTF, a JMAO may be assembled to support the J-4 and serve as the principal MA advisor to the command. The JMAO coordinates directly with the CJMAB on all issues relating to MA support. In FHA missions, the CJMAB must coordinate with the JMAO to develop plans to process local nationals. In most FHA missions, the supported country may lack the necessary infrastructure required to support the local population. Prior to implementing plans for providing MA support, the CJMAB should contact the command SJA for legal guidance concerning the JTF's obligations for providing mortuary support to the local population. The JTF's legal obligations concerning deceased and/or interred human remains found in the JTF's controlled areas derive from the commander's responsibility for health and public hygiene.

(1) For example, mass graves may be contaminating the ground water supply, or uninterred human remains or human remains washed out of shallow graves may constitute a general health hazard. This may require interment of human remains in another location. If the local government will not or cannot perform the reinterment, the commander, following local religion and culture to the extent possible, should do so. The affected commander should request assistance from the JTF-MAO. Upon notification, the JTF-MAO coordinates for an interment site in theater and an MA team will deploy to assist in the reinterment. Upon completion of the reinterment, a report is forwarded to the JTF-MAO by the requesting commander. Sufficient information to identify burial sites and the names of persons buried there should be maintained and forwarded to the

JTF-MAO. Upon termination of the operation, these records are turned over to the legal government representative.

(2) Deaths of persons under the care of the JTF, such as dislocated civilians seeking help at a site under JTF control, create other obligations, such as medical certification and recording of death. Where there is an indigenous governmental infrastructure in place, death records should be registered with it. Where there is none, the JTF should maintain appropriate records for later transmittal to an appropriate governmental office. The same rules apply to persons killed by JTF forces. In these contexts, "identification" is a relative term. It is adequate to attempt to identify such persons through papers in their possession or by witnesses in the immediate area of their death. If the NOK come forward requesting custody of the human remains, the body should be turned over to the NOK only after all legal requirements and processing of the human remains have been completed. Copies of all records pertaining to the deceased and a signed receipt showing transfer of custody of the human remains will be forwarded to the JTF-MAO.

(3) In general terms, legal obligations depend on whether the JTF is simply dealing with a dead body found in a JTF-controlled area or concerned with a death associated with JTF forces action. In either case, the handling of human remains should only be done by MA specialists trained and equipped to avoid contamination from infectious diseases.

d. The JTF-MAO should attempt to coordinate with the members of the Red Cross or Red Crescent for the return of deceased local nationals to local governmental control. Depending on the mission and the political climate of the operation, the JTF may receive limited assistance from the Red Cross or Red Crescent. During hostilities, assistance from the Red Cross or Red Crescent may be limited.

e. In addition to planning for processing of local nationals, the JTF-MAO should develop appendix 3 (Mortuary Affairs), to annex D (Logistics), to the OPLAN that provides the theater concept of MA support. The JTF-MAO recommends tasks for subunits to provide MA support, monitors and coordinates execution, and assists units in obtaining resources required to perform the MA mission. This appendix should include procedures for search, recovery, and evacuation of JTF deceased personnel. The overall objective is to completely recover, positively identify, and transport in a dignified and respectful manner to the final destination determined by the PADD. Multinational forces and other non-US dead will be processed in accordance with existing international agreements or guidance from the CCDR. In cases of foreign nationals or NGOs requesting MA support, the JTF-MAO coordinates with the DOS representative in the affected area.

2. **Assistance to/from Foreign Governments**

a. There is a real possibility that a foreign government may request the assistance of the US military to respond to an MC/FI that occurs in a country where US military are stationed. This likelihood would increase if American fatalities were part of the disaster.

Foreign disaster assistance is covered in DODD 5100.46, *Foreign Disaster Relief.* This directive contains the policy and assigns the responsibilities for employment of DOD resources in foreign disaster relief operations.

b. Foreign governments may provide support for US MA operations overseas. US forces may require HN transportation, medical facilities, mortuaries, security, or other types of services and equipment.

3. Recommended Equipment/Supply Package for Humanitarian Assistance Operations

The list of equipment shown in Figure C-1 is provided as a planning tool when conducting FHA requiring MA support. The list of equipment will allow for initial operations and may require additional items based on the level of support required and the location of operation. Life support items are not included in this list of equipment and supplies. The JMAC can provide current national stock numbers for the items on the list.

RECOMMENDED EQUIPMENT/SUPPLY PACKAGE FOR HUMANITARIAN ASSISTANCE OPERATIONS			
Nomenclature	**U/I**	**Qty**	**Source**
Radio frequency identification tags	EA	As required	
Tent 20 × 32 ft personnel, extendable mod	EA	2	GSA
Tent GP large	EA	2	GSA
Tent GP medium	EA	2	GSA
Generator, 30 kW	EA	1	Unit
Generator, 3 kW	EA	2	Unit
Trailer wtr M149A2 (water 400 gal)	EA	1	Unit
Truck uty cargo trp carrier 1-1/4T M998	EA	2	Unit
Truck, cargo, LMTV, 1078	EA	2	Unit
NTV, 9-passenger van	EA	2	Contract
Light set, general illumination	ST	10	Unit
Refrigeration units (MIRCS, mil reefers, contract) as req	EA	5	Contract
Communications (internal and external as required)			
Container, tri-wall	EA	30	GSA
Ice making machine, cube	EA	2	GSA
Racking system	EA	20	COTS
Case, transfer, human	EA	100	DLA
Human remains pouches (white)	CS	500	COTS
Human remains pouches (black)	CS	500	COTS
Computer	EA	2	GSA
Printer, copier, fax combination unit	EA	2	GSA
Digital camera	EA	6	GSA
Memory card, camera	EA	10	COTS
Cot folding	EA	40	Unit
Litter folding rigid pole	EA	50	Unit
Litter stands (support) folding	EA	100	Unit
Table folding leg	EA	8	GSA
Screen, latrine 18 ft long, 7 ft high, and 9 ft wide	EA	20	GSA
Extension cord (50 ft)	EA	15	COTS
Hammer, sledge	EA	2	Unit
Pick, mattock	EA	6	GSA
Shovel, hand	EA	6	GSA
Pin flags, survey, metal shaft 1 pkg of 100 ea (R, O, Y)	PKG	1	COTS
Tape, engineer	RL	10	GSA
Hats, hard, construction	EA	40	COTS
Vests, reflective	EA	40	COTS

Suit, personal protective, S	CS	20	GSA
Suit, personal protective, M	CS	50	GSA
Suit, personal protective, L	CS	100	GSA
Suit, personal protective, XL	CS	100	GSA
Suit, personal protective, XXL	CS	50	GSA
Gloves, surgical, S	BX	100	GSA
Gloves, surgical, M	BX	100	GSA
Gloves, surgical, L	BX	100	GSA
Gloves, surgical, XL	BX	50	GSA
Gloves, chemical protective, S	PR	100	GSA
Gloves, chemical protective, M	PR	200	GSA
Gloves, chemical protective, L	PR	100	GSA
Gloves, work, S	PR	50	GSA
Gloves, work, M	PR	100	GSA
Gloves, work, L	PR	100	GSA
Gloves, work, XL	PR	50	GSA
Masks, surgical disposable (800 ea)	BX	10	GSA
Masks, N95 respirator (20 ea) in various sizes (small, medium, and large) obtained from at least two different manufacturers	BX	100	COTS
Medical face shields, protective (20 ea)	BX	100	COTS
Bags, plastic, zip-closure, quart	BX	50	GSA
Bags, plastic, zip-closure, gallon	BX	50	GSA
Bags, plastic, zip-closure, 2-gallon	BX	50	GSA
Tag, blank shipping	BX	20	GSA
Tags, stainless steel commercial item 1,000 ea	BX	1	COTS
Bags, PERSONAL EFFECTS	EA	2,000	GSA
Admin supplies (stapler, 3-hole punch, pens pkg 24, pencils pkg 24, paper, scissors, tape, CDs etc.)	BX	2	GSA
Scissors, bandage, surgical	EA	6	GSA
Mortuary affairs forms, asst	EA	1,000	Unit
Towel, industrial wiping	CS	10	GSA
Bleach, liquid, gallon	EA	10	COTS
Cleaning supplies, asst (sponges, mops, buckets, etc.)	BX	2	COTS
Lime, powdered (quick-lime, 50 lb)	BG	50	COTS
Batteries, AA, AAA, C packages	EA	5	COTS

Legend

BG   bag
BX   box
COTS   commercial off-the-shelf
CS   case

DLA	Defense Logistics Agency
EA	each
ft	feet
gal	gallon
GP	general purpose
GSA	General Services Administration
kW	kilowatt
lb	pound
LMTV	light medium tactical vehicle
mil	military
MIRCS	mobile integrated remains collection system
NTV	non-tactical vehicle
PKG	package
PR	pair
Qty	quantity
req	required
RL	roll
ST	set
T	ton
U/I	unit of issue

**Figure C-1. Recommended Equipment/Supply Package for
Humanitarian Assistance Operations**

APPENDIX D
TRANSPORTATION OF CONTAMINATED HUMAN REMAINS

1. Introduction

a. The purpose of this appendix is to provide basic information and guidance for transportation of contaminated human remains. Currently no international or national transportation standards exist specifically for transportation of contaminated human remains from an overseas location back to the US. Also, there are currently no standing agreements in place that address movement of contaminated human remains. Although countries establish requirements for the transport of human remains in or through their country, limited international guidance exists for the transport of contaminated human remains. Contaminated human remains require coordination and approval between countries and carriers prior to transport. The type of contamination and detected levels impact the transportation requirements and safeguards implemented. Transportation of human remains that have been exposed to most contaminants may be able to be transported or evacuated utilizing mortuary evacuation channels once they have been properly processed and packaged for transport.

b. Repatriation of human remains to the US or servicing mortuary requires proof that the human remains pose minimal contamination or infection risk to others. International and national regulations may require that documentation not only cover the type and amount of CBRN material the fatality was exposed to but also any methods used to mitigate, monitor, or detect any internal or external residual contamination associated with the human remains.

c. Transportation of contaminated human remains must comply with all established national and international agreements, laws, and regulations provided by public health authorities and carriers.

d. Within the US there are special agents identified as category "A" agents, by the Centers for Disease Control and Prevention (CDC). Public health authorities mandate quarantine or detention procedures for human remains contaminated with a category "A" agent. Biologically contaminated human remains that have been infected with category "A" agents, as defined by the CDC, require a permit prior to shipment to or within the US. Although this regulation is intended to ensure the safe transport of biological specimens, it also applies to human remains infected with category "A" agents. Obtaining this permit typically requires identifying the safety precautions employed to render the human remains safe for handling and transport. Such safety precautions would include identifying the use of triple layers of leak-proof packaging.

2. General Guidance for Air Transportation of Contaminated Human Remains

DOD aircraft will not transport contaminated human remains that pose a health risk or contamination risk to the air crew or aircraft. An exemption may be authorized to transport small numbers of contaminated human remains. If needed, exemptions to this policy will be addressed to USTRANSCOM on a case-by-case basis. Any remains that pose a threat to public health will be temporarily interred until safe handling procedures and materials can be identified.

3.   General Guidance for Ground Transportation of Contaminated Human Remains

Ground transportation routes within a theater will be determined by Service CBRN specialists. The cargo area should be decontaminated after each delivery of remains to the MACRMS. Ground transportation vehicles will not have any markings on them other than the NATO hazard labels. Any other business markers will be covered or removed. The vehicles will be enclosed or have tarp covers so the contents of the vehicle cannot be seen from outside the vehicle. Human remains will not be stacked in the vehicle under any circumstances. The vehicle should be refrigerated. Air conditioning will not suffice unless there are no refrigerated trucks available. If no refrigerated vehicles are available, then when in high-temperature areas, transport of human remains should take place at night as long as the human remains can be kept refrigerated at 34 to 40 degrees Fahrenheit (1.1 to 4.4 degrees Celsius) while awaiting transport. Loading and unloading of the vehicle shall be accomplished discretely. Tarps or camouflage netting should be used to block the view of the MACRMS from the rest of the installation, entry roads, and other positions that would compromise the dignity of the human remains. The top of the vehicle or transport area should be shielded from the top as well as the sides to prevent observance from the air.   Metal or plastic shelving material is preferred for decontamination purposes.   Decontamination procedures will be followed for all transport vehicles and personnel.

4.   Transportation of Chemically Contaminated Human Remains

a. A chemical incident should not automatically preclude returning human remains. The only variable that directly affects the decision to withhold human remains is the inability to mitigate the contamination to an acceptable level. The AFMES will be notified of a chemical incident resulting in fatalities once the chemical agent has been identified. The AFMES will provide additional guidance on handling, transport, and interment procedures.   The time required to identify, mobilize, and coordinate the resources needed to process chemically contaminated human remains may affect the ability to rapidly return human remains.

b. Once the human remains have gone through the MACRMS, they will be placed in a transfer case if being transported.   The external surface of the transfer case or containment system will be decontaminated and marked with the following information: CBRN hazard label providing dose, agent, and the decedent information. In addition, all appropriate shipping documents will be affixed to the transfer case or containment system. Once human remains have been properly containerized, the containers will not be reopened except by the AFMES or at their direction.

5. Transportation of Biologically Contaminated Human Remains

a. Biologically contaminated human remains are separated into three distinct categories for transportation: Noncontagious pathogens (e.g., anthrax), contagious pathogens (e.g., smallpox), and toxin (e.g., ricin). The AFMES will be notified of a biological contamination incident involving fatalities once the pathogen is identified. The AFMES will provide additional guidance on handling, transportation or interment procedures. Many biological pathogens have been safely handled using standard precautions. Once the human remains have gone through the MACRMS, they will be placed in a transfer case if being transported. The exterior of the transfer case will have the appropriate CBRN label along with all pertinent data and shipping documents. Once the human remains are prepared for shipment, the container will not be opened in transit. Many biologically contaminated human remains can be safely transported to the US once they have been appropriately packaged. Contact and droplet hazards are the primary transportation concern related to biologically contaminated human remains. The transportation of biologically contaminated human remains across national or international borders is a major concern due to the contagion and latency factor in many biological agents.

b. Human remains that meet mitigation standards will be transported through MA evacuation channels. The exterior of the containment system will be decontaminated and marked with the following: a CBRN hazard label providing dose, agent, and the decedent information. In addition, all appropriate shipping documents will be affixed to the transfer case or containment system. Once human remains have been properly containerized, the container will not be reopened except by the AFMES or at their direction. Guidelines to assist the safe handling, mitigation, and management of human remains can be found in USACHPPPM Technical Guide 195: *Safety and Health Guidance for Mortuary Affairs Operations: Infectious Materials and CBRN Handling.*

6. Transportation of Radiological Contaminated Human Remains

a. A radiological incident should not automatically preclude repatriation of human remains. The only variable that directly affects the decision to hold human remains is the inability to mitigate the contamination to an acceptable transportation level. The AFMES will be notified of a radiological incident resulting in fatalities once the type and dose of radiation is known. The AFMES will provide additional guidance on handling, transport, and interment procedures. MA personnel or the ME/C will have a CBRN specialist verify that the human remains are not emitting contamination above the acceptable level of contamination for transport. No loose surface contamination or shrapnel will be present when the human remains are prepared for evacuation.

b. For those human remains that are to be repatriated, a CBRN hazard label will be affixed to the exterior of the containment system. The label will display dose rate and date and time of the measurement, even though the amount of radioactive material is not known. If human remains have internal contamination due to shrapnel, then whenever possible, the shrapnel will be removed prior to shipment.

Intentionally Blank

APPENDIX E
RELIGIOUS SUPPORT TO MORTUARY AFFAIRS

1. Introduction

This appendix provides some basic information and references regarding religious and cultural considerations associated with MA. RS considerations and RS support are critical components of a successful response. US culture places great importance on the ability to provide honor and respect to the deceased. The rituals associated with handling a death help to provide acceptance of the disaster and to the loss of loved ones. Public knowledge regarding the availability of RS during an MC/FI is critical to resiliency. The appendix provides guidance on interment requirements for several of the primary religions. It also addresses considerations when DOD provides DSCA during civilian MC/FIs as part of the NRF ESF #8.

2. General Guidance

a. Beliefs and practices concerning the death of individuals and how their human remains are to be treated differ between religious faiths and may even differ between regions and subcultures within a country (operational area). Details for preparing human remains, mourning, and burial or cremation practices, to include mourning periods and perceptions by belligerents and the local populace on how the deceased are handled by joint forces, may impact joint and multinational operations. History shows us that the treatment of and respect shown to all human remains are newsworthy events that invoke emotion and are open to misrepresentation and propaganda.

b. While MA personnel may be familiar with certain aspects of these issues, they should consult with local authorities and RST personnel on specific religious practices associated with the different populations within the operational area. This is also true for the operational units first coming in contact with the human remains and responsible for their evacuation to an MACP.

c. Chaplains are also capable of assisting commanders in counseling Service members who may be emotionally affected by the loss of comrades or constantly dealing with the deceased.

For additional information on RS considerations to MA, see JP 1-05, Religious Affairs in Joint Operations.

3. General Guidance for Religious Support for Domestic Operations

a. Non-DOD federal fatality management assets under the National Disaster Medical System, to include spiritual care capabilities, may be deployed once a mission assignment has been approved. Upon SecDef approval of DOD assistance, DOD chaplains primarily provide support to DOD personnel. In certain rare and emergency circumstances and in accordance with legal guidelines, DOD chaplains may provide care to civilians (see JP 1-05, *Religious Affairs in Joint Operations*).

b. Chaplains should prioritize RS to personnel conducting mission assignments that place them at great risk from stress (i.e., S&R, family assistance centers, MACPs, or those working at final disposition locations).

c. RS care considerations for interment and disinterment operations. The general role of the chaplain is to offer prayers to consecrate the site, prayers for the dead, as well as prayers for the families.

(1) Catastrophic Temporary Interment. A chaplain, or if needed, an interfaith group of clergy, will offer prayers to consecrate that site as a sacred space prior to the interment of human remains. A chaplain will also offer prayers for the repose of the souls of those placed there. When the temporary site is vacated, a chaplain or group of clergy will offer prayers as the human remains are moved to their final resting place and the space is returned to secular use.

(2) Mass Reinterment. Clergy representing the faith groups of those interred, or if this is unknown, all major faith groups, should be invited to offer prayers prior to and after interment of the human remains at their final resting place.

(3) Mass Burial. The decision for mass burial disposition should consider that there may be people of many faith groups buried together due to circumstances beyond control for any other COA. Clergy leaders from major faith groups should be present at a memorial service to jointly offer prayers for their deceased personnel. It is necessary to build consensus among public health and medical community, faith leaders, and other community leaders in order to maintain the maximum level of dignity and respect possible in this situation.

d. RS considerations for MA following CBRN disasters.

(1) Chemical/Radiological. Human remains must be decontaminated or the contamination mitigated to a safe handling level prior to release to families. In accordance with incident commander instructions, only those personnel trained, equipped, and required in the hot (contaminated) zone will be permitted to enter. Chaplains will not be in the hot zone, but will be present in the cold zone to offer comfort and support.

(2) Biological. Clergy and RS personnel should be aware of the risks of contracting the contagion when performing religious rites, sacraments, and practices such as traditional washing of the dead. Also, personnel attending any large gathering, including a funeral, should be aware of the hazards and precautions necessary to prevent the spread of disease. Consequently, interment or cremation of contaminated human remains should occur close to the place of death and as soon as possible. As an added precaution, the size of the gathering should be restricted and in accordance with public health guidance.

(3) Nuclear. In the event of a nuclear detonation, those close to the impact area may have no recoverable human remains. Thus, mass memorials may be the only means available to honor the dead.

For additional guidance, refer to JP 1-05, Religious Affairs in Joint Operations.

APPENDIX F
MORTUARY AFFAIRS ASSETS AND CAPABILITIES

Mortuary affairs assets are resident in each of the Services to varying degrees. Each Service is responsible for providing MA support for its own personnel. The Army has the preponderance of MA assets in order to accomplish its EA mission as well as provide GS to all DOD forces.

1. United States Army

The US Army capability is task oriented and designed to provide MA support to all Army units as well as GS to all Services. The capability is resident in both the Active Component and Reserve Component. The Army MA companies are intended to provide theater-level support in a multi-Service theater of operation. The Army MA companies can provide any of the following MA support functions:

a. Establish and operate MACPs with refrigeration capability.

b. Establish and operate a TMEP.

c. Establish and operate a MACRMS with equipment sets provided to the units. MACRMS operation requires substantial augmentation of both personnel and equipment.

d. Conduct limited S&R missions, if required.

e. Conduct temporary interment and disinterment operations when directed by the GCC. The interment sites will receive, process, and inter deceased US military, US civilians and others, multinational, local national, and adversary personnel, with associated PE. When interment operations are directed, the company has the ability to set up two temporary interment sites. Engineer equipment must augment the platoons to facilitate interment operations.

f. Produce and maintain essential MA records and reports.

g. Establish and operate an in-theater mortuary with civilian augmentation. When augmented with DOD civilian embalmers, the capability exists to set up and operate one in-theater mortuary. When fully operational, the in-theater mortuary can receive, identify, embalm, and evacuate human remains. However, if the mortuary option is used, the processing and evacuation mission of the TMEP is reduced or eliminated.

h. Establish and operate a theater PE depot to store, safeguard, and coordinate shipment of the PE of human remains processed in theater. A theater PE depot may be required in theater at the beginning of an operation where casualties are anticipated. The theater PE depot will support the JPED by being the single transportation hub for PE to the JPED from the AOR. A theater PE depot may remain in operation throughout an entire conflict to support theater operations. In addition, the company could establish a US PE depot in support of civil authorities as directed by the President or SecDef.

i. Respond to peacetime MC/FIs as requested and authorized.

Note: The company as a whole can perform several MA functions as each platoon could be tasked to provide a different capability. Performing either the TMEP or MACRMS mission greatly reduces the ability to provide other MA functions. Platoons can perform any of the tasks but cannot perform them concurrently.

For additional information, refer to FM 4-20.64, Mortuary Affairs Operations.

2. United States Marine Corps

US Marine Corps MA capability is task oriented and designed to support the Marine air-ground task force in an operational environment, and is not intended to be used for theater-level support in a multi-Service theater of operation. The Marine Corps has one PRP Company within the Reserve Component. The company is trained and equipped to conduct all facets of mortuary support across the range of military operations. PRP is specifically designed to meet an operational gap of tactical S&R. PRP personnel are able to conduct S&R operations in hostile, benign, DSCA, and/or limited contaminated environments. PRP can provide the following MA support:

a. Mortuary affairs collection point operations.

(1) Establish multiple MACPs to support the Marine Corps area of operations.

(2) The MACPs can receive, process, and coordinate evacuation of all personnel and DE authorized MA support.

(3) Establish and operate MACPs with refrigeration capability.

(4) Be prepared to establish and operate a TMEP until relieved.

(5) Conduct S&R missions while simultaneously conducting MACP operations.

(6) Conduct temporary interment and disinterment operations when directed and approved by the GCC.

(7) Maintain essential records and reports.

(8) Respond to MC/FIs as required and authorized.

(9) Each platoon has three MA processing squads.

b. Search and recovery operations.

(1) Conduct S&R operations in a hostile, benign, military support to civil authorities, or limited contaminated environment.

(2) Document S&R operations.

(3) Preserve forensic evidence and perform limited forensic evidence collection.

(4) Recover remains, PE, and government equipment and material from the incident scene.

(5) Coordinate for or provide transportation/evacuation of remains and effects back to the MACP or TMEP.

(6) Each platoon has an S&R squad.

c. The company has two be-prepared-to missions:

(1) Conduct TMEP/TPED operations.

(2) Conduct MA DSCA operations.

For additional information, refer to MCWP, 4-11.8, Services in an Expeditionary Environment, *and Navy Medical Command Instruction 5360.1,* Decedent Affairs Manual.

3. United States Air Force

The Air Force does not have a dedicated MA unit. The Air Force MA capability is resident in the force support squadron. Air Force force support personnel are trained in MA as well as other force support areas. Each Air Force major command commander directs and controls the MA program within the command and designates a supervisor for MA from the directorate, manpower, personnel, and services. At the tactical level, each installation commander appoints, by letter, a mortuary officer. With the exception of Dover AFB, the mortuary officer is the installation's force support commander, director, or deputy. At Dover AFB, Air Force Mortuary Affairs Operations personnel assume the responsibilities of the mortuary officer. The installation force support commander also designates S&R team members who function under the supervision of the mortuary officer as part of the base disaster response force.

For additional information, refer to Air Force Instruction 34-501, Mortuary Affairs Program.

4. United States Navy

The Navy does not have dedicated MA units. At sea, fatalities are handled by the ship's medical department. On shore, fatalities are handled by the installation medical treatment facility staff. The Navy has the Armed Force's only military morticians, stationed throughout the world to support naval operations. The Navy provides peacetime MA support for the Marine Corps. The Navy maintains the capability to evacuate deceased personnel from its units and from other Services. The Navy develops contingency plans to evacuate human remains by surface from an operational area should air evacuation be interrupted.

5. United States Coast Guard

The Coast Guard does not have the force structure capability to provide MA support to Coast Guard units overseas during joint operations and would rely upon the GCC for support. The Coast Guard maintains the capability to accomplish committals at sea. During peacetime, the Coast Guard provides or arranges MA support for Coast Guard deceased personnel worldwide through other services or civilian providers.

6. United States National Guard

The governor of each state commands the NG when performing training or duty in either state active duty or under Title 32, USC. In Title 10, USC, status, the NG is a federal military asset under the C2 of the President and may be assigned to the Commander, USNORTHCOM; Commander, USPACOM; or Commander, United States Southern Command, to mitigate the effects of a CBRNE attack. The NG CERFPs may be deployed in state active duty, Title 32, USC, or Title 10, USC, status. The NG leveraging existing Army National Guard and ANG units, along with designated states, have organized, trained, and equipped NG CERFP units to provide specialized CBRNE capabilities that may be requested by local, tribal, state, or federal authorities. The NG CERFP can be pre-positioned or respond using organic transportation. It is designed with a modular structure, and all elements are comprised of traditional NG (M-Day [term used to designate the unnamed day on which full mobilization commences or is due to commence]) Soldiers and Airmen (supported by a small staff of full-time Guardsmen in Title 32, USC, status) who are trained and equipped to integrate into the NIMS under the ICS construct. CERFP capabilities include FSRTs, at least one of which is located in each of the 10 FEMA regions; the ability to plan and conduct casualty search and extraction; medical triage and treatment; and ambulatory and nonambulatory decontamination, using Occupational Safety and Health Administration, National Institute for Occupational Safety and Health, and National Fire Protection Association PPE and training.

a. When directed, the NG CERFP can be pre-positioned or respond to an incident to support the incident commander using organic transportation. The CERFP is designed with a modular structure; each contains a C2 element and five operational elements. The five operational elements include search and extraction, decontamination, battalion C2, medical, and fatality S&R.

b. The NG CERFP will be assembled and ready to deploy within 6 hours of notification following a validated request for support, and set up for three-lane decontamination operations no more than 90 minutes after arrival at the incident site. The capabilities of the NG CERFP are specifically tailored to augment, support, or relieve existing local, tribal, state, and federal capabilities, and to fill the void when none of these resources is available. The CERFP will, at or near a CBRNE incident site, provide support to the incident commander for casualty search and extraction; emergency medical triage, treatment, and patient stabilization; ambulatory and non-ambulatory casualty decontamination; and the S&R of incident fatalities.

c. The FSRT is an ANG asset within the NG CERFP. It provides the specific MA capability of recovery and transport to designated on-site locations. The FSRT is also capable of deploying independent of the NG CERFP as in the case of a non-CBRNE event (i.e., natural disaster). The FSRT is trained in NIMS courses, which allows for a seamless transition supporting civil authorities under the ICS.

Intentionally Blank

APPENDIX G
KEY POINTS OF CONTACT

1. **Department of Defense**

   Deputy Under Secretary of Defense
   (Military Community and Family Policy)
   The Pentagon, 1B700
   Washington, DC 20318
   Phone: (703) 614-4074 / (DSN 224)

2. **Joint Staff**

   Joint Staff J-4/Medical Readiness Division (MRD)
   The Pentagon, 2C828
   Washington, DC 20318-4000
   Phone: (703) 697-1535 / (DSN 227)

3. **Services**

   a. **Army**

   (1) **Casualty and Mortuary Affairs Operations Center**
   US Army Human Resources Command AHRC-PDC
   1600 Spearhead Division Ave
   Fort Knox, KY 40121
   Phone: (502) 613-9025 / (800) 626-3317

   (2) **Joint Mortuary Affairs Center**
   1840 Quartermaster Rd
   Fort Lee, VA 23801-1606
   Phone: (804) 734-3831 / (DSN 687)
   Web site: www.quartermaster.army.mil/mac

   b. **Air Force**

   (1) **HQ USAF/A1S**
   Directorate of Services
   The Pentagon, 1770 Air Force
   Washington, DC 20330-1770
   Phone: (703) 604-6423 / (DSN 664)

Primary:
Air Force Mortuary Affairs Operations Center (AFMAO)
116 Purple Heart Dr
Dover AFB, DE 19902
Phone: (800) 531-5803, (302) 677-3982 / (DSN 445)

c. **Navy**

Navy & Marine Corps Mortuary Affairs
5720 Integrity Dr, Bldg 457
Millington, TN 38055-6210
Phone: (866) 786-0081
Fax: (901) 874-2611
General e-mail: NAVMORT@NAVY.MIL
Web site: http://www.npc.navy.mil/CommandSupport/CasualtyAssistance

d. **Marine Corps**
HQ USMC
Manpower and Reserve Affairs, Code MRP
3280 Russell Rd
Quantico, VA 22134-5102
Phone: (703) 784-9512 / (DSN 278)

e. **Coast Guard**
USCG Personnel Service Center (PSD FS-Casualty Matters)
4200 Wilson Blvd., Suite 1100, STOP 7200
Arlington, VA 20598-7200
Casualty Matters program manager: (202) 493-1931
USCG Command Center: (202) 372-2100

f. **National Guard**
HQ/USAF/NGB/A1S
Chief, Services
3500 Fetchet Ave
Andrews AFB, MD 20762
Phone: (301) 836-8166 / (DSN278)

4. **Combatant Commands**

a. **US Central Command**
HQ USCENTCOM
Logistics Operations Division, (CCJ4-0)
7115 South Boundary Rd
MacDill AFB, FL 33621-5101
Phone: (813) 827-2162 / (DSN 651)

b. **US European Command**
   HQ USEUCOM
   ECJ4-LS-EMS
   Joint Mortuary Affairs Officer
   Unit 30400
   APO AE 091318
   Phone: 011-49-711-680-5651 / (DSN 314-430-5651)

c. **US Africa Command**
   USAFRICOM HQ
   Attn: OPLOG
   Unit 29951
   APO, AE 09751-9951
   Phone: +49 (0) 711-729-4628
   DSN: (314) 421-4628

d. **US Joint Forces Command**
   HQ USJFCOM
   Attn: JMAO
   1562 Mitschner Ave, Suite 200
   Norfolk, VA 23551-2488
   Phone: (757) 836-5930 / (DSN 836)

e. **US Pacific Command**
   HQ USPACOM
   Attn: J47
   P.O. Box 64020
   Camp Smith, HI 96861-4020
   Phone: (808) 477-6257 / (DSN 315)

f. **US Special Operations Command**
   HQ USSOCOM
   SOAL-J4-O
   7701 Tampa Point Blvd
   MacDill AFB, FL 33621
   Phone: (813) 828-3823 / (DSN 299)

g. **US Southern Command**
   HQ USSOUTHCOM
   SCJ4-LRC
   3511 NW 91st Ave
   Miami, FL 33172
   Phone: (305) 437-1419 / (DSN 567)

h. **USTRANSCOM**
Strategy, Policy, Programs and Logistics (TCJ5/4),
US Transportation Command, Scott AFB, IL
Phone: (618) 229-3999

5. **Other**

a. **Central Joint Mortuary Affairs Board.** The CJMAB functions as a coordinating group of O-6 level representatives from the Army, Navy, Air Force, the Joint Staff J-4, and the AFME, to promote uniform Service policies, procedures, plans, and records for the disposition of human remains and PE. The Army maintains the CJMAB and designates its chairman. See Chapter I, "Mortuary Affairs Program," paragraph 5e, "Central Joint Mortuary Affairs Board," for more detail.

Director, Casualty and Mortuary Affairs Operations Center
CDR, Army Human Resources Command
ATTN: AHRC-PEC
1600 Spearhead Division Ave
Fort Knox, KY 40121
Phone: (703) 325-0489 / (DSN 221)
Web site: https://www.perscomonline.army.mil/tagd/cmaoc/cmaoc.htm

b. **Armed Forces Medical Examiner System.** The AFMES is a tri-service organization under the United States Army Medical Research and Materiel Command (USAMRMC). The AFMES identifies organization, policies, and procedures concerning medicolegal (forensic) investigations for determining positive ID and the cause and manner of death under specific circumstances. The Armed Forces DNA Identification Laboratory is a functional component of the AFMES. See Chapter I, "Mortuary Affairs Program," paragraph 5h, "Armed Forces Medical Examiner System," for more detail.

Armed Forces Medical Examiner's Office
1413 Research Blvd
Rockville, MD 20850
Phone: (301) 319-0000 / (DSN 285-0000)

c. **Joint POW/MIA Accounting Command.** The JPAC's mission is to achieve the fullest possible accounting of all Americans missing as a result of our Nation's previous conflicts. JPAC is responsible for conducting S&R operations worldwide for unaccounted for American servicemen from World War II, the Korean War, the Cold War, and the Vietnam War. See Chapter I, "Mortuary Affairs Program," paragraph 5f, "Joint POW/MIA Accounting Command (JPAC)," for more detail.

Attn: Public Affairs Office
310 Worchester Ave, Bldg 45
Hickam AFB, HI 96853-5530
Phone: (808) 448-1939 or (808) 448-1935
Fax: (808) 448-1998
E-mail: webmaster@jpac.pacom.mil

d. **US Army Medical Research Institute of Chemical Defense**
3100 Ricketts Point Rd
Aberdeen Proving Ground, MD 21010-5400
Phone: (410) 436-3277
Fax: (410) 436-4150
E-mail: usamricd-crp@amedd.army.mil

For assistance during off-duty hours, please call (410) 436-3276.

e. **USAMRIID**
Attn: MCMR-UIZ-R
1425 Porter St
Frederick, MD 21702-5011
E-mail: USAMRIIDpao@amedd.army.mil

6. **Subject Matter Experts**

a. **Centers for Disease Control and Prevention.** The CDC is recognized as the jurisdictional federal agency for protecting the health and safety of people at home and abroad, providing credible information to enhance health decisions, and promoting health through strong partnerships. CDC serves as the national focus for developing and applying disease prevention and control, environmental health, and health promotion and education activities designed to improve the health of the people of the US.

Centers for Disease Control and Prevention
1600 Clifton Rd
Atlanta, GA 30341-3724
Phone: (404) 639-3311
Web site: www.cdc.gov

b. **Armed Forces Radiobiology Research Institute**
8901 Wisconsin Ave
Bldg 42
Bethesda, MD 20889-5603
Phone: (301) 295-0316 Military Medical Operations
Phone: (301) 295-2950 Medical Radiobiology Advisory Team
Phone: (301) 295-0530 Emergency (24 hours)

c. **US Army Medical Research and Materiel Command.** The USAMRMC operates six medical research laboratories and institutes in the US. These laboratories make up the core S&T capability of the command. They are centers of excellence in specific areas of biomedical research, staffed by highly qualified military and civilian scientists and support personnel. The command's in-house S&T capabilities are enhanced by a large extramural contract research program, and numerous cooperative R&D agreements with leading R&D organizations in the civilian sector. The AFMES falls under the higher command of the USAMRMC. The command's headquarters and several of its institutes are listed below.

(1) **HQ, US Army Medical Research and Materiel Command**
504 Scott St
Fort Detrick, MD 21702-5012
Phone: (301) 619-7378 / (DSN 343)
Web site: mrmc.detrick.army.mil

(2) **US Army Medical Research Institute of Chemical Defense**
MCMR-UVA
31 Ricketts Point Rd
Aberdeen Proving Ground, MD 21010-5400
Phone: (410) 436-3276 / (DSN 298)
Web site: www.chemdefapgea.army.mil

(3) **US Army Medical Research Institute of Infectious Diseases**
MCMR-UIZ
1425 Porter Rd
Fort Detrick, MD 21702-5011
Phone: (301) 619-2285 / (DSN 343)
Web site: www.usamriid.army.mil

(4) **US Army Medical Research Institute of Environmental Medicine**
MCMR-UEMZ
Kansas St, Bldg 42
Natick, MA 01760-5007
Phone: (508) 233-4811
Web site: www-usariem.army.mil

d. **US Army Public Health Command.** Organization combines the activities of the Veterinary Command and USACHPPM.

US Army Public Health Command
Army Institute of Public Health
5158 Blackhawk Rd
Aberdeen Proving Ground, MD 21010-5403
Phone: (410) 436-4311/ DSN 312-584-4311

e. **US Army Research, Development, and Engineering Command (USARDECOM).** The USARDECOM leads the military in chemical and biological defense and support to the military forces from daily peace activities to preparing and conducting military operations.

> **HQ, US Army Research, Development, and Engineering Command**
> Attn: AMSRD-PA
> 5183 Blackhawk Rd, Bldg E5101
> Aberdeen Proving Ground, MD 21010-5424
> Phone: (410) 436-4345 / (DSN 298)
> Web site: www.rdecom.army.mil

Intentionally Blank

APPENDIX H
REFERENCES

The development of JP 4-06 is based upon the following primary references:

1. **General**

    a. Title 10, USC, as amended.

    b. Title 32, USC, as amended.

2. **Department of Defense**

    a. DODD 1300.22, *Mortuary Affairs Policy.*

    b. DODD 3025.18, *Defense Support of Civil Authorities.*

    c. DODD 5100.1, *Functions of the Department of Defense and its Major Components.*

    d. DODD 5100.46, *Foreign Disaster Relief.*

    e. DODD 5154.24, *Armed Forces Institute of Pathology (AFIP).*

    f. DODI 1300.18, *Department of Defense (DOD) Personnel Casualty Matters, Policies, and Procedures.*

    g. DODI 2310.08E, *Medical Program Support for Detainee Operations.*

    h. DODI 5505.10, *Investigation of Noncombat Deaths of DOD Personnel and DOD Civilians.*

    i. DODI 6055.05, *Occupational and Environmental Health (OEH).*

    j. DODI 6055.1, *DOD Safety and Occupational Health (SOH) Program.*

3. **Chairman of the Joint Chiefs of Staff**

    a. CJCSM 3122.03C, *Joint Operation Planning and Execution System (JOPES), Volume II, Planning Formats.*

    b. CJCSM 3150.13C, *Joint Reporting Structure - Personnel Manual.*

    c. CJCSI 5120.02B, *Joint Doctrine Development System.*

    d. JP 1-0, *Personnel Support to Joint Operations.*

    e. JP 1-02, *DOD Dictionary of Military and Associated Terms.*

f. JP 1-05, *Religious Affairs in Joint Operations.*

g. JP 3-11, *Operations in Chemical, Biological, Radiological, and Nuclear (CBRN) Environments.*

h. JP 3-28, *Defense Support of Civil Authorities.*

i. JP 3-29, *Foreign Humanitarian Assistance.*

j. JP 3-33, *Joint Task Force Headquarters.*

k. JP 3-34, *Joint Engineer Operations.*

l. JP 3-40, *Combating Weapons of Mass Destruction.*

m. JP 3-41, *Chemical, Biological, Radiological, and Nuclear Consequence Management.*

n. JP 3-57, *Civil-Military Operations.*

o. JP 4-0, *Joint Logistics.*

4. **Service Publications**

a. Army Regulation 638-2, *Care and Disposition of Remains and Disposition of Personal Effects.*

b. FM 4-20.64, *Mortuary Affairs Operations.*

c. FM 4-20.65, *Identification of Deceased Personnel.*

d. Joint Mortuary Affairs Center, *Mortuary Affairs Staff Guide.*

e. US Army Research, Development, and Engineering Command, *Guidelines for Mass Fatality Management During Terrorist Incidents Involving Chemical Agents.*

f. Air Force Instruction 34-501, *Mortuary Affairs Program.*

g. Air Force Instruction 34-511, *Disposition of Personal Property and Effects.*

h. Navy Medical Command Instruction 5360.1, *Decedent Affairs Manual.*

i. Marine Corps Order P3040.4E, *Marine Corps Casualty Procedures Manual.*

j. Marine Corps Order 4050.38D, *Personal Effects and Baggage Manual.*

k. Marine Corps Warfighting Publication 4-11.8, *Services in an Expeditionary Environment.*

APPENDIX J
ADMINISTRATIVE INSTRUCTIONS

1. User Comments

Users in the field are highly encouraged to submit comments on this publication to: Joint Staff J-7, Deputy Director, Joint and Coalition Warfighting, Joint and Coalition Warfighting Center, ATTN: Joint Doctrine Support Division, 116 Lake View Parkway, Suffolk, VA 23435-2697. These comments should address content (accuracy, usefulness, consistency, and organization), writing, and appearance.

2. Authorship

The lead agent for this publication is the US Army. The Joint Staff doctrine sponsor for this publication is the Director for Logistics (J-4).

3. Supersession

This publication supersedes JP 4-06, 5 June 2006, *Mortuary Affairs in Joint Operations*.

4. Change Recommendations

a. Recommendations for urgent changes to this publication should be submitted:

TO: JOINT STAFF WASHINGTON DC//J7-JEDD//

b. Routine changes should be submitted electronically to the Deputy Director, Joint and Coalition Warfighting, Joint and Coalition Warfighting Center, Joint Doctrine Support Division and info the lead agent and the Director for Joint Force Development, J-7/JEDD.

c. When a Joint Staff directorate submits a proposal to the CJCS that would change source document information reflected in this publication, that directorate will include a proposed change to this publication as an enclosure to its proposal. The Services and other organizations are requested to notify the Joint Staff J-7 when changes to source documents reflected in this publication are initiated.

5. Distribution of Publications

Local reproduction is authorized and access to unclassified publications is unrestricted. However, access to and reproduction authorization for classified JPs must be in accordance with DOD 5200.1-R, *Information Security Program*.

6. Distribution of Electronic Publications

a. Joint Staff J-7 will not print copies of JPs for distribution. Electronic versions are available on JDEIS at https://jdeis.js.mil (NIPRNET) and http://jdeis.js.smil.mil (SIPRNET), and on the JEL at http://www.dtic.mil/doctrine (NIPRNET).

b. Only approved JPs and joint test publications are releasable outside the CCMDs, Services, and Joint Staff. Release of any classified JP to foreign governments or foreign nationals must be requested through the local embassy (Defense Attaché Office) to DIA, Defense Foreign Liaison/IE-3, 200 MacDill Blvd., Joint Base Anacostia-Bolling, Washington, DC 20340-5100.

c. JEL CD-ROM. Upon request of a joint doctrine development community member, the Joint Staff J-7 will produce and deliver one CD-ROM with current JPs. This JEL CD-ROM will be updated not less than semi-annually and when received can be locally reproduced for use within the combatant commands and Services.

GLOSSARY
PART I—ABBREVIATIONS AND ACRONYMS

AFB	Air Force base
AFIP	Armed Forces Institute of Pathology
AFME	Armed Forces Medical Examiner
AFMES	Armed Forces Medical Examiner System
AFTTP(I)	Air Force tactics, techniques, and procedures (instruction)
AIT	automated identification technology
AMC	Air Mobility Command
ANG	Air National Guard
AOR	area of responsibility
APOE	aerial port of embarkation
ARC	American Red Cross
ATOC	air terminal operations center
BTB	believed-to-be
C2	command and control
CA	civil affairs
CAAF	contractor personnel authorized to accompany the force
CBRN	chemical, biological, radiological, and nuclear
CBRM-CM	chemical, biological, radiological, and nuclear consequence management
CBRNE	chemical, biological, radiological, nuclear, and high-yield explosives
CCDR	combatant commander
CCMD	combatant command
CDC	Centers for Disease Control and Prevention
CERFP	chemical, biological, radiological, nuclear, and high-yield explosives enhanced response force package
CIIRP	contaminated human remains pouch
CJCS	Chairman of the Joint Chiefs of Staff
CJCSM	Chairman of the Joint Chiefs of Staff manual
CJMAB	Central Joint Mortuary Affairs Board
cm	centimeter
CMAOC	Casualty and Mortuary Affairs Operations Center
COA	course of action
CONOPS	concept of operations
CONUS	continental United States
COTS	commercial off-the-shelf
CP	collection point
CSSB	combat sustainment support battalion
DCO	defense coordinating officer
DD	Department of Defense (form)

DE	decedent effects
DHHS	Department of Health and Human Services
DHS	Department of Homeland Security
DMORT	disaster mortuary operational response team
DNA	deoxyribonucleic acid
DOD	Department of Defense
DODD	Department of Defense directive
DODI	Department of Defense instruction
DOS	Department of State
DS	direct support
DSCA	defense support of civil authorities
DTD	detailed troop decontamination
EA	executive agent
EFAC	emergency family assistance center
EOD	explosive ordnance disposal
ESF	emergency support function
FBI	Federal Bureau of Investigation
FCO	federal coordinating officer
FEMA	Federal Emergency Management Agency
FHA	foreign humanitarian assistance
FM	field manual (Army)
FSRT	fatality search and recovery team
GCC	geographic combatant commander
GPS	Global Positioning System
GS	general support
HA	humanitarian assistance
HEPA	high efficiency particulate air
HN	host nation
HNS	host-nation support
HRC	Human Resources Command (Army)
HRF	homeland response force
HRP	human remains pouch
ICS	incident command system
ID	identification
J-1	manpower and personnel directorate of a joint staff
J-4	logistics directorate of a joint staff
JFC	joint force commander
JFO	joint field office
JMAC	Joint Mortuary Affairs Center (Army)
JMAO	joint mortuary affairs office

JOPES	Joint Operation Planning and Execution System
JP	joint publication
JPAC	Joint POW/MIA Accounting Command
JPED	joint personal effects depot
JTF	joint task force
JTF-MAO	joint task force–mortuary affairs office
LNO	liaison officer
m	meter
MA	mortuary affairs
MACP	mortuary affairs collection point
MACRMS	mortuary affairs contaminated remains mitigation site
MARTS	Mortuary Affairs Reporting and Tracking System
MC/FI	mass casualty/fatality incident
MCRP	Marine Corps reference publication
MCWP	Marine Corps warfighting publication
ME/C	medical examiner and/or coroner
MILAIR	military airlift
MIRCS	mobile integrated remains collection system
MOPP	mission-oriented protective posture
NATO	North Atlantic Treaty Organization
NCOIC	noncommissioned officer in charge
NG	National Guard
NGB	National Guard Bureau
NGO	nongovernmental organization
NIMS	National Incident Management System
NOK	next of kin
NRF	National Response Framework
NTSB	National Transportation Safety Board
NTTP	Navy tactics, techniques, and procedures
OAFME	Office of the Armed Forces Medical Examiner
OCONUS	outside the continental United States
OIC	officer in charge
OPCON	operational control
OPLAN	operation plan
OPORD	operation order
PADD	person authorized to direct disposition of human remains
PE	personal effects
PEIO	personnel effects inventory officer
PERE	person eligible to receive effects
POC	point of contact
POE	port of embarkation

PPE	personal protective equipment
PRP	personnel retrieval and processing
QC	quality control
R&D	research and development
RFA	request for assistance
RFID	radio frequency identification
RS	religious support
RST	religious support team
S&R	search and recovery
S&T	science and technology
SCO	state coordinating officer
SecDef	Secretary of Defense
SECHS	Secretary of Homeland Security
SF	standard form
SJA	staff judge advocate
SME	subject matter expert
SOP	standard operating procedure
SSN	Social Security number
STANAG	standardization agreement (NATO)
TACON	tactical control
TMAO	theater mortuary affairs office
TMEP	theater mortuary evacuation point
TPED	theater personal effects depot
TTP	tactics, techniques, and procedures
USACHPPM	United States Army Center for Health Promotion and Preventive Medicine
USAF	United States Air Force
USAMRMC	United States Army Medical Research and Materiel Command
USARDECOM	United States Army Research, Development, and Engineering Command
USC	United States Code
USG	United States Government
USNORTHCOM	United States Northern Command
USPACOM	United States Pacific Command
USTRANSCOM	United States Transportation Command
UXO	unexploded ordnance
WMD	weapons of mass destruction
WMD-CST	weapons of mass destruction–civil support team

antemortem data. Medical records, samples, and photographs taken prior to death. These include (but are not limited to) fingerprints, dental x-rays, body tissue samples, photographs of tattoos, or other identifying marks. These "pre-death" records would be compared against records completed after death to help establish a positive identification of human remains. (Approved for replacement of "antemortem identification media" and its definition in JP 1-02.)

believed-to-be. In mortuary affairs, the status of any human remains until a positive identification has been determined. Used interchangeably with tentative identification. Also called **BTB.** (Approved for inclusion in JP 1-02.)

Blue Bark. US military personnel, US citizen civilian employees of the Department of Defense, and the dependents of both categories who travel in connection with the death of an immediate family member. It also applies to designated escorts for dependents of deceased military members. Furthermore, the term is used to designate the personal property shipment of a deceased member. (Approved for incorporation into JP 1-02 with JP 4-06 as the source JP.)

collection point. A point designated for the assembly of personnel casualties, stragglers, disabled materiel, salvage, etc., for further movement to collecting stations or rear installations. Also called **CP.** (Approved for incorporation into JP 1-02.)

commercial items. Articles of supply readily available from established commercial distribution sources which the Department of Defense or inventory managers in the Services have designated to be obtained directly or indirectly from such sources. (Approved for incorporation into JP 1-02 with JP 4-06 as the source JP.)

commercial vehicle. A vehicle that has evolved in the commercial market to meet civilian requirements and which is selected from existing production lines for military use. (Approved for incorporation into JP 1-02 with JP 4-06 as the source JP.)

contaminated remains. Remains of personnel which have absorbed or upon which have been deposited radioactive material, or biological or chemical agents. (JP 1-02. SOURCE: JP 4-06)

decedent effects. Personal effects found on human remains. Also called **DE.** (Approved for inclusion in JP 1-02.)

emergency interment. None. (Approved for removal from JP 1-02.)

escort. A member of the Armed Forces assigned to accompany, assist, or guide an individual or group, e.g., an escort officer. (JP 1-02. SOURCE: JP 4-06)

graves registration program. None. (Approved for removal from JP 1-02.)

joint mortuary affairs office. Plans and executes all mortuary affairs programs within a theater. Provides guidance to facilitate the conduct of all mortuary programs and to maintain data (as required) pertaining to recovery, identification, and disposition of all US dead and missing in the assigned theater. Serves as the central clearing point for all mortuary affairs and monitors the deceased and missing personal effects program. Also called **JMAO.** (JP 1-02. SOURCE: JP 4-06)

M-day. See **times.** (Approved for incorporation into JP 1-02 with JP 4-06 as the source JP.)

mortuary affairs. Provides for the search, recovery, identification, preparation, and disposition of human remains of persons for whom the Services are responsible by status and executive order. Also called **MA.** (Approved for incorporation into JP 1-02.)

personal effects. All privately owned moveable, personal property of an individual. Also called **PE.** (JP 1-02. SOURCE: JP 4-06)

personal property. Property of any kind or any interest therein, except real property, records of the United States Government, and naval vessels of the following categories: surface combatants, support ships, and submarines. (Approved for incorporation into JP 1-02.)

person authorized to direct disposition of human remains. A person, usually primary next of kin, who is authorized to direct disposition of human remains. Also called **PADD.** (JP 1-02. SOURCE: JP 4-06)

person eligible to receive effects. The person authorized by law to receive the personal effects of a deceased military member. Receipt of personal effects does not constitute ownership. Also called **PERE.** (JP 1-02. SOURCE: JP 4-06)

personnel effects inventory officer. An officer appointed to establish clear chain of custody for all personal effects of an individual from the time they establish control of the effects until they release the effect to mortuary affairs personnel. Also called **PEIO.** (Approved for inclusion in JP 1-02.)

search. 1. An operation to locate an enemy force known or believed to be at sea. 2. A systematic reconnaissance of a defined area, so that all parts of the area have passed within visibility. (JP 4-06) 3. To distribute gunfire over an area in depth by successive changes in gun elevation. (Approved for incorporation into JP 1-02 with JP 4-06 as the source JP for Definition #2.)

temporary interment. A site for the purpose of: a. the interment of the remains if the circumstances permit; or b. the reburial of remains exhumed from an emergency interment. (JP 1-02. SOURCE: JP 4-06)

JOINT DOCTRINE PUBLICATIONS HIERARCHY

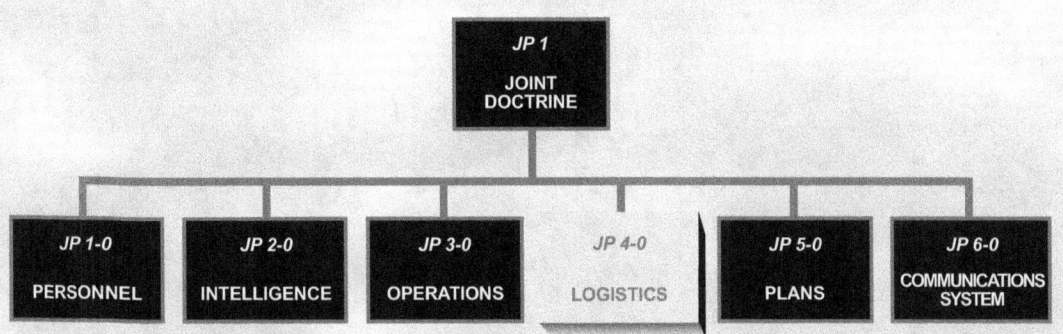

All joint publications are organized into a comprehensive hierarchy as shown in the chart above. **Joint Publication (JP) 4-06** is in the **Logistics** series of joint doctrine publications. The diagram below illustrates an overview of the development process:

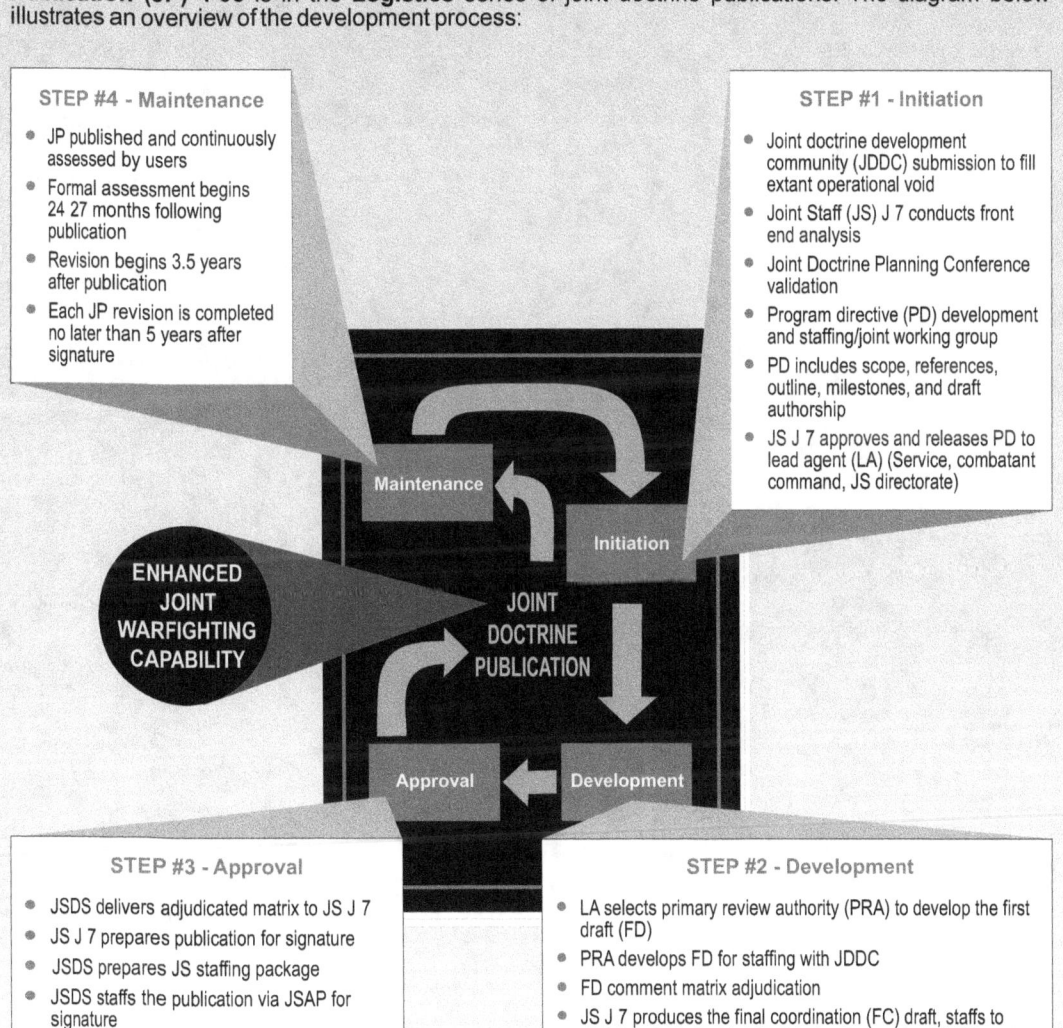

STEP #4 - Maintenance

- JP published and continuously assessed by users
- Formal assessment begins 24 27 months following publication
- Revision begins 3.5 years after publication
- Each JP revision is completed no later than 5 years after signature

STEP #1 - Initiation

- Joint doctrine development community (JDDC) submission to fill extant operational void
- Joint Staff (JS) J 7 conducts front end analysis
- Joint Doctrine Planning Conference validation
- Program directive (PD) development and staffing/joint working group
- PD includes scope, references, outline, milestones, and draft authorship
- JS J 7 approves and releases PD to lead agent (LA) (Service, combatant command, JS directorate)

STEP #3 - Approval

- JSDS delivers adjudicated matrix to JS J 7
- JS J 7 prepares publication for signature
- JSDS prepares JS staffing package
- JSDS staffs the publication via JSAP for signature

STEP #2 - Development

- LA selects primary review authority (PRA) to develop the first draft (FD)
- PRA develops FD for staffing with JDDC
- FD comment matrix adjudication
- JS J 7 produces the final coordination (FC) draft, staffs to JDDC and JS via Joint Staff Action Processing (JSAP) system
- Joint Staff doctrine sponsor (JSDS) adjudicates FC comment matrix
- FC joint working group